OVERSEAS BUSINESS ACTIVITIES

The International
Conference on
Business
History **9**

OVERSEAS BUSINESS ACTIVITIES

Proceedings of the Fuji Conference

edited by
AKIO OKOCHI
TADAKATSU INOUE

UNIVERSITY OF TOKYO PRESS

© Committee for the International Conference on Business History, 1984
All rights reserved
Published by
University of Tokyo Press
Printed in Japan

ISBN 4–13–047019–1 (UTP 47197)
ISBN 0–86008–325–X

HD
2755.5
I555
1982

ORGANIZING COMMITTEE FOR THE SECOND SERIES
INTERNATIONAL CONFERENCE ON BUSINESS HISTORY
1979–1983

Chairman:	Okochi, Akio	(University of Tokyo)
Treasurer:	Watanabe, Hisashi	(Kyoto University)
Secretary:	Yuzawa, Takeshi	(Gakushuin University)
	Daito, Eisuke	(University of Tokyo)
	Hara, Terushi	(Waseda University)
	Ishikawa, Kenjiro	(Doshisha University)
	Kita, Masami	(Soka University)
	Miyamoto, Matao	(Osaka University)
	Udagawa, Masaru	(Hosei University)

Advisory Board:

Nakagawa, Keiichiro	(The International University of Japan)
Kobayashi, Kesaji	(Ryukoku University)
Morikawa, Hidemasa	(Hosei University)
Yasuoka, Shigeaki	(Doshisha University)
Yonekawa, Shin-ichi	(Hitotsubashi University)

Participants

Project Leader for the Fourth Meeting:
Inoue, Tadakatsu (Kobe University)

Blainey, Geoffrey
(University of Melbourne)

Caron, François
(University of Paris-Sorbonne)

Cusumano, Michael A.
(University of Tokyo)

Daito, Eisuke
(University of Tokyo)

Fujita, Nobuhisa
(Konan University)

Hara, Terushi
(Waseda University)

Inoue, Tadakatsu
(Kobe University)

Ishikawa, Kenjiro
(Doshisha University)

Jones, Geoffrey
(University of London)

Kinugasa, Yosuke
(Yokohama City University)

Kita, Masami
(Soka University)

Kobayashi, Keishi
(Waseda University)

Miyamoto, Matao
(Osaka University)

Nakagawa, Keiichiro
(The International University of Japan)

Okochi, Akio
  (University of Tokyo)
Schneider, Jürgen
  (University of Erlangen-
  Nürnberg)
Udagawa, Masaru
  (Hosei University)
Watanabe, Hisashi
  (Kyoto University)
Yamada, Makiko
  (Sangyonoritsu University)

Yang, Tien-yi
  (Asia University)
Yasumuro, Ken'ichi
  (Kobe University of
  Commerce)
Yoshihara, Hideki
  (Kobe University)
Yoshino, Michael Y.
  (Harvard University)
Yuzawa, Takeshi
  (Gakushuin University)

CONTENTS

PREFACE

The fourth meeting of the Second Series International Conference on Business History was held January 5–8, 1982, at the Fuji Education Center, Shizuoka, Japan, under the joint auspices of the Business History Society of Japan and the Taniguchi Foundation.

The original plan of the Organizing Committee was to investigate the overseas business activities of banking and trading companies, which have created their own international network. Accordingly, the Organizing Committee asked Professor Tadakatsu Inoue to accept the role of Project Leader. After exchanging opinions on the subject, the Organizing Committee agreed with Prof. Inoue's proposed frame work for the meeting, and finally we decided that international direct and portfolio investments would be the central theme for the fourth meeting. Professor Inoue, in cooperation with the Organizing Committee, designed and organized the fourth meeting.

The following proceedings are a record of the meeting. On behalf of the Organizing Committee, I would like to express my thanks to Professor Inoue for his effort in editing these proceedings and preparing a summary of the discussions. We regret that Professor Y. Yoshino of the U.S.A. was unable to attend the meeting due to illness; his paper was presented by a colleague, and is included in these proceedings. We also wish to express our warm thanks to Ms. S. Schmidt and Mr. W. Izumi of the University of Tokyo Press for all their labors in editing and producing this volume.

March 1983

Akio Okochi
General Editor and Chairman of the Organizing Committee for the International Conference on Business History

INTRODUCTION

Early in 1981 the Organizing Committee for the International Conference on Business History asked Tadakatsu Inoue to organize the 4th meeting of the second five-year series of the Conference under the theme "Overseas Business Activities." One of the tasks assigned to him was to compile a proposal to participants who were expected to read papers at the meeting. The following is the summary of it acknowledged by the Organzing Committee.

Proposal

A. *Types of "Overseas Business Activities" and our intentions*
1. Our primary concern is with foreign direct investment. Yet portfolio investment, another important type of foreign investment, will not be ignored.
2. We will place emphasis on foreign direct investment in manufacturing. Yet we shall not prevent participants from referring to the other sectors which attracted foreign investment, such as agriculture, mining or petroleum.
3. It goes without saying that foreign direct investment in manufacturing is connected with the other aspects of overseas activities of manufacturers such as exporting and licensing.

B. *Two viewpoints*
We approach the subject from two viewpoints. Participants from France, the United Kingdom, the United States, West Germany, and Japan are expected to deal with the phenomena associated with foreign direct investment from the point of view of the home country, while those from Australia, China or Thailand are expected to examine them from the viewpoint of the host country.

C. *Period to be referred to*
The formative years of the present-day multinational enterprises in Europe and America go back to the decades prior to World War I. It

was not until the late 1960s, in contrast, that Thailand induced foreign capital to its industry. This makes it impossible to prescribe the time period to be referred to by every participant. We rather hope each will select the time period that gives the best understanding of the problems mentioned next.

D. Problems to be discussed

1. Causes and processes of multinational manufacturing

In the case of extractive industries, the motivation for foreign investment is fairly straightforward. In the case of manufacturing industries, however, it is not so easy to find the factors bearing on a decision to invest abroad. Why, for example, should a corporation choose to serve a foreign market through the establishment of a local subsidiary rather than by exporting or licensing?

2. Managerial problems of multinational manufacturing

Both organizational problems of a multinational manufacturing corporation and operational problems of its subsidiaries in alien lands fall within the field of international management. Comparative analyses of the operating methods adopted by foreign subsidiaries in a particular host country must arouse our interest.

3. Effects of multinational manufacturing on a host country

Foreign direct investment in manufacturing has effects not only upon the host country but also upon the investor nation. Here we shall be mainly concerned with its effects on the host country, however.

Our expectation is that participants from the European countries, the United States, and Japan will concentrate on Problems 1 and 2, and the rest on Problems 2 and 3.

In the course of correspondence between the Organizing Committee and possible participants, the original program for the meeting was somewhat altered. An accident made it impossible for the invited Thaischolar to attend and read a paper on foreign direct investment in Southeast Asian countries. Fortunately, Tien-yi Yang, Asia University, was able to substitute for him by presenting a paper on foreign business activities in China before World War II. Just before the meeting, M. Y. Yoshino of Harvard Business School was attacked by influenza and advised by a doctor not to travel. His paper was read by Makiko Yamada.

During the four-day session, ten papers were read. An introductory paper by Inoue on the causes and processes of foreign direct investment in manufacturing was followed and supplemented by Kinugasa, who explained how and why Japanese manufacturers established their subsidiaries in the United States. The changing role of the sogo shosha in the multinationalization of Japanese industrial firms was explored by Yasumuro. Yoshihara discussed the Japanese style of multinational growth in comparison with the U.S. and the European multinational manufacturing enterprises. Jones traced the origins and spread of British multinational manufacturing before 1939 by examining the performance of Courtaulds, Dunlop, Gramophone and others. Schneider dealt with German investments in the United States between 1871 and 1914 and compared them with those in Latin America. Yoshino attempted to present a synthesis of the patterns of evolution of the strategy, organization, and management system of U.S. -based multinational enterprises.

Unlike these seven papers written from the viewpoint of investor countries, the last three papers considered foreign direct investment from the vantage point of the host countries. Blainey gave a full description of multinational factories in Australia. Caron analyzed the changes in French government policies on foreign capital in the 1950s and 1960s. And Yang examined the activities of Standard Oil, British-American Tobacco, and Japanese-owned cotton mills in China and their impact on the Chinese economy.

This volume contains all but one of the conference papers, comments on them, and a summary of the concluding discussion on the final day. We hope this will be a milestone for the historical study of overseas business activities.

Tadakatsu Inoue

OVERSEAS BUSINESS ACTIVITIES

A Comparison of the Emergence of Multinational Manufacturing by U.S., European, and Japanese Firms

Tadakatsu Inoue
Kobe University

When asking how and why a certain manufacturer began foreign direct investment, we face many problems awaiting solution. Suppose, for example, he was a market-oriented investor who sought to sell mainly within a foreign nation. Then why was the market abroad served not by local entrepreneurs but by him? On what basis of capability could he serve the market? And why did he seek to serve the market through the establishment of a local plant rather than through exports?

To explore these problems, I shall compare the emergence of multinational manufacturing by U.S., European, and Japanese firms. Although I have depended upon scholars in each country for data and facts and have not conducted independent research, I hope this paper will offer some suggestions to explain the causes and processes of foreign direct investments in manufacturing.

I.

A few American manufacturers made foreign direct investments before the Civil War,[1] but it was not until the decades prior to World War I that many American manufacturing enterprises became involved in foreign operations. According to Cleona Lewis's estimate, in the years from 1897 to 1914, the United States remained a debtor in international accounts, yet the book value of the U.S. direct investment in foreign manufacturing increased from $94 million in 1897 to $296 million in 1908 and to $478 million in 1914.[2] More significant is Mira Wilkins's list of the U.S. enterprises that built or acquired manufacturing plants in two or more foreign countries between 1890 and 1914.[3] This list includes thirty-seven companies. Their names and the locations of their foreign plants are as follows:

Name	Location of Foreign Plants
Alcoa	France, Canada
American Bicycle	Germany, Canada
American Chicle	Britain, Canada
American Cotton Oil	Holland, Canada
American Graphophone	Britain, Germany, France, Canada
American Radiator	Britain, Germany, France, Austria, Italy, Canada
American Tobacco*	Britain, Germany, Canada, Japan, Australia, Puerto Rico, Korea, China, Argentina
Armour	Canada, Argentina
British-American Tobacco (see American Tobacco)	
Carborundum	Britain, Germany
Chicago Pneumatic Tool	Britain, Germany, Canada
Coca-Cola	Canada, Cuba
Crown Cork and Seal	Canada, Mexico
Diamond Match	Britain, Germany, Switzerland, Canada, Brazil, Peru, South Africa, Australia
Eastman Kodak	Britain, France, Canada, Australia
Ford	Britain (mainly assembly), France (only assembly), Canada
General Electric**	Britain, Canada***
Gillette	Britain, Germany, France, Canada
Heinz (H.J.)	Britain, Spain, Canada
International Harvester	Germany, France, Russia, Sweden, Canada
International Steam Pump	Britain, Germany, France, Austria, Canada
Mergenthaler Linotype	Britain, Germany, Canada
National Cash Register	Britain, Canada
Norton	Germany, Canada
Otis Elevator	Britain, Germany, France, Canada
Parke, Davis	Britain, Russia, Canada***
Quaker Oats	Britain (only bulk packaging), Germany, Canada
Sherwin-Williams	Britain, Canada
Singer	Britain,*** Germany, Russia, Canada***
Stearns & Co. (Frederick) (later part of Sterling Drugs)	Canada,*** Australia
Swift	Canada, Argentina, Uruguay, Australia, Mexico
Torrington	Britain, Germany
United Shoe Machinery	Britain, Germany, France, Canada
United Drug	Britain, Canada

Western Electric	Britain, Germany,*** France, Austria, Italy, Belgium,*** Russia, Canada, Japan
Westinghouse Air Brake	Britain,*** Germany, France,*** Russia, Canada
Westinghouse Electric	Britain, Germany, France, Russia, Canada

    *:   According to a market-sharing agreement of 1902, practically all these plants were transferred to Imperial Tobacco and a new concern, British-American Tobacco.

  **:   Excluding agreements with German, French, Austrian, Italian, and Japanese manufacturing companies in which G.E. did not have controlling interest.

***:   Plant built prior to 1890.

In a paper published in a Japanese journal, I attempted to examine how and why these thirty-seven pioneers began foreign direct investments.[4] Some conclusions I reached were as follows.

1. Almost all the companies possessed either a novel or seemingly novel product or production process, or special marketing skills, or a combination of these. Among the innovators of novel products[5] were such companies as American Graphophone in phonographs and graphophones, American Radiator in sectional radiators and boilers, Chicago Pneumatic Tool in pneumatic tools and air compressors, Crown Cork and Seal in bottlecaps and bottling machinery, Eastman Kodak in photographic goods, Ford in public or utility cars, G. E. in electrical products and equipment, Gillette in safety razors, International Harvester in agricultural machinery, International Steam Pump in heavy steam power machinery, Mergenthaler Linotype in linotype, National Cash Register in cash registers, Otis Elevator in hydraulic and other elevators, Singer in sewing machines, Stearns in family medicines in popular-sized packages with a statement of ingredients, Swift in refrigerated meat, United Shoe Machinery in shoe machinery, Western Electric in telephone equipment, Westinghouse Air Brake in air brakes and signal equipment, and Westinghouse Electric in the alternating current system.

Examples of firms with new production processes include Alcoa, one of two inventors of the electrolytic process for the production of aluminum; American Bicycle, the oligopolistic producer of a European product that had become known by the close of the century for its high degree of standardization and mechanization; Ford, the pioneer in introducing the moving assembly system for the mass production of cars; and American Tobacco, Diamond Match, and Quaker Oats, who were innovators in devising continuous process machinery and plants for the production of packaged goods.

Of these innovative producers, the manufacturers of new types of mass-produced machines, such as Singer, International Harvester, and National Cash Register, were also pioneers in building large distributing networks of their own and offering specialized services such as demonstration, continuing service and repair, and consumer credit. Likewise American Tobacco, Diamond Match, and Quaker Oats, the mass-producers of small packaged products, pioneered in the development of modern marketing techniques, such as branding and advertising, through which the flow of goods from the factories to distributors or ultimate consumers was coordinated.

2.   Most companies on the list concentrated on market-oriented manufacturing investments that sought to sell mainly within the host nation. Exceptions such as the Chicago meatpackers Armour and Swift made both market-oriented manufacturing investments in Canada and supply-oriented manufacturing investments in Argentina and other countries that aimed to export dressed beef from the capital-recipient countries.[6]

3.   While the market-oriented investors did not ignore Asia, Oceania, and Africa,[7] they established their foreign stakes first in neighboring Canada and Europe where there was little or no demand lag for products that were often associated with the labor-saving and high-income needs of the U.S. economy.[8]

4.   Prior to direct investments in foreign manufacturing, many of the U.S. companies sought to serve the overseas markets through exporting.[9] Singer's foreign operations started with the creation of international sales networks and then developed into the establishment of its first factory in Glasgow in 1867.[10] Similarly, American Radiator, National Cash Register, Westinghouse Air Brake, Ford, and Eastman Kodak began the process of involvement in foreign manufacturing by exporting their dominant products through independent agents, salaried export managers, salaried representatives abroad, or foreign sales branches.[11]

5.   What were the major reasons for the U.S. manufacturers seeking to serve the overseas markets through the establishment of local assembly or manufacturing plants rather than through exporting?

An answer to this question can be found by dividing the investors into two groups. The first group includes a smaller number of manufacturers who aggressively made foreign direct investments even though they could have maintained their market positions through exporting. One example is Ford Motor. Seeing the mounting sales of the Model T in England, the company was convinced that it would be sensible to build an assembly plant there. Although there would be no savings on custom duties in this free trade country at that time, transportation costs were expected to be substantially reduced, since "ten knocked down cars occupy the (cargo) space of one completely assembled car."[12] Thus, the Manchester assembly plant was built in 1911–12.

The other group includes those manufacturers who were compelled to set up production plants abroad because they perceived the threat of losing their established export markets. The threat often took the form of the rise of their competition in local markets where the relevant technology was becoming available through diffusion or imitation. Foreign government actions such as custom duties and patent requirements also increased the threat. Thus, to maintain their market share and forestall competition, the American manufacturers had to establish foreign subsidiaries to exploit what remained of their competitive advantages. For example, by 1911, faced with high tariffs and the possibility of competition developing behind the tariff walls, International Harvester had built a total of five plants in Canada, Sweden, France, Germany, and Russia.[13]

In short, many American manufacturing enterprises, by 1914, were involved in foreign operations. As a whole they had competitive advantages accruing mainly from their technological superiority. To exploit their advantages outside their domestic market, they first sought to create and fill foreign demand through exporting and later switched from exporting to foreign manufacturing. While some were aggressive in doing so, many others did not begin to manufacture abroad until being threatened by the rise of foreign competition.

II.

When World War I broke out, Britain held the highest international position in foreign investments. The book value of her investments abroad was estimated at $18.3 billion, more than five times U.S. foreign investments.[14] Concerning direct investments abroad, however, the proportion in the aggregate was very small. According to John M. Stopford's estimate, it was only 10 percent of the total.[15] This must be compared with the lion's share of U.S. direct investments accounting for 75 percent of the total stock of her foreign investments.[16] By far the larger category in British foreign investments was portfolio investments that controlled 68 percent of the total. The remaining 22 percent was for "expatriate" investments.[17] It may be said that while British businessmen and business firms in those days would readily make portfolio investments abroad simply to obtain added revenue, they would not readily make foreign direct investments that involved managerial responsibility, the possibility of a voice in management, and a direct business purpose.

There were, nevertheless, a significant number of firms that had established manufacturing plants abroad by 1914. Based on a search of materials on the largest 100 manufacturing firms in Britain in 1970, Stopford produced a list of fourteen enterprises that had invested abroad on a significant scale before 1914[18]:

Firm	Location of Major Foreign Manufacturing Investment
British-American Tobacco	Dominion (Australia, Canada*), Rest of British Empire (India,* Trinidad), Europe (Germany, Denmark), Japan, Korea, Puerto Rico, China
Bryant and May (later British Match)	Dominion (Australia, S. Africa, N. Zealand*), Brazil*
J. and P. Coats (later Coats Patons)	Dominion (Canada), Europe (Belgium, Italy), U.S., Russia, Japan
Courtaulds	Europe (Belgium), U.S.
Dunlop	Dominion (S. Africa, Canada), Europe (Germany), Argentina, Japan
English Sewing Cotton (later Tootal)	Dominion (Canada), Europe (Spain, France), U.S.
The Gramophone Co. (later EMI)	British Empire (India), Brazil, Europe (Denmark)
Lever Brothers (later Unilever)	Dominion (S. Africa, Australia, Canada), Europe (Germany, Austria, Belgium, France), U.S., Japan
Liebig Extract of Meat (later Brooke Bond Liebig)	Europe (Belgium), Argentina,* Uruguay*

Nobel Explosives (later part of ICI)	Dominion (Australia, Canada)
Pilkington	Dominion (Canada), Europe (France, Germany)
Reckitts (later Reckitt and Colman)	Dominion (Australia, S. Africa), Europe (Germany), U.S., Argentina
Royal Dutch Shell	Europe (Germany), U.S.,* Russia,* Indonesia,* Mexico,* Borneo,* Romania,* Egypt*
Vickers	Dominion (Canada), Europe (Italy, Spain, Turkey), Japan, Russia

*: A manufacturing investment closely tied to local sources of raw materials.

Like their counterparts in the U.S., all these companies had special skills which were technological, marketing, or—in the case of Shell—logistical. Courtaulds in viscose silk, Dunlop in pneumatic tires, Gramophone in records, Nobel in explosives, and Vickers in armaments all possessed new technology. J. and P. Coats and English Sewing Cotton, both in cotton thread, and Pilkington in glass had also established their strong positions by specialization of products and by continuously introducing new lower cost methods of production. Lever Brothers in soaps, Reckitts in starch, and Bryant and May in matches also had special marketing techniques.

These companies had the energy and ability to take advantage of their special skills. A company wishing to undertake direct investment in a foreign country must have an oligopolistic advantage over existing or potentially competitive firms in that country.[19] But such an advantage is by no means a sufficient condition for international expansion. In fact, there were many other British companies that had established oligopolistic positions based on their special skills yet still remained at home. Thus, a company going abroad also needed to have the entrepreneurship to exploit its advantage even outside the domestic market. As Stopford notes, the fourteen pioneers were all led by men who shared a global vision.[20]

Apart from foreign manufacturing investments closely tied to local sources of raw materials, major investments of British companies were in high-income countries. Investments even in the British Empire were almost exclusively restricted to "white" dominions, where the burgeoning populations had income levels sufficient to provide markets for British goods.

Like their U.S. counterparts, most of these British pioneers had established overseas networks of agencies, branch houses, and sales subsidiaries before setting up manufacturing plants overseas. The threatened loss of an export market and the rise of foreign competition was often the stimulus for this transition from exporting to foreign manufacturing. In the case of Courtaulds, for example, a threat to its export position, in the form of a sharp rise in U.S. tariffs on imported artificial silk, precipitated the decision to set up its first U.S. subsidiary in Pennsylvania in 1910.[21]

III.

On the eve of World War I, Continental European enterprises had never been behind their American and British counterparts in undertaking direct investments in foreign manufacturing. According to Lawrence G. Franko, no fewer that thirty-seven of the eighty-five largest industrial firms in the western part of Continental Europe in 1970 owned one or more foreign manufacturing subsidiaries by 1914,[22] and the total number of these subsidiaries well exceeded the number of those owned by American firms.[23] Moreover, Continental European multinational manufacturing began considerably earlier than did American. Antedating a Yankee armsmaker's pioneering venture in London by thirty-seven years, Cockerill of Belgium constructed its first foreign manufacturing plant in Prussia in 1815.[24]

Of the thirty-seven Continental European firms that owned one or more foreign manufacturing subsidiary by 1914, the earliest pioneers and the locations of their foreign manufacturing operations are cited by Franko in the following table:

Country and Parent Firm	Location of Foreign Manufacturing Operations
Switzerland	
Ciba	Russia, France, Germany, U.K.
Geigy	Russia, France, Germany, U.S., U.K., Austria
Brown-Boveri	France, Germany, Austria, Italy, Norway
Nestlé	Germany, U.S., U.K., Spain, Holland, Norway
Germany	
Siemens	Russia, France,* U.S.,* U.K., Spain, Austria
AEG	Russia, Spain, Austria, Italy, Belgium*
Degussa	U.S., Spain, Belgium

Bosch	France, U.S., U.K., Japan
BASF	Russia, France, U.K., Norway
Hoechst	Russia, France, U.K.
Bayer	Russia, France, U.S.
Agfa	Russia, France
Metallgesellschaft	France,* U.S., U.K., Austria, Holland, Belgium, Mexico
Daimler-Benz	U.S., U.K., Austria
France	
Cie De St Gobain	Germany, Spain, Austria, Italy, Belgium
Netherlands	
Margarine Uni (later Unilever)	Germany, U.S.,** U.K., Belgium, Denmark
Belgium	
Solvay	Russia, France, Germany, U.S., U.K., Spain, Austria, Italy
Sweden	
SKF	Russia,** France, Germany, U.S.,** U.K.

*:   Failed or abandoned prior to World War I.
**:   Entered between the years 1914 and 1918.

Out of a total of eighteen parent firms, ten were German and four were Swiss. Eight firms were based in the chemical industry, and four were active in electrical equipment. The eighteen firms located a majority of their foreign manufacturing operations in Europe, including the United Kingdom. When they manufactured outside of Europe, they did so in the Western Hemisphere. The Continental enterprises rarely went to Asia.

Like most of their American and British counterparts, these Continental European manufacturers had competitive advantages based on their technological superiority. But the products and processes developed by them tended to be unlike those introduced by U.S. manufacturers. While American innovations were typically biased toward goods and processes that appealed to the labor-short and high-income American market, European innovations seem to have been directed toward material substitutes, material-saving processes, and goods oriented either to a luxury market of aristocratic elites or a large low-income market of peasants and workers. The ammonia soda process by Solvay, alizarine and ammonia synthesis for fertilizer by BASF were European innovations, as were luxury cars by Benz and margarine by a predecessor of Unilever. As Franko notes, even when Continental and American firms produced similar products, Continental firms often did so with different, material saving processes.[25]

Also, like their U.S. and U.K. counterparts, Continental European firms began the process of becoming multinational by exporting. For example, exports of synthetic dyestuffs from Germany and Switzerland increased from about eight thousand tons in 1880 to about fifty thousand tons in 1900, and to about ninty thousand tons in 1910. BASF, Hoechst, Bayer, and Agfa in Germany, and Ciba and Geigy in Switzerland could exploit their innovative advantages in foreign markets where there were almost no locally-owned chemical dyestuff producers. Trade barriers, such as increased French duties in the 1880s, the Franco-Swiss tariff war in 1892–95, and the 1907 Patent Act of England also led German and Swiss companies to set up foreign manufacturing plants.[26]

IV.

I do not have figures for Japanese direct foreign investments around 1914, but, judging from an estimated yearly average of Japan's foreign investments for 1902 to 1915 amounting to ¥20 to ¥30 million—most of which fell in the category of portfolio investments—it is safe to say that the size of Japanese direct investments abroad was very small compared with those of U.S., Britain, and Continental European nations.[27] Moreover, the substantial Japanese direct investment abroad was concentrated in trading, shipping, banks, mining, and colonial development, such as the Southern Manchurian Railway Company, a mixed enterprise formed in 1906.[28] Except for a few cotton mills built or purchased in China by trading companies such as Mitsui Bussan, Nihon Menka, and Naigaimen in the early 1900s, Japanese direct investments in manufacturing before 1914 were insignificant.[29]

It was in the years just after World War I that a number of the leading Japanese manufacturing companies were involved in foreign operations. These companies were Dainippon Spinning, Osaka Consolidated Spinning, Nisshin Spinning, Kanegafuchi Spinning, Fuji Gas Spinning, Toyo Spinning, Nagasaki Spinning, and Fukushima Spinning. As their names show, they were all cotton spinners; they planned and established local mills in Shanghai and

Tsingtao in the years 1917–22. By 1926, when these mills had been completed, Japanese cotton mills in China, including those owned by Japanese traders, controlled about 1.3 million spindles, equivalent to 36 percent of the total spindles.[30] In comparison, Chinese spinners and English cotton mills in China held, respectively, 58 and 6 percent of the total.

The modern Japanese cotton spinning industry was started by the introduction of Western technology. Take, for example, the Osaka Spinning Company (later Toyo Spinning) founded in Osaka in 1882. This first successful cotton mill in Japan was equipped with Pratt's 10,500 spindles and was managed by Manchester-trained *samurai*. The industry thus initiated grew so rapidly that the first export of thirty-one bales of cotton yarn began in 1890. Seven years later exports well exceeded imported cotton yarn, which were once the greatest volume of all imports. When the First World War broke out, Japanese spinners found the Asian markets left to them. Yarn exports in 1915 reached about five hundred and seventy-six thousand bales, of which about 80 percent was for the Chinese market.

After World War I, however, Chinese spinners increased their production capacity from about six hundred and fifty thousand spindles in 1916 to about nine hundred thousand spindles in 1919 to about 2.1 million spindles in 1921. This increase was partly due to the revision of Chinese customs rates in 1919, the first step toward Chinese customs autonomy of 1930. To respond to this self-sustaining tendency in the Chinese market, the leading Japanese spinning firms decided to switch their overseas strategy from exporting to local manufacturing.

V.

As noted, particularly by Charles Kindleberger and Stephen Hymer, a firm that undertakes direct investment in a foreign country must have an advantage over existing or potentially competitive firms in that country.[31] If not, the firm would be put out of business by those local firms that do not have the additional costs accompanied with foreign operations. The advantages necessary for direct investments may consist of technological superiority, managerial expertise, better sources of finance, or a combination of these advantages.

The U.S. and European firms that early invested abroad all possessed such advantages. In general, the advantages of the U.S. firms lay in the ownership of novel products and processes that appealed to the high-income, labor-saving needs of the American consumers, while those of the European firms were based on the innovations typically directed toward material-saving processes and substitutes and products designed for either low-income or luxury consumers.

What then could we say about the advantages of Japanese spinning companies that invested and succeeded in China? In contrast to the sequence from *innovation* to export to foreign production for typical U.S. and European companies, Japanese spinners started with Western technology and seemed to follow a sequence from *imitation* to export to foreign manufacturing. If Japanese spinning companies had been mere technological followers, possessing no advantages that could be transferred to China and that could not be acquired by local spinners, they would have had much trouble combating local competition. What advantages did Japanese spinners enjoy over their local competitors? Professor Tien-Yi Yang will give an elaborate explanation of these advantages in his paper on foreign investments in China, and Professor Yosuke Kinugasa will explain the nature of the Japanese advantages by dealing with the evolution of Japanese overseas business after World War II.[32]

It should be noted, however, that an advantage over foreign competitors is a necessary though by no means sufficient condition for international expansion. One must add to this advantage the entrepreneurial energy and ability to exploit the advantage in an international setting. In addition to the earliest British pioneers who had made foreign direct investments by 1914, there were many other companies, including leaders of oligopolies, who might have done the same with their special skills and accumulated capital but chose not to do so and remained at home. Is it too much to say that a slackening of entrepreneurial drive among them produced this result?

Even if a firm possesses an advantage over foreign competitors and the energy to use this advantage, it does not necessarily develop overseas activities in the form of direct investment. The firm may have an alternative of selling products through exporting. In fact, most of the companies observed first sought to serve overseas markets through exporting from their home countries and then began to manufacture abroad. But the process of switching from exporting to foreign manufacturing was not the same. It seems that, while some firms went aggressively into foreign direct investments even though they could have maintained their overseas markets through exporting, many others were compelled to set up overseas plants because of the threat of losing their export market positions. The causes and processes of being involved in multinational manufacturing should cause further discussion during this conference.

NOTES

1. It is well known that Samuel Colt, the famous Yankee arms maker, set up Colt's Patent Repeating Arms Manufactory in Thames Bank, London, in 1852. Mira Wilkins calls this the first foreign branch plant of any American company, see *The Emergence of Multinational Enterprise: American Business Abroad from the Colonial Era to 1914* (Cambridge, Mass., 1970), pp. 29–30, 259. Four years later, however, the enterprise was sold to a few Englishmen. One of the reasons why Colt abandoned his British manufacturing project was his trouble with workmen who, as full-fledged gunsmiths, disliked Colt's new methods of production based upon the interchangeable parts system developed in the United States. For further information, see Jack Rohan, *Yankee Arms Maker: The Story of Sam Colt and His Six-shot Peacemaker* (New York, 1935) and Charles T. Haven and Frank A. Belden, *A History of the Colt Revolver* (New York, 1940).

    Another case of U.S. participation in foreign manufacturing by the time of the Civil War was a vulcanized rubber factory set up in Edinburgh in 1856 by five Americans who were partners in the U.S. firm of J. Ford and Company of New Brunswick, New Jersey. Like Colt's case, the entire U.S. shareholding was repatriated in the second half of the 1860s. See W. Woodruff, "The American Origin of a Scottish Industry," *Scottish Journal of Political Economy* (February 1955), John Dunning, *American Investment in British Manufacturing Industry* (London, 1958), and Mira Wilkins, *op. cit.*

2. The table below presents the book value of America's foreign lia-
    bilities, America's foreign investments, and America's foreign direct
    investments by types of industries in the years 1897, 1908, and 1914.

U.S. foreign liabilities (millions of dollars)

Items	1893	1908	1914
Securities	3145	6000	5440
Direct investments			1310
Short-term credit	250	400	450
Total	3395	6400	7200

U.S. investments abroad (millions of dollars)

Items	1893	1908	1914
Securities	50	886	862
Direct investments	635	1639	2652
Total	685	2525	3514

U.S. direct investments abroad (millions of dollars)

Types of industries	1893	1908	1914
Sales organization	56.5	83.5	169.5
Purchasing	5.0	5.0	9.0
Banking	10.0	20.0	30.0
Oil distribution	75.0	148.0	200.0
Oil production	10.5	75.5	143.0
Mining			
Precious metals	88.0	193.6	232.7
Industrial minerals	46.0	251.0	487.0
Agricultural enterprises	76.5	186.5	355.8
Manufacturing	93.5	296.0	478.0
Railways	143.4	161.4	255.1
Public utilities	22.1	85.0	133.2
Miscellaneous	8.0	133.0	159.0
Total	634.5	1638.5	2652.3

Source: Cleona Lewis, *America's Stake in International Investments* (Washington, D.C.,
          1938).

Some of these figures should attract our special attention. First,
while the size of U.S. foreign investments was small compared with
that of the major creditor nation of Great Britain ($18.3 billion in
1914), 75 percent of the total was by direct investments. Second,

the size of direct investments in 1914 was small compared with that of about \$78 billion in 1970. But, as Mira Wilkins pointed out in her book mentioned in footnote 1, it comprised a sum equal to 7.28 percent of the U.S. GNP for that year. This was about the same as the percentage of 8.03 in 1970. Third, manufacturing ranked below mining in the book value of U.S. direct investments abroad in 1914. But, it should be noted that although large minimum investment was needed to get the mining project started, U.S. foreign investments in manufacturing grew gradually, using reinvested profits in many cases.

3. Mira Wilkins, *op. cit.*, pp. 212–13. The list excludes the many corporations with single manufactories in foreign nations, such as the Burroughs Adding Machine Company in England. It also omits the numerous companies that established one or more plants in Canada, such as Computing-Tabulating-Recording Company (later IBM).

4. Tadakatsu Inoue, "Amerika no Kigyō ni yoru Shoki no Kaigai Seizōgyō Tōshi ni tsuite" (The emergence of multinational manufacturing by U.S. firms), *Kokumin Keizai Zasshi* (December 1980).

5. The word innovation as used here refers to first commercial introduction rather than the first invention of a product.

6. Mira Wilkins divides direct foreign investments into market-oriented and supply-oriented investments. While the former seeks to sell mainly within the host nation, the latter seeks to export from the host nation. See *The Maturing of Multinational Enterprise: American Business Abroad from 1914 to 1970* (Cambridge, Mass., 1974).

   In the case of supply-oriented manufacturing, the explanation of direct foreign investments is fairly straightforward. Such investments are based on available and relatively cheap resources. When we turn to market-oriented manufacturing, however, the situation becomes more complicated. Why, for example, should a corporation seek to serve a particular market through the establishment of a local subsidiary rather than through exporting or licensing?

7. As seen in the list, they were limited to a few companies such as American Tobacco or British-American Tobacco and Diamond Match.

8. For the concept "the demand lag," see Michael Posner, "International Trade and Technical Change," *Oxford Economic Papers* (October 1961) and Louis T. Wells, Jr. ed., *The Product Life Cycle and International Trade* (Boston, 1972), pp. 23–24.

9. According to Raymond Vernon's *Sovereignty at Bay* (New York, 1971), all of the ten specified U.S. firms (Colt, Singer, ITT, G. E. and its predecessors, Westinghouse Air Brake, Westinghouse Electric, Eastman Kodak, United Shoe Machinery, Davis Park, and American Radiator and Standard Sanitary's predecessor) that established their foreign manufacturing plants before 1900 had substantial exports prior to their foreign investments.

10. For information on Singer's overseas operations, see Robert B. Davies, "Peacefully Working to Conquer World Markets," *Business History Review* (Autumn 1969) and Mira Wilkins, *The Emergence of Multinational Enterprise* (Cambridge, Mass., 1970).

11. American Radiator opened its first overseas sales branch in London, in 1895, prior to investments in the French and British plants in 1898 and 1905. See Mira Wilkins, "An American Enterprise Abroad: American Radiator Company in Europe, 1895–1914," *Business History Review* (Autumn 1969).

    National Cash Register started in European business with the appointment of sales agents in 1885, then developed sales subsidiaries in London, Berlin, and Paris in the late nineties, and built its first European factory in Berlin in 1903. See Samuel Crowther, *John H. Patterson: The Romance of Business* (New York, 1924).

    Ford's export business was first conducted through R. M. Lockwood in New York, who was appointed export agent in 1903. Seven years later his position was replaced by a new foreign department manager whose office was in New York. About the same time, sales branches were set up in Paris and London. In 1911–12 an assembly plant to handle a small amount of manufacturing was built in Manchester, England. See Mira Wilkins and Frank Ernest Hill, *American Business Abroad: Ford on Six Continents* (Detroit, 1964).

12. Frank A. Southard, Jr., *American Industry in Europe* (Cambridge, Mass., 1931), p. 119. See also Mira Wilkins and Frank Ernest Hill, *op. cit.*, pp. 46–47.

13. Mira Wilkins, *op. cit.*, pp. 102–03.

14. W. S. Woytinsky and E. S. Woytinsky, *World Commerce and Governments* (New York, 1955), p. 191.

15. John M. Stopford, *op. cit.*, pp. 310, 326.

16. See footnote 2.

17. Imagine an entrepreneur who emigrates, starts a firm in his new homeland, finances the venture with money raised in his old homeland, then creates what John M. Stopford calls "expatriate"

investment. For a fuller description of this concept, see Stopford, *op. cit.*, pp. 305–06.

18. Stopford, *op. cit.*, pp. 316–17. Besides these fourteen companies, many other British companies had manufacturing facilities abroad before 1914. These facilities were often extremely small and represented little more than "outposts" in a network of selling agencies. For a list of typical "outpost" factories established by selected fifteen U.K. firms, see Stopford, *op. cit.*, p. 324.

19. Charles P. Kindleberger, *American Business Abroad* (New Haven, 1969), pp. 11–14.

20. Stopford, *op. cit.*, p. 318.

21. D. C. Coleman, *Courtaulds: An Economic and Social History* (Oxford, 1969), p. 105.

22. Lawrence G. Franko, *The European Multinationals: A Renewed Challenge to American and British Big Business* (London, 1976), p. 8.

23. The foreign manufacturing subsidiaries established or acquired before 1914 by parents from the U.S., U.K., and Continental Europe are respectively estimated at 122, 60, and 167. For further details, see Franko, *ibid.*, p. 10.

24. See footnote 1 and *ibid.*, p. 3.

25. *Ibid.*, p. 77.

26. *Ibid.*, pp. 24–25, 86–88.

27. Gen Numaguchi, "Nihon no Kaigai Jigyō Tōshi" (A Study of Japan's Foreign Investments), *Chiba Shodai Ronso* (December 1970), pp. 249–51. Also see Susumu Takamiya, ed., *Kaigai Keiei Senryaku* (Overseas Business Strategy) (Tokyo, 1970), pp. 293, 297.

28. For example, see Mitsuo Fujii and others, ed., *Nihon Takokuseki-kigyō no Shiteki Tenkai* (A Historical Study of Japan-based Multinational Enterprises), vol. I (1979).

29. Milagros C. Guerrero, *A Survey of Japanese Trade and Investments in the Philippines, with Special References to Philippine-American Reaction, 1900–1941* (Quezon City, 1967) provides insights into the prewar Japanese investments in Philippine manufacturing as well as mining. Of the limited manufacturing activities, one of the earliest was the O'Racca Confectionary established in 1907. See also M. M. Moorman, "The Emergence of Multinational Corporate Strategy in Japanese Manufacturing Companies" (Ph.D. diss., University of Washington, 1974).

30. Tetsuya Kuwahara, "Senzen ni okeru Nihon Bōseki Kigyo no Kaigai Katsudō" (The Overseas Operations of Japanese Cotton Spin-

ning Firms prior to the Second World War: The Case of Kanegafuchi Cotton Spinning Co.), *Rokkodai Ronshū* (April 1975). See also
his "The Business Strategy of Japanese Cotton Spinners: Overseas
Operations 1890–1931" in Akio Okochi and Shin'ichi Yonekawa,
ed., *The Textile Industry and its Business Climate: The Proceedings of
the International Conference on Business History 8* (Tokyo, 1982).

31. Charles Kindleberger, *op. cit.*, pp. 11–14. See also Stephen Hymer,
    "The International Operations of National Firms: A Study of
    Direct Foreign Investment" (Ph.D. diss., MIT, 1960).

32. See also M. Y. Yoshino, *Japan's Multinational Enterprises* (Cam-
    bridge, Mass., 1976), p. 69, which states, "The Japanese, unlike
    Americans, could hardly compete on the basis of innovative tech-
    nologies. Japanese manufacturers, however, . . . did have a unique
    advantage in the Keiretsu, the network of small independent manu-
    facturing firms loosely organized by a large trading company or
    manufacturing firm to complement one another's skills in perform-
    ing a variety of specialized manufacturing and distribution func-
    tions."

Japanese Firms' Foreign Direct Investment in the U.S.
—The case of Matsushita and others—

Yosuke Kinugasa
Yokohama City University

I. Purpose and Viewpoints of This Paper

Through case studies this paper aims to clarify both the actual conditions and the characteristics of Japanese firms' direct investment in the U.S. Studies on firms' foreign direct investment still need to be developed that remains premature. What is required most is to set up adequate viewpoints for analysis.

My viewpoint in this paper is based on the following points:

(a) Japanese firms' direct investment must be grasped systematically not only in the U.S. but also in other countries.

(b) The pattern of Japanese firms' direct investment must be compared with those of the U.S. or West European firms.

A number of case studies which I've done lead me to several contentions. And they can be summarized into two analyses.

1. Analysis 1

To analyze from the viewpoint of marketing, especially "product-market analysis," is effective and indispensable.

Marketing Approach

The pattern of foreign direct investment is strongly influenced both by the product characteristics and by the market characteristics. Therefore, it is necessary to make patterns clear through "product-market analysis" and marketing analysis. Marketing analysis further demands research on export marketing and exporting stage.

Application of PLC Model on an International Basis

The PLC (Product Life Cycle) model is a basic model developed in the field of marketing. By dividing the product life from birth to death into several stages, characteristics of products (including technology), market and competitive conditions can be made clear, and guidelines in applying proper marketing tools on each stage can be shown.

Application of the PLC model was originally limited to within one nation; but in line with firms' internationalization, this model has come to be used at a multi-national or international level. This can be regarded as a matter of course and will lead us to a new approach.

Japanese firms' products can be divided into three types:
(1)   Products with the PLC starting point in Japan
(2)   Products with the PLC starting point in Europe
(3)   Products with the PLC starting point in the U.S.

In considering Japanese firms' direct investment in the U.S., whether a product has the PLC starting point in Japan or in the U.S. is a matter of great importance. In this sense, the above classification is quite essential for this paper's analysis, and I have proved its validity through a considerable number of case studies. This classification is one of the results of applying the PLC model on an international basis. A clue is given to questions such as how products with the PLC starting point in the U.S. came to be manufactured in Japan, why Japan became a large exporter of those products, and why those have become objects of direct investment by Japanese firms. Concerning these questions, it suffices to say that the PLC model is applicable to understanding international transfer of technology, shifts of production location, and changes in the direction of the flow of international product transactions.

Three Types of Product

Proposed cases on this paper are selected according to the above classification. (Caution: the staring point in PLC does not refer to where research and development was initiated but where the product started to be massively produced and put on a commercial basis.)

(1)   Products with the PLC starting point in Japan

Typical examples are soy sauce and "Ajinomoto" (here, not the company's name, but the brand name for monosodium glutamate). Most of products of this type have been seen in the foodstuff industry. Recently the number of both products and industries of this type have been increasing. Video tape recorders (VTRs) can be regarded as such a product. This paper will deal Kikkoman Co., a soy sauce company, for a case study.

(2) Products with the PLC starting point in West Europe

Watches, cameras, motorcycles, small-sized cars, beer and whisky are among the products of this type. They were introduced in the early stage of Japanese industrialization. After their introduction, "originality" (mass-production method is a part of it) has been at-tributed to those products, and now many of them are regarded as Type 1 products. Honda, a vehicle-manufacturing company, will be a supplementary example of Japanese firms' direct investment in the U.S. in Type 2 products.

(3) Products with the PLC starting point in the U.S.

The majority of products that Japanese firms have dealt in since World War II are of this type, ranging from home electric appli-ances to computers. After World War II, products with the PLC starting point in Europe were often transferred into Japan by way of the U.S., and these are also regarded as products of this type. In this case study, Matsushita is an appropriate example.

2. Analysis 2

Foreign direct investment (in manufacturing) and exporting are closely interrelated. It is not until exporting is fully considered that a proper understanding of direct investment in the U.S. will be made possible.

The trend in recent studies is to put so much emphasis on foreign direct investment in manufacturing that the importance of export-ing activities is overlooked. But analysis of exporting is a key factor in a systematic grasp of foreign direct investment. By deepening this analysis, we can ascertain close the relationship between exporting and direct investment.

Degree of Maturity of Exporting

Exporting activities vary according to the degree of maturity, ranging from a primitive level to a highly elaborate one.

Direct exporting is regarded as the higher level in comparison with indirect exporting. Direct exporting takes forms ranging from exporting through orders by foreign importers to exporting on the basis of firms' own local marketing systems with overseas sales subsidiaries, and further, to exporting based on international marketing systems set up by linking sales subsidiaries together throughout the world. In this way, the degree of maturity of exporting differs from one case to another. Its determining factors are necessity of exporting, firms' competence, experience, know-how inherent to export and, what's more, the types of products. Regarding Japanese firms, exporting has been fixed as the core of growth strategy. In most cases, highly sophisticated development in exporting can be found. This is the reason why research on Japanese firms' exporting provides us with a large amount of important data.

Here, attention must be paid to the fact that direct foreign investment is usually defined only as the establishment and operation of overseas manufacturing subsidiaries; but where overseas sales subsidiaries have already been operated at the exporting stage, the question arises whether the establishment (and operation) of overseas sales subsidiaries is included in foreign direct investment or not. From the standpoint that exporting and foreign direct investment are interrelated, as a necessity we must consider the establishment (and operation) of overseas manufacturing subsidiaries and sales subsidiaries at the same time. Both are supposed to belong in the category of foreign direct investment. In this paper, however, according to the common terminology, the term "foreign direct investment" is applied only to the establishment (and operation) of overseas manufacturing subsidiaries, and not to that of overseas sales subsidiaries.

Capabilities at Exporting Stage

The relationships between exporting and foreign direct investment are usually recognized as: exporting → import restrictions → foreign direct investment.

In case import restrictions are imposed or predicted in advance, both belong in the category of defensive (=market-protective) foreign direct investment. The opposite type is aggressive (=positive) foreign direct investment, aiming at effective utilization of local management resources, reduced transportation costs, higher profitability and efficiency (cf. the case of Kikkoman).

As for defensive foreign direct investment, however, a detailed analysis shows that not all exporting firms make foreign direct investment by overcoming import restrictions. The fact is that restrictions work as screening: some firms give up exporting and others select a new alternative of setting up production plants abroad. It is important to check the capabilities which leads to go through the screening or drop out. The capabilities accumulated during the exporting stage must be paid much attention. The analysis of these capabilities will be a major task of this paper and will be expected to shed light on the reason why Japanese firms were much later in making direct investment in advanced countries than in less developed countries (cf. the case of Matsushita).

II. Case Study: Matsushita

1. Before World War II
1-1. Characteristics of Matsushita's overseas activities

Matsushita's overseas activities were thoroughly based on the characteristics of the companies domestic activities. They can be summarized as follows:
- Exporting products closely related to the masses needs in foreign countries
- Setting Matsushita's own market segments and targets which meet the needs of local markets
- Thorough product differentiation
- Developing overseas markets under Matsushita's own brand
- Arranging a marketing network with a system of "one agency for each country"
- Price setting for export, adding a considerable amount of margin
- Positive and comprehensive utilization of marketing tools in the area of home electric appliances. In prewar days Matsushita's policies mentioned above were quite unique in the Japanese electric industry.

Matsushita has rapidly grown to gain the top rank in the domestic market, dealing in both Matsushita's pioneer products and follower ones. Matsushita's strategy which had taken major role in the success of its domestic marketing was fully applied to the development of overseas markets in each country.

1–2.   Foundation of export division (in 1932)

Getting away from unplanned trade, Matsushita took the first step toward direct export in 1932. At first, its exporting system was just nominal, and the real development was made after the establishment of Matsushita Trading Company. Until then Matsushita had concentrated on building its ready gained domestic business base and it attempted further growth in both domestic and overseas markets.

Major export products included almost all kinds of Matsushita's manufactured goods: dry batteries, battery lamps, radios, etc., which were acceptable in the South-east Asian markets.

Main export target areas were at first China and Manchuria, later all South-east Asian nations, such as Indonesia, the Philippines and Thailand.

1–3.   Establishment of Matsushita Trading Company

Through the rapid popularization of electric home appliances in Japan and the arrangement of Matsushita's nation-wide marketing channel, a mass-production system was required, and consequently the head office and new factories were founded in Kadoma, Osaka.

This led to large-scale reorganization, that is, the adoption of divisional organization in 1933, and Matsushita shifted from a private business to a joint-stock corporation in 1935. Under these circumstances it became necessary for Matsushita to undertake direct and planned exporting.

Matsushita Trading Company acted as both export agency for Matsushita's products and importer of electric appliances and materials.

1–4.   Administrative organization of overseas sales and production
        activities

At first, Matsushita set up sales offices one after another in Manchuria (1935–1937), and these offices were integrated into Matsushita, Manchuria in 1938.

Next, Matsushita set up sales offices and production plants in various parts of China (1938–1942) and Korea (1941–1942). Later, these sales offices and production plants were integrated into Matsushita-Dengyo Co. (Matsushita, China) and Matsushita, Korea, respectively.

In the case of Matsushita-Dengyo, it established itself out of the

Shanghai Plant when the plant, which had been under the direct control of Matsushita Dry Battery Co. (Matsushita's domestic subsidiary), began to manufacture many other products besides dry batteries.

In Korea, some production plants took the forms of Matsushita Dry Battery, Korea (Matsushita Dry Battery's subsidiary), and Matsushita Wireless, Korea (Matsushita Wireless's subsidiary). When in Japan Matsushita Dry Battery and Matsushita Wireless were integrated into Matsushita (parent company), all the production plants in Korea were also integrated into Matsushita, Korea.

These facts prove that Matsushita strictly applied the principle of divisional organization to overseas as well as domestic activity, and that it properly connected product division organization with area division organization. These characteristics in Matsushita were also found after World War II.

2. Post-World War II

2-1.   Establishment of world-wide perspective in business policy

After Japan's defeat, Matsushita lost its bases of foreign activity and had to start from nothing. Matsushita's business policy of prewar days was adapted in a more elaborate form to foreign countries as well as to Japan.

Kōnosuke Matsushita, president of Matsushita Electric Co. emphasized a world-wide perspective. In this policy, Matsushita intended to reduce remarkable gap during and after the war by means of the introduction of technology and know-how from abroad, and to make Matsushita's products the best in the world.

The results of those efforts included the following:

1) Establishment of Matsushita Electronic Industry Co. as a joint-venture with Phillips (1952). This company has contributed to the field of applied electronics.

2) Positive introduction from abroad of technology and know-how on products and production.

3) Establishment of the Central Research Institute (1953), which led to the reversal of the technological gap and the improvement of product quality and of the mass-production system. This made Matsushita's products among the best in the world.

4) Establishment of a group of the most advanced new plants in

the world. These plants operated efficiently during the period of
the boom in domestic home electric appliances. Matsushita won
the top share in Japanese electric industry through its positive
and elaborate marketing activities. And these domestic activities
made its exporting brisk.

2–2.   Establishment of a global image for Matsushita Electric Co.

VIPs in the politic and business from foreign countries visited the
above-mentioned group of new plants. Such visitors from abroad
amounted to about 3000 in a year. They recognized the superiority
of Matsushita's new plants, and that became influential PR to both
Japan and foreign countries, and thus remarkably heightened
Matsushita's corporate and brand image.

The quality and performance of Matsushita's products remarkably advanced through both operating the new plants and strengthening the examination system of products. In those days, Japanese
firms' products were generally thought of as cheap and inferior
("low-quality, low-price" products). But Matsushita's products
overcame this evaluation.

Several American publications carried articles on Matsushita's
chairman Kōnosuke Matsushita: *Time* (cover story, 1962), *Life* (in
a special issue on Japan, Kōnosuke's business philosophy was introduced in detail), *The New York Times* (a special report on Japan).

3. Exporting Activity

3–1.   The start of a new exporting system (1954)

1)   As key products in the exporting system, radios and dry batteries were selected. They were Matsushita's important products
and had stable demand abroad. In the case of radios, Matsushita
developed a novel approach to product design, quality, performance, mass-production technology and marketing channels. This
approach was unique in the Japanese electric industry at that
time and led Matsushita to gain the biggest market share in
Japan. Matsushita applied to overseas activities those methods
and know-how on business acquired through domestic activities.
This approach was also applied to Matsushita's other later products.

2)   Matsushita regarded the establishment of overseas marketing
channels as the key factor in expotring and tried through the ex-

port of radios to set up channels which would be available for other later products.

3)   Planned manufacturing of all radios for export was carried out. This is worthy of notice in that export shifted from spot-type to long-run and continual type. In the case of vacuum-tube radios, compared with those of other types, product planning and planned manufacturing exclusively for foreign markets, especially for the U.S., were achieved. This approach came to be used in exporting all other products.

4)   Radios were exported through close cooperation between the Radio Division and Matsushita Trading Co. Afterwards, when other kinds of products were exported, the close relationship was established between each division and the Trading Co.

It was not until this new exporting system was established in 1954 that Matsushita's exporting activity took off. Matsushita's new exporting system led itself to the solution of the following problems with which all the Japanese industries were confronted in those days:

1.   There were very few competitive products.
2.   There were a large number of limitations on exporting.
3.   Practically no products were feasible for exporting without modification of Japanese standards.
4.   Foreign marketing channels were very poor.

Matsushita took the initiative in foreign activities not only in less developed countries (LDCs) but also in the U.S. through the new exporting system started in 1954 and the selection of vacuum-tube radios as exporting products.

3–2.   Product policy for exporting to the U.S.

In the export of vacuum-tube radios, Matsushita decided the U.S. as its core market and established its basic exporting policy. The U.S. market was characterized by a high level and diversity of consumption and use. Even in the same product market, there were a large number of market segments: a segment which accepted products from LDCs with low quality and capacity, bad design and low price; a segment which accepted products with average level of quality, capacity and design and low price; a segment which accepted products with high quality and high price. This last segment newly appeared with the changes in life-style.

Matsushita exported to the U.S. products manufactured with the latest high technology, in conformity with the changes of life-style rather than "low-quality, low-price" products whose key competitive tool was price.

Matsushita's products which became popular in the U.S. market were fitted for the changes of life-style in the U.S. and built with the most up-to-date technology.

The new exporting system was a great success for a radios: the amount of exported radios reached 80% of the total sales in the Radio Division. In this stage, exporting was very important for the Radio Division and merchandising of radios was carried out corresponding with diversified consumption and use in the U.S. And these radios later came to be sold all over the world. In the new exporting system, Matsushita used the U.S. markets as a pilot farm for product diversity and an index of forecast for sales all over the world. So the characteristic point is that from the beginning Matsushita directed its export to the U.S. and advanced countries. This is shown in Table 1.

This approach was later successful in exporting tape recorders, black-and-white and color TV sets, and Matsushita's other products. Each division followed the exporting method pioneered by the Radio Division.

3-3.   Establishment of Local Marketing Systems

As obviously shown in its exporting policy, Matsushita laid the groundwork enforcing product differentiation in order to set the higher prices through products' originality. For that reason, the adaptation to changing life-styles and the possession of both the latest high technology and devices were required. This meant getting away from standardized products.

When the degree of standardization was not so high, Matsushita tried to establish local marketing systems by means of high pricing, promoting its own brand, and strengthening local marketing channels.

The promotion of Matsushita's own brand reflected Matsushita's overall marketing abilities (product, price, channel, advertising, PR, etc.). Nearly 80% of Matsushita's products were sold with Matsushita's brand, while very few other Japanese electric firms (except SONY) sold their products under their own brand in 1972.

TABLE 1   Matsushita's Local Sales Subsidiaries.

Area (country)	Year of establishment	Products
U.S.	1959	R, D, B, S, CTV, B/W TV
West Germany	1962	R, TV, TR, etc.
Hawaii	1963	R, TV, TR, S, etc.
Peru	1966	DB, R, TV, TR, EA
Canada	1966	R, TV, TR, S, EA
Costa Rica	1967	DB, R, TV, TR, EA
France	1968	R, TV, TR, S, etc.
Mexico	1970	T, VTR, CTV
Panama	1970	R, TV, TR, EA
Thailand	1970	DB, R, TV
Sweden	1972	R, TV, DB
West Germany	1972	commodity for PX electronic parts
Italy	1972	DB, Shaver
U.K.	1972	R, TV, TR, EA
Venezuela	1972	R, TV, TR, S
San Salvador	1973	DB, R, TV, Anp
Belgium	1973	Wireless, EA
Brazil	1974	TV, TR, DB, Wireless, R, Electric Calculator DB
Guatemala	1974	EC, DB, R, TV, TR
Singapore	1974	DB, R, TV, Parts
Belgium	1975	DB
Sweden	1975	Supplemental parts
Denmark	1975	EA
Malaysia	1976	TV, S, EA
Panama	1976	R, TV, TR, EA
Ecuador	1976	Wireless, EA
Switzerland	1976	Wireless, EA

Notes: R: Radios,   TV: Television sets,   CTV: Color TV sets,   B/W TV:
Black-and-white TV sets,   EA: Electric Applicances,   DB: Dry Batteries,
TR: Transistors,   S: Stereos.

As an important means of strengthening overseas marketing channels, Matsushita at first founded a sufficient number of foreign
sales subsidiaries in advanced countries: such as Matsushita, U.S.
(1960), Hamburg (1962), Hawaii (1964) and Canada (1967). In
less developed countries, the spread of sales subsidiaries was slower.

Later I will describe how local marketing systems developed with
a sales subsidiary as the center.

4. Overseas Production

4–1. Direct investment in LDCs

After the start of the new exporting system, the field of products rapidly expanded and their exporting was promoted. Exports were directed not only to the U.S. but to the whole world. Subsequently, like other Japanese electric industry firms, Matsushita began to undertake direct investment in LDCs.

Most of the subsidiaries in LDCs initially produced dry batteries, because (1) they were highly standardized and technologically simple, (2) they needed a limited number of parts, and (3) they easily reached at an appropriate size of production. Then the items and volume of production gradually increased.

The motive of direct investment in LDCs was usually to defend the market against the protective tariff (or import restrictions) by local governments. At first it was usual for Matsushita to undertake local-market-oriented, joint-venture-type and small-scale direct investment. However, in the 1970s Matsushita achieved a considerable growth in production size, selling products to both local markets and third-country markets.

Matsushita also founded wholly-owned subsidiaries, as in Singapore and Malaysia (1972) to deal in compressors for refrigerators. When Matsushita dispatched managers or engineers to overseas subsidiaries, it made the subsidiaries pay management or technology instruction fees, just as it did in Japan.

4–2. Matsushita's Direct Investment (manufacturing) in the U.S.

Matsushita's direct investment for selling in the U.S. was realized in the form of Matsushita, U.S. in 1959. But it was a local sales subsidiary aimed only to expand exporting to the U.S. It was not until the establishment of Matsushita Electric, Puerto Rico in 1965 that Matsushita's direct investment (manufacturing) in the U.S. was begun.

1) The establishment of Matsushita, Puerto Rico (1965)

The first step in Matsushita's direct investment in the U.S. was investment in Puerto Rico, a self-governing commonwealth. This investment can be understood as investment in an underdeveloped area near the U.S. (as in the case of Mexico), rather than investment to advanced country. Matsushita's investment in Puerto Rico deserves high praise, in that it was made before the reinforcement

TABLE 2   Matsushita's Local Manufacturing Subsidiaries.

Area (Country)	Year of establishment	Products
Thailand	1961	R, DB, Parts, CTV
Thaiwan	1962	R, S, EA, Parts
Puerto Rico	1965	R, S, B/W TV
Mexico	1965	R
Peru	1966	DB, R, CTV, TR
Costa Rica	1966	DB, R, S
Taiwan	1966	Carbon Bar
Malaysia	1966	DB, S, EA, Parts
Tanzania	1966	DB, R, TR
Brazil	1967	DB, R, S, TR, CTV
Philippines	1967	DB, R, S, TR, EA
Australia	1968	CTV, B/W TV, S
Venezuela	1969	S, Parts, B/W TV
Indonesia	1970	T, TR, Parts, EA
Belgium	1970	DB
Vietnam	1971	B/W TV, R
Singapore	1972	Refrigerator Compressors
Malaysia	1972	Room airconditioning
India	1972	DB
India	1972	DB
Malaysia	1972	Parts
Canada	1972	CTV
Spain	1973	Vacuum cleaner, air-cooling and heating facilities
Iran	1973	Rice cooker, juicer
Korea	1973	R, CTV, B/W TV
Brazil	1974	CTV, R, S, DB, TR
U.S.	1974	CTV, B/W TV
U.K.	1974	CTV
Philippines	1975	Refrigerators, washers

Notes: R: Radio,   TV: Television sets,   CTV: Color TV sets,   B/W TV: Black-and-white TV sets,   DB: Dry Batteries,   S: Stereos,   EA: Electric Appliances,   TR: Transistors.

of import restrictions by the U.S. and when other Japanese electric firms took no notice of that country. Major advantages of this direct investment were as follows:

1.   Although the market of Puerto Rico itself was not large, it was near the large U.S. market.

2. Puerto Rico was in the same tariff area as the U.S., and products made in Puerto Rico were regarded as "Made in U.S.A." and could be sent to the continental U.S. market tariff-free.

3. New companies in Puerto Rico could receive government aids of various kinds.

4. In Puerto Rico, it was possible for Matsushita to utilize comparatively cheap labor.

Matsushita's investment in Puerto Rico at that time aimed not merely to pursue comparative cost advantage but also to cope with the uncertainty of the U.S. market and to penetrate the U.S. market with products regarded as "Made in U.S.A." The investment in Puerto Rico may be regarded as a prestage of Matsushita's direct investment (manufacturing) in the U.S. But the establishment of Matsushita, Puerto Rico cannot be understood as full-scale direct investment (manufacturing) in the U.S.

2) Acquisition of Motorola's TV Division (1974)—Full-scale direct investment in manufacturing in the U.S.

As a result of the U.S. government's strengthening of import restrictions in the 1970s, the interest in manufacturing in the U.S. grew very remarkably among Japanese electric firms. Each firm made efforts at planning direct investment in the U.S., but Sony and Matsushita were able to carry out direct investments in the U.S. at an early stage. Why did Matsushita and Sony succeed in this direct investment so early? To answer these questions will make it clear what capabilities are required of Japanese firms in making direct investment in the U.S., a key factor for my analysis.

Sony was the first Japanese electric firm to realize direct investment in the U.S. Sony constructed new plants for color TV in San Diego, California, and started production in 1972. Matsushita's direct investment was realized by taking over Motorola's TV Division and its plants.

The difference was that Sony realized its investment by means of construction of new plants, and Matsushita by means of takeover. But these two firms had far more common points than differences, in direct investment in the U.S.

4-3. Characteristics of Matsushita's direct investment (manufacturing) in the U.S.

1. Matsushita established a new export system after World War II, in 1954. Since that time, Matsushita has regarded the U.S. market as the most important area for exporting and has concentrated on product development for the U.S. market.
2. Matsushita realized synergy (joint effects) through kinds of know-how that it acquired at the exporting stage. It is a very important requirement for success in overseas production to manufacture those products which a company has already accumulated experiences and know-how in its own country. In case of Matsushita, this requirement was fully satisfied. Matsushita realized much synergy through combining those advantages in products and technology which have been acquired at the exporting stage with its own marketing systems in the U.S. market.

    In addition, experiences in its U.S. sales subsidiary, which was in the core of Matsushita's own marketing system in the U.S., brought about much synergy to the establishment (and operation) of Matsushita's manufacturing subsidiaries in the U.S.
3. Matsushita's basic policy of direct investment in the U.S. was to establish a full-scale production system for parts as well as finished products. Matsushita produced not only TV sets but also stereo and video tape recorders (VTRs) and other products.

III. Capabilities Necessary for Direct Investment in the U.S.
(Comparison among Japanese electric firms)

1. General Characteristics of Growth Strategies of Japanese Firms

A number of Japanese firms have manufactured "products with the PLC starting point in the U.S.", and put them at a core of growth strategies and attained high-level growth. This applies best to electric firms including Matsushita. Here, through comparison between Matsushita and other Japanese electric firms, I would like to clarify general characteristics of growth strategies of Japanese electric firms, particularly of strategies of direct investment in the U.S. Figure 1 shows the characteristics of growth strategies of Japanese firms, in particular, electric firms. The following major points are shown in Fig. 1.

1) Introduction of technology and importance of its timing.

TABLE 3. Three Types of Product Exporting by Japanese Firms.

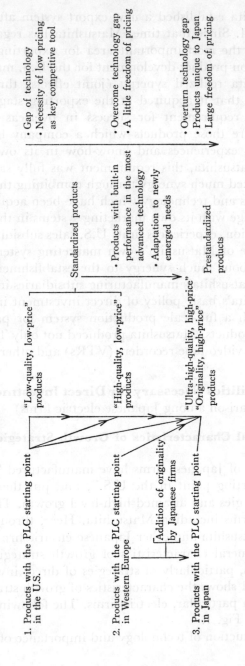

- Gap of technology
- Necessity of low pricing as key competitive tool

- Overcome technology gap
- A little freedom of pricing

- Overturn technology gap
- Products unique to Japan
- Large freedom of pricing

Standardized products
- Products with built-in performance in the most advanced technology
- Adaptation to newly emerged needs

Prestandardized products

"Low-quality, low-price" products

"High-quality, low-price" products

"Ultra-high-quality, high-price"
"Originality, high-price" products

1. Products with the PLC starting point in the U.S.

2. Products with the PLC starting point in Western Europe

Addition of originality by Japanese firms

3. Products with the PLC starting point in Japan

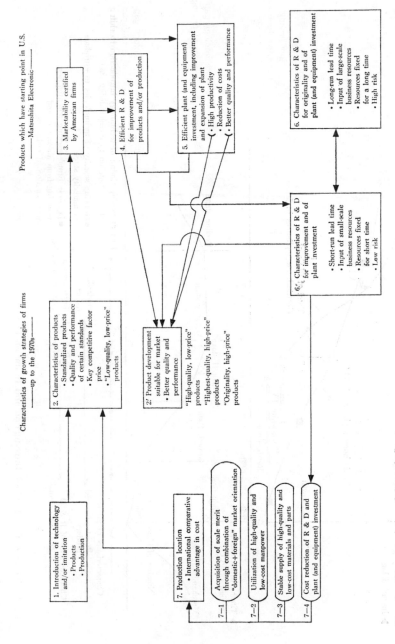

FIG. 1.   Characteristics of Growth Strategy.

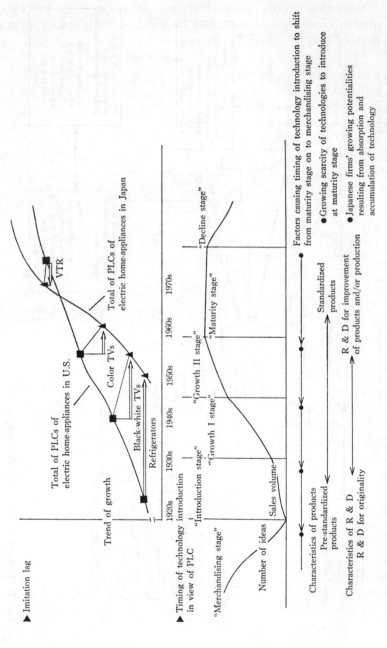

Fig. 2. Timing of Technology Introduction and Imitation Lag.

2) Shift away from "low-quality, low-price" products to "high-quality, low-price" ones, and further, to "originality (ultra-high-quality), high-price" ones.

3) Marketing strategies for each type of product.

4) Secrets of high-level growth of Japanese firms

I will make clear these problems, using Fig. 1.

1-1. Introduction of technology and its timing

[BOX 1] Introduction of technology from abroad or imitation. This is necessary whenever products with the PLC starting point in the U.S. or in other countries are manufactured in Japan. Japanese firms succeeded in introducing smoothly and intensively for a short term the technology of products and/or production which had been developed in the U.S. or in other countries.

Factors which made this possible were the following (compared with those in developing countries today):

1) Technological education was high-level in Japan.

2) Capacity for absorption of technology (including accumulation of technology in the past) was very high.

3) Introduction of technology was the core of top management's policy in Japanese firms.

4) U.S. firms easily transferred technology to other countries.

5) Japanese management systems also contributed much to introduction of technology. For example, the lifetime employment system suppressed the oppositions to the introduction of technology, and ringi system had the effects of obscuring where responsibility lay for the introduction of technology.

When we analyze introduction of technology, its timing is very important. As shown in Fig. 2, Japanese electric firms introduced or imitated technology of products with the PLC starting point in the U.S. After World War II, refrigerators, washers and cleaners were products that brought about an electric home-appliances boom in Japan. These products spread rapidly in the 1920s in the U.S. The imitation lag for these products is about 30 years. Here imitation lag means the time lag at the start of manufacturing between the U.S. and Japan. But afterward, the imitation lag of black-and-white TV and that of color TV was remarkably shortened. In the case of color TV, Japan started to adopt mass-production system earlier than did the U.S. It was worthy of notice that the complete reversion of imitation lag is shown in the case of VTR. Shortening of imitation lag means that the timing of Japanese firms' introduction of technology shifted forward to an earlier stage, that is, from the maturity, growth I, II stage, to the introduction, R & D stage. When introduction of technology occurs at the maturity stage of PLC in the U.S., as in the case of refrigerators, products and technology of production usually get standardized and leveled among other firms. We call such products standardized products. It is notable that such standardization and leveling promote international technology transfer. Products in [BOX 2] are such standardized products. As timing of technology introduction shifts to introduction stage or R & D stage of PLC in the U.S., characteristics of products come to be prestandardized. Factors which promote to shift timing of introduction of technology from maturity stage to R & D stage are: 1) growing scarcity of technologies to introduce at maturity stage and 2) Japanese firms' growing potential for introduction of more advanced technology through absorption and accumulation of introduced technology. In addition, the shift of timing from maturity stage to R & D stage has a great influence on the characteristics of R & D, causing a shift from R & D for improvement to R & D for originality. R & D for originality, unlike R & D for improvement is very risky, but has much more possibilities of attributing originality to products. This shift of timing also causes a shift from "low-quality, low-price" products to "high-quality, low-price" products and to "originality (ultra-high-quality), high-price" products.

Most products at the early stage of electric home-appliances boom in Japan were at the maturity stage of PLC in the U.S. They were standardized products. It is not too much to say that the main products which made Japanese firms' high growth possible after World War II were these standardized products. Let us analyse the growth strategies of Japanese firms, with special reference to these standardized products.

1–2. Characteristics of products

[BOX 2] When products and technology of production are standardized and leveled, low pricing is vitally important, but only if products are of a certain level of quality and performance. In the case of "products with the PLC starting point in the U.S.," Japanese firms began to manufacture after U.S. firms, so that products and other marketing tools, such as marketing channels, advertisement and sales promotion, were inferior to those of U.S. firms. Japanese firms had to make low pricing the only key competitive tool. These are general characteristics found at the growth II stage and the maturity stage in PLC (See Fig. 2).

1–3.   Certified Marketability

[BOX 3]   In case of standardized products (where introduction of technology occurs at growth II stage and maturity stage in the PLC in the U.S.), marketability of products is generally certified by American firms, and on a world-wide scale, because in growth II stage in the PLC in the U.S. domestic production scale (P_D) becomes larger than domestic market scale (M_D). Then U.S. firms export positively $[P_D < M_D + M_F$ (overseas market scale)] and/or intend to make direct investments $[P_D + P_F$ (overseas production scale)$< M_D + M_F]$. In this way, they make efforts to solve market problems with their products from a world-wide perspective.

Through introduction of technology for products with certified marketability, Japanese firms were able to attain to the utmost the efficiency of R & D, of plant (and equipment) investment, and of overall business activities. It is not too much to say that the most important key to high growth of Japanese firms was in "certified marketability of products" [BOX 3], which is a property of standardized products. ¡Though this point has never been adequately discussed, it is of vital importance.

If marketability of products had had to be certified by Japanese firms, as was done by U.S. firms, then the situation would have been entirely different. As shown in [BOX 6], characteristics of R & D and plant (and equipment) investment are as follows: ① long-run lead time is necessary; ② input of large-scale business resources including funds is needed; ③ these resources are tied up for a long time; ④ Japanese firms are forced to take a high risk as to whether a product will be accepted or not.

In fact, Japanese firms avoided these risks and operated very efficiently.

1–4.   Efficient R & D for improvement

[BOX 4]   For products with certified marketability, R & D means

R & D for improvement corresponding to certified marketability. In the case of products at the maturity stage in PLC in the U.S., evaluation of technologies in the U.S. was low and U.S. firms tended to transfer technologies to other countries at relatively cheap prices without evaluating them from a world-wide perspective. Japanese firms acquired technologies for products with the PLC starting point in the U.S., at the maturity stage in the U.S., at relatively cheap prices, and at the same time they were able to take full advantage of R & D for improvement of products and technologies of production at the introduction and growth stage in PLC in Japan. For efficiency of R & D and high morale for it are the highest at the introduction and growth stage of PLC.

Japanese firms acquired technologies of "products with the PLC starting point in the U.S." and at the same time made R & D for improvement of products and technologies of production corresponding to certified marketability. So Japanese firms have gained much benefit by means of small-scale R & D expenditure. Compared with R & D for originality, R & D for improvement has the advantages of ① reduction of lead time, ② curtailment of business resources to be inputted, ③ mitigation of fixed resources, and ④ risk avoidance.

Japanese firms have emphasized both improvement of technologies for the sake of reduction of cost (positive improvement of production system including manufacturing technology and process) and improvement of products corresponding to the needs of the market.

1–5. Efficient plant investment

[BOX 5] For products with certified marketability, a mass-production system can be used from the beginning, and so plant (and equipment) investment is made positively. Products when manufactured by such mass-production system at a low price have good marketability.

Japanese firms realized efficient plant (and equipment) investment ([BOX 5]) on the basis of the conditions both of certified marketability ([BOX 3]) and of R & D for improvement which aims to reduce manufacturing cost ([BOX 4]) and to develop products corresponding to market needs. Plant (and equipment) investment as well as R & D often spoils elasticity of business administration. Plant (and equipment) investment of Japanese firms was made to products with certified marketability, and so high efficiency was maintained.

1-6. Development of products suitable for market and improving
      quality and performance

[BOX 2'] "Efficient R & D for improvement" ([BOX 4]) puts emphasis on ① reducing cost, on ② improving quality and performance of products, and ③ increasing their marketability; ② and ③ leads to "development of products suitable for market and improvement of quality and performance" ([BOX 2']), which contributes much to strengthening Japanese firms' international competitive power. This point will be discussed in detail below.

1-7. Realization of comparative cost advantage

[BOX 7] International comparative cost advantage—Production location in Japan

For standardized products, the key competitive tool is low pricing. Japanese firms manufacturing in Japan realized international comparative advantages in costs and consequently low pricing. Factors which brought about international comparative advantage in cost are ① pursuit of economies of scale through "domestic+foreign" market orientation, ② utilization of high-quality and low-cost manpower, ③ stable supply of high-quality, low-cost materials and parts, ④ cost reduction of R & D and plant (and equipment) investment. The most vital factor of these is pursuit of economies of scale through "domestic+foreign" market orientation based upon world-wide certified marketability ([BOX 3]). Characteristics of Japanese firms' growth strategies can be understood as "establishment of a world-wide supply base of standardized products."

Japanese firms realized competitive power through repetitive application of the circulatory process from [BOX 1] to [BOX 7] (Fig. 1) and established "a world-wide supply base of standardized products." The key factor which made Japanese firms' high growth possible was intensively introducing products one after another for a short run and putting them into this circulatory process.

But Japanese firms' growth strategies aiming to establish a world-wide supply base of standardized products suffered a hard blow from import restrictions of both less developed and advanced countries, and they were driven to drastic reorientation.

1–8.   Getting away from standardized products: Shift from [BOX 2] to [BOX 2′]

Today, Japanese firms are gradually getting away from standardized products.

Export products of Japanese firms, as shown in Table 4, are divided into three types. These three types are classified of products with the PLC starting point in the U.S. on the basis of technological and marketing gaps between U.S. and Japanese firms.

1) "Low-quality, low-price" products: products of this type are characterized technological gaps between Japanese and U.S. firms, so that low pricing has to be made a key competitive tool in order to cover gaps in quality and performance of products and marketing competence. Most Japanese firms started by exporting these products, which had the image of "cheap and inferior."

At an early stage, Matsushita got away from "low-price, low-quality" products. Matsushita's pricing policy was that whenever there were leading firms whose products' quality and performance and brand image excelled those of Matsushita, at first it strove to fill technological gaps, then developed its own original products, and finally made the highest pricing in the electric industry. We can find these characteristics in the case of radios. Matsushita began to produce radios in the 1930s. In those days, radios often went out of order. Matsushita attempted to produce "radios without trouble" by completely revising product specification and succeeded in attaining high quality and performance; as a result, it could charge the highest pricing in the industry. A few years later, after Matsushita reached the top in the sales of radios, it adopted a penetration pricing policy. These radios with high quality and performance can be classed as the above-mentioned "high-quality, low-price" products or "originality, high-price" products. And we can find these facts in Matsushita's activities.

2) "High-quality, low-price" products: products of this type show technological gaps between Japanese and the U.S. firms, or sometimes Japanese firms' technology is superior to that of U.S. firms. The major competitive tool in these products is low pricing, which is achieved through reduction of cost by mass production. Compared with "low-quality, low-price" products, this type of products gives greater freedom in pricing.

Table 4 Shift from Exporting Stage to Overseas Production Stage.

	Standardized products	"High-quality, low-price" products	Pre-standardized products
(1) Exporting stage			
1. Characteristics of products	"Low-quality, low-price" products	"High-quality, low-price" products	"Ultra-high-quality, high-price" products and/or "originality, high-price" products
2. Characteristics of market (in foreign countries)	Established market	Established market	New market (new needs)
3. Characteristics of competition	Competition with local firms Competition among Japanese firms	Competition with local firms Competition among Japanese firms	No competition with local firms Competition among Japanese firms
	Necessity of low pricing as a key tool No freedom of pricing	Necessity of low pricing as an important tool Freedom of pricing	No necessity of low pricing as a key tool Large freedom of pricing
4. Establishment of firms own marketing system (cf. Table 5)	Less efforts for firms to establish X →	→ Δ	More efforts for firms to establish → O
Import restrictions	Exist	Exist	Possibly exist
(2) Overseas production stage			
1. Key factor	On condition that is will meet the terms of international comparative advantage in cost	On condition that is will meet the terms of international comparative advantage in cost	Existence of market (more penetration to local market) No need to acquire international advantage
	Comparatively easy to attain	Difficult to attain	Easy to attain if there is a market
2. Location of production	In LDCs	In ACs	In both LDC and AC
3. Firm's effort	Risk dispersion joint venture pursuit of multinational market	Labor saving to avoid high wages improvement of productivity pursuit of multinational market	

The shift from "low-quality, low-price" products to "high-quality, low-price" products was what all Japanese firms aspired to, and they positively pursued this shift through "efficient R & D improvement" ([BOX 4]).

Matsushita's basic policy of getting away from Type 1 products dates from prewar days. After World War II, Japanese electric firms competed to introduce products with the PLC starting point in the U.S. and to produce them. They plunged into fierce price competition in the case of radios, which were at the maturity stage of radios in Japan, and even in the case of washers, refrigerators, and black-and-white TVs, which were at the introduction stage in the PLC in Japan.

3) "Originality (ultra-high-quality), high-price" products; this type of product was produced by filling and/or reversing the technological gap between Japanese and U.S. firms, and by means of Japanese firms' unique devices. Japanese firms have great freedom of pricing on products of this type, because of their "originality." In the 1970s many Japanese firms succeeded in developing and merchandising products of this type, and Matsushita was a pioneer. Matsushita merchandised various kinds of products with the most up-to-date device as a result of technological innovation. Matsushita's such basic merchandising policy was adopted in Matsushita's all products. Matsushita and SONY can be regarded as the earliest Japanese electric firms that developed "originality, high-price" products. But from an international point of view almost all Japanese electric firms today have entered the stage of Type 3 products.

After World War II, the drastic, concentrative and competitive introduction of products with the PLC starting point in the U.S. drove Japanese electric firms into violent price competition at the introduction stage in PLC in Japan. Other Japanese electric firms persistently chased Matsushita and SONY, which pioneered in producing Type 3 products. As the result, the product level of the Japanese electric industry was raised drastically. Today "originality, high-price" products are not the possessions only of Matsushita and SONY, but from an international point of view, they are the common property of Japanese firms group as followers against U.S. firms group as forerunners. This is true not only of Japanese electric firms but also of many other Japanese industries.

Originally, "originality, high-price" products of Japanese firms should be found among products with the PLC starting point in Japan. But in fact there are only a few such products, like miso, soy sauce, 'Ajinomoto' (monosodium glutamate), etc. Conversely, products to which originality has been attributed by Japanese firms, such as cameras, watches, motorcycles, VTRs, transistor radios, and radio-TV cassette-tape recorders, have come to be Japanese firms' main products.

2. "Originality, high-price" Products and Direct Investment in the U.S.

The export products of Japanese firms shifted from "low-quality, low-price" products to "high-quality, low-price" products, and to "originality, high-price" products. During the exporting stage Japanese firms gradually developed advanced and sophisticated marketing systems. The above-mentioned three types of products have exerted a serious influence on export marketing. Setting up a firm's own local marketing systems abroad and developing marketing strategy on the basis of those systems can be achieved successfully in the case of "originality, high-price" products.

At first Japanese firms have positively exported standardized products: "low-quality, low-price" products and "high-quality, low-price" products. These standardized products are subject to import restrictions by host countries, because in LDCs such products are located in the first stage of the industrialization plan, and because in the U.S. and other advanced countries, Japanese products exert pressure on domestic firms. Foreign direct investment is the important alternative to import restrictions. In the case of standardized products, low price is the most effective marketing tool, so it is necessary for direct investment to secure the international comparative advantage in cost. With production located in the U.S. and other advanced countries, it is practically impossible to satisfy this condition. Generally, Japanese firms coped with the import restriction of advanced countries by changing their export products from standardized products to "originality (ultra-high-quality) high-price" products, while they coped with the import

48   Y. Kinugasa

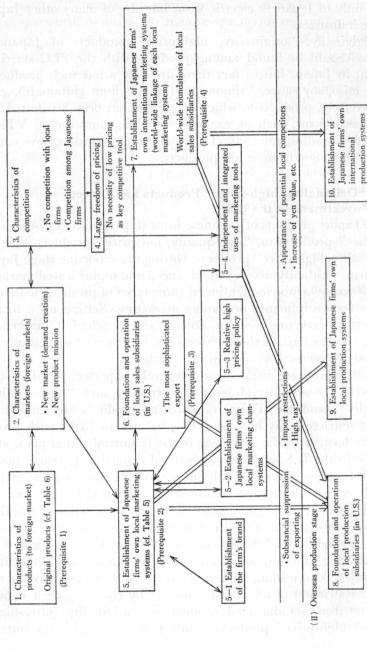

Fig. 3.   Direct Investment in the U.S. (Integrated Analysis of Three Cases).

restrictions of LDCs by means of direct investment. That was the reason why foreign direct investment of Japanese firms was concentrated LDCs.

"Originality, high-price" products can scarcely be the object of import restrictions. Even if such restrictions should be applied, Japanese firms could cope with them by direct investment. As the key factor for direct investment in the case of "originality, high-price" products, the penetration into the local market is far more important than the securing of international comparative advantage in cost. So direct investment in the U.S. is impossible for standardized products, but possible for "originality, high-price" products. This is reflected in the fact that most Japanese firms' direct investment in the U.S. is concentrated on "originality, high-price" products. It can be said that the basic prerequisite for direct investment in advanced countries is the development of "originality, high-price" products.

3. Prerequisites for Direct Investment in the U.S.

Figure 2 shows the major prerequisites for direct investment in the U.S. As stated above, the basic prerequisite is to develop "originality, high-price" products. When products are "originality" or "prestandardized" ([BOX 1]), the market can be characterized as new market and/or new product mission ([BOX 2]), the characteristics of competition can be shown as ① Japanese firms' strong competitive power, ② no strong local competitors, and ③ if any, competitors among Japanese firms ([BOX 3]).

In case of "originality, high-price" products, "establishment of Japanese firms' own local marketing systems" ([BOX 5]) is made possible; this consists of "establishment of firms' own brand" ([BOX 5–1]), "establishment of firms' own local marketing channel" ([BOX 5–2]), "adoption of high pricing policy" ([BOX 5–3]), which is made possible by "Japanese firms' large freedom of pricing" ([BOX 4]), and "firms' own integrated application of all marketing tools" ([BOX 5–4]).

It is the second prerequisite to establish Japanese firms' own local marketing system.

It must be noted here that local marketing systems take far more lead time than local production systems to put into full operation.

TABLE 5   Feasibility of Establishment of a Firms' Own Marketing System.

	"Low-quality, low-price" products	"High-quality, low-price" products	"Ultra-high-quality, high-price" products
Establishment of the firm's brand	×	× ←— △ —→ ○	○
Competitive technology	×	× ←— △ —→ ○	○
Establishment of the firm's marketing channel	×	× ←— △ —→ ○	○
Exporting countries → Importing countries	×	△ →	○
Local marketing channel	×	× ←——— △ → ○	○
Great freedom of pricing	×	× ←— △ —→ ○	○
Independent and integrated uses of marketing tools	×	× ←— △ —→ ○	○
		↑ Less effort for firms to establish	↑ More effort for firms to establish

So it is necessary for local marketing systems to be operated in advance to keep pace with local production systems.

Most Japanese firms already established their own local marketing systems at the exporting stage; consequently, when their production systems were started, their marketing systems were in full operation, so that Japanese firms had only to set up their production systems in those countries where their marketing systems were in full operation.

This was an advantage financially as well as administratively, since the investment in a marketing system could be made at a different time from that in a production system.

The third prerequisite is to establish local sales subsidiaries at exporting stage ([BOX 6]). Most successful Japanese exporting firms founded local sales subsidiaries at the exporting stage ([BOX 6]). The foundation and operation of local sales subsidiary reflects the development of the most sophisticated exporting activity. The accumulated experience and know-how (in such field as financial management, personnel management and R & D) gained through its foundation and operation can be applied to the foundation and operation of local production subsidiaries. For instance, in the field of financial management, know-how for international financial operation (foreign exchange risk hedge or tax saving by means of "leads and lags" and/or "transfer pricing") acquired through the utilization of local sales subsidiaries, is applicable to local production subsidiaries. In personnel management, local sales subsidiaries recruit and train local sales managers, salesmen, or clerks, financial staff, and service engineers. In setting up production subsidiaries all newly required is to recruit workers, foremen, engineers, or production managers. Even then know-how that has been acquired through the operation of local sales subsidiaries is applicable.

The fourth prerequisite is existence of firm's own international marketing system ([BOX 7]). International marketing system is set up by linking sales subsidiaries founded throughout the world, each of which is the core of local marketing system.

When local marketing systems are linked with an international marketing system, the size of local production subsidiaries is not restricted by the size of each local market. So an international marketing system functions as both a prerequisite and a spur to establishment of local production subsidiaries. Moreover, it offers substantial know-how for establishment of an international production system by linking production subsidiaries in different locations.

With special reference to Matsushita, a typical Japanese electric firm, we have analyzed the capabilities for making direct investment in the U.S. for products with the PLC starting point in the U.S. The focus of the analysis is on how a firm has developed its growth strategy. For comparison, the case of two other firms will be described: Kikkoman, a manufacturer of soy sauce and the other is Honda, a manufacturer of motorcycles and small-sized cars.

IV. Other Cases of Direct Investment in the U.S.

I would like to describe how Kikkoman and Honda have satisfied the prerequisites defined in Fig. 2, in comparison with Matsushita. Three firms were among the first Japanese firms to undertake direct investment in the U.S. and they deal with different types of products, Matsushita, products with the PLC starting point in the U.S., Kikkoman, products with the PLC starting point in Japan, and Honda, products with the PLC starting point in Europe.

1. Common Characteristics of the Three Firms

Top management in each of these firms had an international perspective and from the beginning regarded the U.S. market as the most important area for exportation.

a) In 1951 Matsushita set forth "management based on world-wide perspective." Since the establishment of new exporting system in 1954, Matsushita has a consistent policy to make both product development and planned production for the U.S. market, considering that the U.S. market plays a role of a pilot farm for product development and product diversification. (cf. the case of Matsushita)

b) In case of Kikkoman it restarted exports of soy sauce in 1954. Soy sauce is one of the originality products with the PLC starting point in Japan. At first, soy sauce was first introduced abroad by Dutch and Chinese buyers in the Edo period. Kikkoman began to export soy sauce for itself in the Meiji Era. In prewar days, target areas for soy sauce were China, Manchuria, Southeast Asia, North America, Brazil, etc., and its market target was mainly Japanese emigrants and settlers. But after World War II, Kikkoman focused on the U.S. market as its most important target area from the beginning, and changed its market target from Japanese-Americans to all Americans. Main reasons for the change of its market target were as follows:

1. In post-war days, Isseis (Japanese emigrants to the U.S. who had been major consumers of soy sauce) were becoming outnumbered by Niseis and Sanseis (second- and third-generation Japanese-Americans, who had assimilated into American life-style), and so the increase of consumption of soy sauce was quite hopeless.

2. In post-war days, American people in military service came to Japan from every parts of the U.S. and they knew soy sauce and used it.

Not only among all Japanese soy sauce firms, but also all Japanese firms, Kikkoman's top management has had a distinguished international perspective. As early as 1873, Kikkoman won an honorable prize at Vienna contest, and subsequently prizes were awarded in many international exhibitions. It can be said that these facts reflected Kikkoman's distinguished international perspective.

    c) Honda, like SONY, was founded after World War II. Honda emphasized "Management with world-wide perspective," and asserted: "To become No. 1 in Japan, Honda must become No. 1 in the world." And Honda made the U.S. market its most vital market area, like Matsushita and Kikkoman.

    These were striking similarities among these firms in business philosophy, international perspective and major export target area. The same can be said of many other firms doing positive business around the world, like SONY, Canon, Nikon, and many others.

2. "Originality, High-Price" Products—Prerequisite 1

How is "originality" attributed to products? As is shown in Table 6, there are various ways to attribute "originality" to products. "Products unique to Japan," are typical products manufactured in Japan, such as soy sauce and "Ajinomoto."

TABLE 6   Characteristics of "Originality" Products of Japan.

	Products unique to Japan	Innovative products	Ultra-high-quality mass-production and/or (improved type)	New product mission and/or new needs	Most advanced (mass) production technology (process)
Products with the PLC starting point in Japan					
Soy sauce	O	O	O	O	O
VTRs		O	O	O	O
Products with the PLC starting point in Western Europe					
Motorcycles			O	O (the U.S. market)	O
Cameras				O	O
Small cars				O	O
Products with the PLC starting point in the U.S.					
Color TVs (VTR)				O	O

Next, "innovative products" include such products as transister radios, radio-TV cassette-tape recorders, VTR, etc. To these products "originality" attributed through new devices as a result of technological innovation. The majority of Japanese firms' products are those which are only partially innovative.

"Ultra-high-quality products" are those which have reached the highest level in quality and performance through the improvement of existing products. Typical Japanese export products have the PLC starting point in the U.S. but are successful in filling and/or reversing the technological gap. "Products with new missions" are those to fill new needs or requirements. Japanese firms' motorcycles in the U.S., for example, have changed the image of motorcycles from vehicles for people in black leather jackets to vehicles for the general public.

Some put emphasis on originality of production technology when they talk about "originality products." Yet "originality" matters most only when the originality of technology brings forth original products. Details of "originality" products of the above three firms are shown in Table 6.

3. Establishment of Firms Own Local Marketing Systems and Sales Subsidiaries—Prerequisites 2 and 3

Each of the above three firms, making the U.S. market its most important target area and attributing "originality" to its products, was able to set up high-level and well-organized marketing systems in the U.S.

a)   Matsushita established its U.S. sales subsidiary (Matsushita, U.S.) in 1960 and, based on this subsidiary, set up its own marketing systems in the U.S. Matsushita's local marketing systems (both at home and abroad) were among the most sophisticated for Japanese firms.

b)   The uniqueness of soy sauce enabled Kikkoman to start positive efforts to establish its own brand ("Kikkoman") early in the Meiji Era. Awarded prizes in several international exhibitions, Kikkoman made efforts to establish its product image at home and abroad; it registered its trademark in California in 1879, Germany in 1886, and the entire continental U.S. in

1906. Further efforts were made to set up marketing channels in a "one agency for one nation" method.

There was, after World War II, a kind of turning point where Kikkoman began to shift its market target from Japanese-Americans to all Americans.

Then Kikkoman started positive advertising through TV, radio and magazines, and positive demonstration sales at stores. This promoted Americans to know more about soy sauce and, at the same time, about the superiority of Kikkoman's soy sauce. As a result, Kikkoman became a synonym for soy sauce in the U.S.

With the establishment of Kikkoman International Incorporated (1957), Kikkoman's marketing channels in the U.S. were expanded nationwide. In 1958 the Los Angeles Branch was established as the base for the West; in 1960 the New York Branch as the base for the East; and in 1965, the Chicago Branch as the base for the Midwest. Kikkoman's national channel network was realized, and sales balanced in each branch, 70 percent of sales were to Americans. In these respects, Kikkoman was different from other Japanese soy sauce distillers, which limited customers to Japanese residents in the West Coast market.

Like Matsushita, Kikkoman has set up elaborate marketing systems in the U.S. through exporting activities.

c) Honda established its own brand and thereby succeeded in setting up marketing systems in the U.S. The export of motorcycles to the U.S. was initiated by Honda on a full scale at the same time as the foundation of Honda, U.S. in 1959. At that time, the total sales volume of motorcycles was only 50,000 to 60,000 a year, and the motorcycle industry in the U.S. was regarded as a declining one. The image of motorcycles was extremely bad and unhealthy. Motorcycles were looked upon as a vehicle for people in black leather jackets, and dealers' shops were very small and difficult for the general public to visit. The first task for Honda, U.S. was to clear away such prejudice against motorcycles and to establish a healthy image for motorcycles.

The basic policy set forth by Honda, U.S. was to popularize motorcycles as the general public's new-type sports or leisure vehicles and as ways to cope with traffic congestion and parking difficulties.

Continuous efforts were made to familiarize the general public with the new image by means of advertising in well-known magazines such as *Life* or *Look*, to demonstrate motorcycles as modern commodities through exhibitions, and to recruit dealers who agreed with Honda's basic policy.

The process of popularizing motorcycles in the U.S. by Honda is quite similar to the case of soy sauce by Kikkoman. New missions or new uses were attributed to motorcycles by Honda and thus those motorcycles were brought to the U.S. as new products with new missions. Both Honda's motorcycles and Kikkoman's soy sauce were new products with new missions in the U.S. market, and their popularization required new market development or demand creation.

Honda's major competitors in the U.S. were Japanese firms, such as Kawasaki, Yamaha and Suzuki; there were only a few American or European firms in the market. The same situation could also be seen in the case of soy sauce, where Japanese firms took a major role, and there were only a few competitors with the Chinese brands.

It was characteristic for Honda to have constructed well-organized marketing systems in the U.S., including firms' own brand and marketing channels.

Again I would like to suggest that the establishment of marketing systems in the U.S. and the foundation (and operation) of U.S. sales subsidiaries have made an important contribution to the establishment and operation of U.S. production subsidiaries.

4. Establishment of International Marketing Systems

All the three firms set up excellent international marketing systems, though they differed in its scale. In Matsushita's case, it operated the largest number of overseas sales subsidiaries (cf. Table 1), and international marketing system which resulted from linking those subsidiaries together covered the world. Honda also set up such systems, while Kikkoman, compared with the other two, covered limited areas (advanced countries only) through its international marketing system.

The establishment of international marketing system is not only a prerequisite for foundation and operation of overseas production subsidiaries but also a prerequisite for the establishment of international production systems through the linking of production subsidiaries together.

The three cases give us sufficient information on the transition of firms' strategies from exporting to direct investment to U.S.

5. Full-scale Direct Investment in the U.S.

a) In the case of Matsushita, as mentioned above, it made a direct investment in Puerto Rico, the self-governing commonwealth territory of the U.S., in 1965. In 1974 it made full-scale direct investment in the U.S. itself, taking over Motorola's TV Division.

b) Kikkoman's direct investment in the U.S. actually began through the construction of a factory in Denver, Colorado, in 1892. But this factory, negligibly small-sized, produced soy sauce solely for Japanese emigrants.

After World War II, as a result of Kikkoman's marketing efforts, its sales of soy sauce in the U.S. increased remarkably by five times in ten years (1957–1966). In response to such a rapid increase, Kikkoman consigned local bottling to Wesley Salt Corp., California, in 1967. Through this consignment Kikkoman aimed to realize efficient transportation, to reduce transportation cost (in the case of soy sauce, transportation costs occupying a great part in price), and to develop products suitable for local needs.

Such consignment is, as it were, a stepping stone to local production, and this local bottling stage can be regarded as transitional stage to local production.

Kikkoman's full-scale direct investment started with the establishment of integrated production systems for soy sauce in Walworth, Wisconsin, and Kikkoman Foods International (manufacturing subsidiary) in 1971. Its planning of direct investment in the U.S. had already started in the early 1960s, on

the advice of Kikkoman International Incorporated (sales subsidiary in the U.S.) and of American food importers. In 1965
Kikkoman formally organized a special committee on direct
investment in the U.S., and in 1970 dispatched a survey mission.

And Kikkoman's direct investment in U.S. was accelerated
by Nixon Shock in 1971.

Kikkoman had made a prudent investigation, taking time
to arrive at an intercompany consensus for the firm's direct
investment in the U.S. Once the decision for direct investment
in the U.S. was made, the first steps were taken very swiftly.

Kikkoman had two product policies: (1) to manufacture ex-
actly the same soy sauce as it produces in its factories in Japan,
and make its soy sauce appeal to Americans' taste, and (2) to
develop and introduce products like "Teriyaki sauce" suitable to Americans' needs.

The merits of Kikkoman's direct investment in the U.S.
were as follows: (1) effectiveness in coping with the increase of
transportation costs and the decrease of Japan's exports owing
to the rise in value of the yen after 1971, (2) overcoming the
shortage of land for plants in Japan (average only 132,000–
165,000 m^2 per plant in Japan, 792,000 m^2 in Walworth,
Wis.), (3) availability of a cheap and stable supply of materials
(soybeans), (4) cutting down transportation costs of both importing raw materials and exporting products, (5) further
penetration into the local market.

Kikkoman made remarkable efforts (1) to build a plant
causing no environmental pollution, (2) to concentrate the
most advanced production technology in the most up-to-date
integrated production plant, (3) to contract not with a large-
sized consulting firm but with one offering specialized and
elaborate consultation in view of the uniqueness of soy sauce,
and (4) to gain more U.S. patents before direct investment in
the U.S. (562 patents in 1968, 875 in 1969, and 675 in 1970).

Kikkoman's direct investment in the U.S. was made not
because there were import restrictions but because it was
more profitable than exporting. The experience and know-
how which Kikkoman gained through its direct investment in

the U.S. were fully applied to its later direct investment in West Germany.

c) As for Honda, it well satisfied prerequisites for direct investment in the U.S. at a very early stage. But Honda's direct investment in advanced countries was begun with the establishment of Honda, S.A. (Belgium) in 1962. Honda started local production much earlier in Europe, at first mainly with KD (knock down), than in the U.S.

The reasons why Honda made no direct investment in the U.S. at first, though the prerequisites for production in the U.S. had been fully satisfied, are as follows: (1) for motorcycles, unlike electric home-appliances, there were no import restrictions for Japan (since there were hardly any U.S. competitive firms); (2) exporting to the U.S. was far more profitable than manufacturing there, because there was no need for low pricing of export products; and (3) Honda chose to make heavy new investment in entering the automobile industry in Japan instead of investing in production in the U.S.

In the field of small-sized cars, into which Honda had made a new entry, the situation was quite different from that for motorcycles. The production of small-sized cars in the U.S. was rapidly became necessary because of the import restrictions on Japanese cars.

Thus Honda attempted at first to manufacture motorcycles in the U.S.; later, it started producing small-sized cars there. That was because the production of motorcycles was far earlier in the U.S. than that of cars so that small-scale operation was enough, and because know-how and experience acquired through the production of motorcycles were also applicable to that of cars. Honda owed its success in its early start of the production of cars in the U.S. to its production of motorcycles. On the other hand, Toyota, Nissan and other Japanese firms without such experience hesitated to start the production of cars in the U.S.

I have described how three Japanese firms with quite different kinds of products, Matsushita, Kikkoman and Honda, made direct investment in the U.S. at a very early stage and fully satisfied the prerequisites for direct investments in

the U.S. These prerequisites are applicable equally not only
to direct investments in the U.S. but also to those in other
advanced countries.

To fully satisfy these prerequisites for direct investments in
the U.S., it is indispensable for firms to have capabilities of ex-
ceedingly high level, which can be gained and accumulated
only through firms' consistent efforts; therefore, whether firms
can satisfy these prerequisites depends solely on their own
capabilities.

Nowadays the capabilities of many Japanese firms have
reached the level of the above three firms through their sophisticated exporting activities, and there is no doubt that
Japanese firms' direct investments in all advanced countries
(including the U.S.) will become more active in future.

COMMENTS

Keiichiro Nakagawa
The International University of Japan

Professor Inoue's paper is a good summary of the development of overseas activities of American and European business enterprises. Professor Kinugasa's statements are also very useful for understanding the Japanese experiences in comparison with Western ones. In the following, I shall summarize my feelings mainly on Professor Inoue's paper.

First, Professor Inoue emphasizes that, in both the United States and Europe, overseas activities started with innovations of new products or new production processes. Thus he focuses his analysis on product-oriented or marketing-oriented overseas activities. However, before 1914, American enterprises actively engaged in overseas activities not only of marketing new products but also exploiting natural resources. They invested in mining and lumbering in Canada. In Mexico and South America also, they developed many kinds of natural resources. As is well known, the United Fruit Company invested in agricultural industry. In fact, before 1914, in the total amount of direct foreign investment by U.S., the share of mining was the largest and that of manufacturing was the second largest. Investment into agriculture and oil occupied the third and fourth positions respectively. In sum, in the early stage of overseas activities of American enterprises, the development of natural resources was of great importance.

At the first meeting of this conference, Professor Charles Wilson emphasized that European multinational enterprises did not develop along the same lines as their American counterparts, maintaining that, while American firms developed their overseas activities mostly through exporting their products, European multinational enterprises emerged to exploit overseas natural resources. However, Professor Wilson seems to have overemphasized the difference between

Europe and America. As is pointed out by Professor Inoue, European firms also developed their overseas activities by exporting their products. It seems to me that both in the U.S. and Europe the two types of overseas activities developed side by side. At any rate, these aspects should be considered in detail at this meeting.

My second comment is on the difference between Professor Inoue's paper and Professor Yoshino's. Professor Yoshino contends that in the U.S. the multinational enterprises rapidly developed in the 1960s and that in the 1940s and 1950s they were just at the starting line. In contrast, according to Professor Inoue, in the 1910s there were already many well-developed multinational enterprises. Here is a big gap between the two interpretations. What was the situation between the two world wars? How can we relate the above two stages of the development of overseas activities of multinational enterprises? In my understanding, the total amount of direct foreign investment by U.S. in 1929 was about 7.2 billion dollars, and in 1946 it was just 7.5 billion. In other words, during the interwars period, American direct foreign investment did not increase. Why not? What was the situation of overseas activities of American enterprises during the interwar years? This is my second question, to which I would like to have an answer in this meeting.

Third, Professor Inoue emphasizes the imitative activities of Japanese enterprises at the starting stage of their overseas operations. This view may be slightly modified by Professor Kinugasa's study of the Kikkoman case. But I do not think that Japanese and Western firms developed their overseas activities in the same way. What were the characteristics of overseas activities of Japanese firms? Are they imitative or not? This is my third question.

Lastly, Professor Kinugasa maintains that the stage of overseas sales branches is very important to understanding the overseas business activities of multinational enterprises. In this respect, I agree with Professor Kinugasa. Even in the case of the U.S. multinational enterprises, as is underlined by Professor M. Wilkins, this stage is very important. American multinational enterprises, such as Singer Manufacturing Co. and National Cash Register, exported their products first through domestic exporters and then appointed their overseas sales agencies. In the next stage, they developed the agencies into their own overseas sales branches owned by their head offices;

and after that, they established overseas factories for local productions. Without correct understanding of the overseas marketing activities, we cannot grasp the real features of overseas production activities.

The Contribution of Sogo Shosha to the Multinationalization of Japanese Industrial Enterprises in Historical Perspective

Ken'ichi Yasumuro
Kobe University of Commerce

During the last hundred years, Japanese industrial enterprises have successfully penetrated the world market by trade, and the vital task of promoting foreign trade has mainly rested with large general trading companies known as *sogo shosha*.[1] The core business of the sogo shosha has always been in trade. Sogo shosha are not only trade intermediaries but also active creators of trade flows. They create demand and supply by establishing joint ventures abroad with Japanese and local partners in raw materials as well as in manufacturing. According to M. Y. Yoshino, "the general trading companies have played and will continue to play important roles in the multinationalization of Japanese industries."[2]

Some Japanese scholars insist that joint ventures with sogo shosha are an indispensable means of facilitating the multinationalization of Japanese industrial firms, because sogo shosha have the knowledge of doing business in foreign countries which industrial enterprises lack. Thus, they often assert that from the viewpoint of national trade policy, sogo shosha and industrial enterprises should create joint ventures overseas. Joint ventures of this type are referred to as "sogo shosha participated joint ventures."[3]

If we accept the sogo shosha participated joint venture as a uniquely Japanese approach to the multinationalization of industrial enterprises, it should have existed in the past and will continue to exist as a dominant style of direct foreign investment. In my paper, I will examine the changing role of the sogo shosha in the multinationalization of Japanese industrial firms from an historical perspective.

I will describe the background of foreign direct investment before World War II, explain the ownership policy and the joint ventures with trading companies before World War II, and discuss the postwar spread and decline of sogo shosha participated joint ventures.

I. The Background of Foreign Direct Investment before World War II

1. Early Stage of Foreign Direct Investment

In the early stage of industrialization, Japan's major export items were raw materials such as coal, copper, and agricultural products. The *zaibatsu* [financial cliques], which were Japan's first large enterprises, built their foundations on the mining industries, shipping industry, and trading companies to export their products. In the 1870s foreign trading companies were handling about 95 percent of Japan's import and export business, because Japanese firms at that time were unable to carry out transactions without the assistance of foreign traders who could negotiate with buyers and sellers in overseas markets and handle documents written in foreign languages for foreign exchange transactions.

To prevent the ultimate domination of all trade by foreign trading firms, the Japanese government and zaibatsu cooperated to set up shipping industry and trading companies to handle the functions being performed by foreign companies. In February 1875 Mitsubishi Goshi Kaisha (which latter became the Mitsubishi zaibatsu holding company) established its Shanghai branch for shipping operations. Mitsui & Co., Ltd. established a Shanghai branch in 1877, a Tientsin office in 1878, and a London branch in 1880 to promote the exports of raw materials.

By the 1890s the first industrial revolution began to appear with the emergence of the cotton spinning industry. A modern spinning mill was established in Osaka in 1888 and created a need for trading firms to keep the industry supplied with imported raw cotton. Mitsui & Co., Ltd. had already been importing raw cotton since 1886 and, for refining, it established a joint venture with British and German investors. This joint venture was named the Shanghai Cotton Cleaning and Works Co., Ltd. and started operations in 1889.

The cotton textile market was growing rapidly in China. In response to this new growing market, Johtaro Yamamoto, Shanghai branch manager of Mitsui & Co., purchased a Chinese cotton mill and reestablished it under the name of the Shanghai Cotton Spinning Co., Ltd. in 1902. Mitsui & Co. also purchased another Chinese cotton mill, Santai Cotton Spinning Co., Ltd., in 1906 and expanded its productive capacity. The responsibility for the investments and risk taking rested with Johtaro Yamamoto. The chief executive of Mitsui & Co., Takashi Masuda, was adverse to risk and preferred to earn commissions by acting as an intermediary between buyers and sellers.[4]

The early investments in manufacturing plants made by the trading companies were rather short lived. Mitsui & Co. sold its interest in the Shanghai Cotton Cleaning and Works in 1899 in spite of its profitable operation. The trading company's foreign direct investments in raw material production as well as manufacturing plants in the Meiji period were also provisional. The major strategy they pursued was to expand their sales networks around the world. From 1877 to 1914, Mitsui & Co. established 28 branches in Japan, 46 in Asia (especially in China), 5 in Europe, 2 in the U.S. and 1 in Australia. There were only 26 expatriates in the overseas branches in 1893, but the number increased to 395 in 1909. In 1919, there were 1,414 expatriates—37 percent of the employees of Mitsui & Co., Ltd.—serving in overseas branches.

2. The Rise of the Japanese Cotton Textile Industry from the 1890s to 1914

Japanese cotton textile companies began to export in the 1890s under the economic pressure of the depression. In 1906, Japanese cotton textile companies organized two export promotion associations: the San'ei Gumi and the Nippon Menpu Yushutsu Kumiai. Mitsui & Co. was the agent of these associations and sold textile goods in the Korean and north China markets. While the Japanese cotton textile companies were expanding their export markets through the two associations, Naigaimen Co., an importer of raw cotton, built a new and powerful spinning mill in Shanghai in 1909. This subsidiary was equipped with the most advanced machinery and was managed by some experienced Japanese staffs sent from the parent company. The Shanghai mill was successfully developed and became very profitable. The success of Naigaimen Co. also motivated competitors, who found that with advanced technology and a system of Japanese management the production cost of textiles was much cheaper in China than in Japan. During this period, the Japanese cotton textile industry was depressed, and during the 1900s, it cut down its operations sevenfold.

When World War I broke out in 1914, the British, who were the most dominant force in the Asian market, retreated. The Japanese and Chinese cotton textile industry scrambled for the Chinese market and achieved rapid growth during the war. The Japanese captured the major share of the British cotton textile market in China.

3. Changing Environment after World War I

During World War I, the pace of economic growth accelerated in Japan. The gross national product of Japan increased nearly threefold, and the volume of industrial production expanded nearly fivefold. Consequently, Japanese industries, especially the trading companies, grew. The total sales volume of Mitsui & Co., for example, leapt from $214 million in 1914 to $1,057 million in 1919.

When World War I ended in 1919 special procurement demands suddenly dropped and the Japanese economy slid into a full-fledged recession. Negative growth rates continued from 1920 to 1927, and the volume of foreign trade in 1931 declined to half of the volume of 1920. However, the damage of the recession was not equally felt by the trading companies. Table 1 shows the financial positions of the major trading companies in 1925. Although most of the Japanese trading companies were faced with a serious shortage of liquid assets, Mitsui & Co. and Ohkura Shoji had excess liquidity. Mitsui & Co. therefore began providing finance to industrial firms that were in financial difficulties and eventually integrated these firms into its zaibatsu organization.

It soon become clear that the real causes of the recession were not only the imbalance of supply and demand but also the structural defects of the Japanese economy. Yūnosuke Yasukawa, who

TABLE 1   The Financial Positions of Major Japanese Trading Companies in 1925.
(per $1,000)

Company	Capital	Debt
Mitsui & Co., Ltd.	57,716	51,992
Suzuki Shoten Co.	26,866	40,050
Nichimen Co.	20,246	34,950
Mitsubishi Trading Co.	7,992	20,997
Ohkura Shoji Co.	4,812	900
Iwai Shoten Co.	3,623	5,758
C. Itoh & Co.	3,315	3,009
Itoman Shoten Co.	3,195	604

Note: ￥100 – $40.75.
Source: Tokyo Kohsinjo, ed., *Ginko Kaisha Youroku* (30th Tokyo Koshinjo), 1925.

became the chief executive of Mitsui & Co. in 1924, referred to these structural defects in the following manner.

The major Japanese industries today are textiles, sugar, brewing, cement, flour milling and chemical fertilizer. These industries are already mature in Japan and cannot expand any further. Originally, these industries were introduced from the advanced countries. Consequently, almost all the materials and equipment were imported and Japanese industries exported their products because of the cheaper labor costs. However, the improvement of the standard of living in Japan will bring demands for higher wages. Japanese industries that are competing with foreign counterparts because of their cheap labor cannot expect further development in the world market. Moreover, those industries which do not require sophisticated technology are growing in number in countries such as China, India, and Southeast Asia which possess cheaper labor than in Japan. We must recognize that it is only a matter of time before those countries start to export standardized products which are now Japan's major exports.[5]

Yasukawa had already understood the meaning of the "product life cycle" and decided to behave according to the "trade cycle theory" which he developed from his business experiences in foreign countries. He established a new policy of investing excess liquidity into industrial fields. At the ninth committee meeting of branch managers held in 1926, he stated that investments in new business ventures should be made to expand Mitsui & Co. Thus, Mitsui & Co. took part in new ventures with foreign partners in Japan from 1925 to 1931.[6]

4. Deterioration of the International Environment since 1931

William W. Lockwood, the famous U.S. economic historian, wrote that "the most conspicuous feature of the early thirties in Japan, so far as the rest of the world was concerned, was the boom in Japanese exports after 1931."[7]

The immediate stimulus came from the swift depreciation of the currency. The value of one hundred yen plummeted from $49.40 in November 1931 to $20.70 a year latter, and the volume of Japanese exports nearly doubled from 1930 to 1936. Textiles, which were long dominant in Japan's export trade, again lead the way in penetrating world markets. The flood of Japanese goods into foreign markets after 1931 brought frantic outcries from the West because most other countries—particularly Japan's major industrial competitors—were struggling in a depression. Antagonism was further increased by the political reactions to the Japanese army's invasion of north China and especially Manchuria in 1931.

After 1932, tariffs were raised or quotas were established in almost every country against Japanese goods, although at their peak, Japan's exports were less than 4 percent of world exports.[8]

In 1933 Yūnosuke Yasukawa commented, "it is impossible to expect further growth in the commercial sector because of a declining tendency in world trade and tightening of import restrictions on our exports. Consequently, it is necessarily to expand our investments into industrial fields abroad."

At this time, a more serious problem had arisen between China and Japan. When World War I broke out in 1914, the Chinese government fought with the Allied Forces. After World War I, the Chinese government made an attempt to recover its autonomy to set tariffs. Negotiations with Japan began in 1919, and agreement was concluded in 1930. During this period, the Chinese government gradually increased tariff rates and by the end of 1930, it had succeeded in setting up a prohibitive tariff wall against the Japanese cotton textile industry and trade companies. The tariff rates on cotton textile goods ranged from 40 to 70 percent. But to protect the Chinese market, Japanese cotton textile companies had begun direct investments and local production since the end of the war, so that about 40 percent of all Chinese spindles were under the control of Japanese cotton textile companies, until 1930.[9] However, the high rates of tariff were a source of conflict, and the Japanese military clique used this problem as an excuse to attack China.

II. Ownership Policy and Joint Ventures with Trading Companies before World War II

As noted above, the general trading companies contributed to the development of Japanese industries by foreign trade. Exporting had become so difficult because of the import restrictions in many countries in the 1930s that Japanese industrial enterprises rushed to invest directly in China and Manchuria after the 1930s. In this period, however, the sogo shosha did not play a major role in establishing joint ventures abroad with Japanese manufacturers, contrary to the opinions of some scholars who claim that the sogo shosha led the way in direct foreign investments.

Table 2 shows the number of direct investments of Japanese industrial enterprises and military controlled and occupied plants in China. Table 3 shows the ownership policy of Japanese industrial enterprises in Manchuria.[10]

1. Ownership Policies in China

The total number of affiliates in China was 719 in 1938. Five hundred and twenty-two were directly controlled (wholly owned or majority owned) by Japanese industrial enterprises. Joint ventures with Chinese enterprises numbered only thirty-five. However, some of these joint ventures were very large projects, especially in mining, and total investments were very large. Another 159 were Japanese military controlled and occupied, and their management was entrusted to Japanese enterprises. Apart from government and military controlled plants, the textile industry had the largest number of subsidiaries (24), followed by the mining and chemical industries (21).

TABLE 2   Number of Direct Investments and Military Controlled Plants in China in 1938.

Industry	Direct control (wholly or majority owned)	Joint venture with China (50%)	Government controlled	Military controlled and management entrusted
Mining	11	10	3	26
Coal	(6)	(7)	(1)	(21)
Iron	(1)	(1)	(1)	(5)
Gold Mine & Others	(4)	(2)	(1)	(0)
Textile	22	2	0	33
Cotton Spinning	(18)	(1)	(0)	(33)
Other Textiles	(4)	(1)	(0)	(0)
Foodstuffs	8	4	0	39
Brewing	2	0	0	0
Tobacco	6	0	0	2
Metals & Machinery	12	5	0	8
Matches	5	3	0	9
Rubber Products	7	1	0	2
Chemicals	20	1	0	15
Stone, Clay & Glass	7	4	0	9
Miscellaneous Products	22	3	0	12
Unknown	400*	2	0	4
Total	522	35	3	159**

Notes: * Small scale, personally managed concerns.
** Chinese plants occupied by the Japanese Army whose management was entrusted to Japanese industrial enterprises.

Source: Toa Kenkyūjyo, ed., *Nihon no Tai Shi Tōshi* (Japan's Investments in China), rev. ed. (Tokyo: Harashobō, 1974). Hiroshi Higuchi, *Nihon no Tai Shi Tōshi no Kenkyū* (Investigation of Japan's Investment in China) (Seikatsusya, 1939), Toa Dobunkai Chōsa, ed., *Shina Kaikōjō Shi* (The History of Treaty Ports in China) (Tokyo: Toa Dobunkai Shuppan, 1921).

2.   Ownership Policies in Manchuria

Japanese direct investments in Manchuria numbered 322 in 1942 (see Table 3). The zaibatsu groups made 244 investments, and the residual 78 investments were made by non-zaibatsu (independent) enterprises. Of the 322 investments, 103 (32%) were wholly owned by Japanese parent companies, and 38 (11.8%) were majority owned by Japanese parent companies. The characteristics of direct investments in Manchuria compared with that of China were:

1)   In Manchuria, the zaibatsu—especially Mitsubishi, Mitsui,

TABLE 3   Direct Investments and Ownership Policies of Japanese Industrial Enterprises in Manchuria in 1942.

Enterprise	Wholly owned (100%)	Majority owned (99–50%)	Minority owned (49–10%)	Investment (less than 10%)	Unknown
Zaibatsu Group's Total	74	33	49	64	24
Mitsui	24	9	9	9	2
Mitsubishi	7	1	7	9	0
Sumitomo	0	3	6	6	0
Tōyōtakushoku	3	1	7	3	2
Nitchitsu	4	0	3	0	0
Asano	2	4	2	0	0
Ohkura	9	2	6	6	0
Nezu	0	3	1	6	0
Nomura	3	1	0	6	0
Suzuki-Ajinomoto	3	0	1	3	0
Yasuda	1	1	2	4	0
Nissan	7	3	3	5	0
Local Zaibatsu Group					
Takada	2	0	1	2	1
Ueshima	1	0	0	2	0
Aioi	8	5	1	3	19
Non-Zaibatsu Enterprises					
Total	29	5	18	26	0
Heavy Industry (including chemicals)	13	5	9	18	0
Brewing	4	0	2	0	0
Sugar	4	0	0	2	0
Stone, Clay and Glass	1	0	1	3	0
Textiles	7	0	6	3	0
Total	103	38	67	90	24

Source: Manshū Keizai, ed., *Manshū Kigyō no Zenmenteki Kenkyū* (Investigation of the Manchurian Enterprises) (Tokyo: Manshū Keizai-sha, 1939). Tsuyoshi Monma, "Manshū Dotchaku Shihon no Kigyōteki Tokushitsu," (Corporate Characteristics of Local Business in Manchuria), *Manchu Keizai*, vol. 1, no. 6 (1937), pp. 38–83. Shukei Kikuchi, *Manshū Juyō Sangyō Kōsei* (The Composition of Manchu Major Industries) (Tokyo: Toyo Keizai-sha, 1939).

Ohkura and Nissan—had taken the initiative in direct investments, whereas in China, independent companies—especially the textile companies—played an important role in direct investment.

2)   In Manchuria, investment was concentrated in the heavy

industries, including chemicals, in line with government policy. Investment in China was concentrated in the light industries such as textile and manufacturing.

3) In Manchuria, companies with a less than 10 percent ownership were mostly state owned or controlled.

In spite of these differencies, Japanese industrial enterprise preferred wholly owned or majority owned affiliates abroad.

3. Ownership Policy of the Trading Companies in the Manufacturing and Extractive Industries

Table 4 shows the number of foreign direct investments made by

TABLE 4 Foreign Direct Investments Manufacturing and Extractive Industries by Mitsui & Co., Ltd. and Mitsubishi Trading Company before 1942.

Company	Manu-factur-ing	Ex-trac-tive	Ownership of Parent Company					
			1–24%	24–49%	50%	51–94%	94–100%	Un-known
Mitsui & Co., Ltd.								
Directly affiliated	12	5	3	3	2	2	6	1
Sogo shosha participated joint ventures								
with Japanese partners	4	4	2	2	2	2	0	0
with Japanese and local partners	3	0	1	2	0	0	0	0
Other investments to government controlled enterprises	11	4	15	0	0	0	0	0
Mitsubishi Trading Company								
Directly affiliated	13	5	0	0	3	0	12	3
Sogo shosha participated joint ventures								
with Japanese partners	6	2	1	2	0	1	0	4
with Japanese and local partners	2	0	1	0	0	0	0	1
Other investments to government controlled enterprises	4	2	6	0	0	0	0	0
Total	55	22	29	9	7	5	18	9

Source: Nihon Keieishi Kenkyūjo, ed., *Mitsui Bussan Hyaku Nen Shi, I* (Nihon Keiei-shi Kenkyujo, 1978), p. 432, and Yasuo Mishima, "Sogo Shosha no Shihon Yushutsu Nenpyo" (The Capital Export of Sogo Shosha) *Konan Keiei Kenkyu*, vol. 12, no. 3 (1971), pp. 143–60.

TABLE 5   Foreign Direct Investments in Manufacturing by Four Trading Companies before 1942.

Company	Direct investments	China	Manchuria	Southeast Asia
Nichimen Co., Ltd.	8	6	2	0
Iwai Industry Co., Ltd.	10	7	0	3
Gosho Co., Ltd.	7	4	3	0
Sanko Co., Ltd.	12	4	8	0
Total	37	21	13	3

Note: The ownership percentage by parent companies is unknown.
Sources: *Nichimen Nanajū Nen Shi* (Seventy Years of Nichimen Co., Ltd.) (Tokyo, 1961).
   Iwai Hyaku Nen Shi (One Hundred Years of Iwai Industry Co., Ltd.) (Tokyo, 1964).
   Gosho Rokujū Nen Shi (Sixty Years of Gosho Co., Ltd.) (Tokyo, 1967).
   Marubeni Zen Shi (Early Period of Marubeni Co., Ltd.) (Tokyo, 1978).

Mitsui & Co., and Mitsubishi Trading Company before 1942 in the manufacturing and extractive industries. Table 5 shows the number of direct investments in manufacturing made by other trading companies.

Mitsui & Co., Ltd. had invested in forty-three affiliates, and Mitsubishi Trading Company had invested in thirty-four affiliates by 1942. The other trading companies—Nichimen, Iwai Industry, Gosho, and Sanko (which later split into Marubeni and C. Itoh)—had made thirty-seven direct investments in China, Manchuria, and Southeast Asia.

The foreign direct investments in manufacturing and extractive industries made by the trading companies were large and costly. Therefore, we cannot talk about Japan's investments abroad before World War II without considering these cases.

The investment and ownership policy preferred by the trading companies was directly affiliated and majority owned subsidiaries rather than minority owned joint ventures. Ten of Mitsui & Co.'s forty-three joint ventures and thirteen of Mitsubishi Trading Company's were wholly or majority owned subsidiaries. On the other hand, joint ventures with Japanese industrial enterprises and local partners, namely, sogo shosha participated joint ventures, were few.

Mitsui & Co. had eight joint ventures with Japanese partners and three joint ventures with Japanese and local partners. Mitsubishi Trading Company had eight joint ventures with Japanese partners and two joint ventures with Japanese and local partners. One-half or more of these jointly owned subsidiaries were small in size and unsuccessful. The jointly owned large subsidiaries that had a long history were rather few: Manchuria Onoda Cement Co., Ltd., 80 percent owned by Onoda Cement Co., Ltd. and 20 percent by Mitsui & Co., Ltd.; Harbin Cement Co., Ltd., 58 percent owned by Onoda Cement, 23.6 percent by Mitsui & Co., and 18.4 percent by local partners; and Manchuria Mitsubishi Machinery and Equipment Co., Ltd., which was jointly owned by Mitsubishi Heavy Industries Co., Ltd. and Mitsubishi Trading Company.

Japanese industrial enterprises and trading companies showed a strong preference for wholly owned or majority owned subsidiaries, thus the issue of ownership and control appeared to be paramount before World War II. In this period, Japan's exports were so restricted in many countries that the only way left for enterprises to safeguard their markets was to aggressively promote local production. Although the contributions of trading companies and local partners may have been of value to the industrial enterprises, retaining control of foreign operations was critical if the strategy of export substitution by local production was to succeed.

Japanese industrial enterprises and trading companies eagerly pursued strategies to survive in a deteriorating international environment and didn't share the benefits among themselves. Consequently, the sogo shosha participated joint ventures in which a partner's interests would coincide with that of the trading company's, were rare. Sogo shosha participated joint ventures were a minor device in promoting the multinationalization of Japanese industrial enterprises before World War II; they began play an important role after World War II, especially in the period of Japan's double-digit economic growth.

III.   Postwar Spread and Decline of Sogo Shosha Participated Joint Ventures

1.   Foreign Trade after the 1950s

World War II came to an end in 1945, and Japan lost a great amount of foreign investment, estimated at roughly ¥219 billion ($51.4 billion, at the rate of 100 yen=$23.47),[11] three times the value of the GNP in 1944. Looking at the geographical distribution of Japan's foreign investment at that time on a country basis, 61.1 percent was invested in Manchuria, 30.1 percent was in China and the remaining 8.8 percent was invested in other regions—especially in Southeast Asia (excluding Taiwan and Korea).[12]

Japanese investment abroad was forbidden until 1951, but when it was again permitted, the circumstances were unfavorable to Japanese investors, because Japanese industries were preoccupied with rebuilding their war-torn factories. In the case of the textile industry, its productive capacity was only 7 percent of its prewar level. Foreign exchange was scarce, so "processing trade" was the only strategy to feed the 100 million hungry war sufferers. Consequently, Japanese industries again intensified export orientation strategy and toward the end of the 1950s, Japanese manufacturing industries again began asserting themselves in the world market.

Japanese industries pursued an aggressive strategy of expansion in the export market and began to face import restrictions, especially in the Southeast Asian countries, in the late 1950s and the early 1960s. Japanese export-oriented firms were particularly vulnerable to these restrictions.

Threatened by the possible loss of finished goods export markets, Japanese manufacturing firms decided to establish small-scale manufacturing factories locally, especially in Southeast Asia. These factories were most often built to handle the very last stage of fabrication—in other words, they were downstream processing factories. From a Japanese parent company's point of view, such factories were necessary to overcome import restrictions and to preserve its market in foreign countries. These subsidiaries often were part of the export strategy of the parent company—in other words, these investments were included in the costs of exporting. Such foreign operations could be performed on a small scale, required little capital and technical input, and the operations were ordinarily performed by Japanese subcontractors. Despite such small-scale investment, Japanese manufacturing companies were reluctant to take any risks, especially in the Third World, and preferred joint ventures with local partners.

2. Reaction of the Sogo Shosha

The export supplementary investment of Japanese manufacturing industries was threatening to the sogo shosha, because they exported many finished goods made by the manufacturing firms. However, the sogo shosha had overlooked these investments in the early period, because investments did not contribute to their immediate profits. When Japanese cotton textile companies such as Toyobo, Kanebo, and Kurabo invested in Brazil and other Latin American countries in the early 1950s, the sogo shosha lost their export markets in these countries. Threatened by the possible loss of export

TABLE 6   Sogo Shosha Participated Joint Ventures by Years and Regions.

Region	Pre-1959	1960–64	1965–69	1970–74	1975–78	Total
Asia	3	34	97	234	28	396
Near East and Africa	1	6	7	21	7	42
Oceania	2	4	6	29	1	42
Brazil	2	4	3	70	13	92
Middle East	2	7	17	29	1	56
North and Latin America (except Brazil)	0	3	17	52	8	80
Europe	0	5	7	37	3	52
Total	10	63	154	472	61	760

Notes: The ten largest general trading companies (Mitsui & Co., Ltd., Sumitomo Shoji Kaisha Ltd., Marubeni Corporation, C. Itoh & Co., Toyomenka, Nichimen Company, Ltd., Ataka & Co., Nisho-Iwai Co., Ltd. and Kanematsu-Gosho Ltd.) are included with the smaller, general trading companies (Chōry, Toyoda Tsusho, Tokyo Bōeki, and Nomura Bōeki). Years refer to when the establishment of joint ventures was permitted by local governments; jointly owned subsidiaries include those in manufacturing and sales. After 1975, the joint ventures are mostly those in the planning stages but already permitted by local governments.

Source: Tōyō Keizai-sha, ed., *Kaigai Shinshutsu Kigyō Sōran* (Japanese Multinationals: Facts and Figures) (Tokyo: Tōyō Keizai-sha, 1976).

markets, the sogo shosha decided to participate in the investments with the intention of protecting their overseas business. These export supplementary investments presented an opportunity to export equipment and intermediary materials to be used in overseas ventures. Many Japanese manufacturing firms wished to limit risks, so they welcomed the sogo shoshas' participation in these ventures. Moreover, Japanese manufacturing firms thought that small overseas factories were only a device to deal with import restrictions abroad and, since they were not the major business of the company, they did not need tight control.

The sogo shosha, however, decided to participate in jointly owned subsidiaries and pursued an aggressive strategy of expansive foreign direct investments. Table 6 shows the sogo shosha participated joint ventures, classified according to the year in which they were established or acquired by the parent companies.

Sogo shosha participated joint ventures began to increase in the early 1960s. From 1960 to 1964, sogo shosha participated joint ventures increased to keep pace with Japan's double-digit economic growth, which peaked in 1973. In this year the first oil crisis occurred and soon serious inflationary pressures followed. Encouraged by this "inflation psychology," Japanese industrial enterprises as well as general trading companies rushed to invest directly in foreign countries, especially in cheap labor cost countries such as Southeast Asia. After a frenzied inflationary period, the boom in business slowed and demand fell off. The Japanese economy was faced with stagflation. Consequently, the number of newly established sogo shosha participated joint ventures rapidly declined (see Appendix A).

Oil prices were constantly raised, and Japan seemed to be beating inflation. Foreign direct investment again grew in 1978. When the second boom of foreign direct investment came in 1978, the number of newly established sogo shosha participated joint ventures did not reach its previous level.

3. The Changing Role of the Sogo Shosha in the Multinationalization of Japanese Enterprises

After 1978, Japan's leading high technology, marketing-oriented industries, which had innovative products or processing techniques, began to invest abroad on a large scale. Their outlooks seemed to resemble the U.S. multinationals, and their business behavior was different from their Japanese ancestors.

The typical newcomers were electronics and precision machinery industries whose strategy was different from their predecessors. They manufacture highly technological and marketing-intensive products that need a technical service network worldwide. The general trading companies, having neither technical service knowledge nor marketing knowledge about these new products, had only treated standardized products that were less intensified in technology and in marketing. Thus, they could not trade these new technological products. When the Japanese electronics and precision industries decided to export their products, they had to invest their own effort and money to achieve their objectives. They built

TABLE 7 Industry Concentration of Sogo Shosha Participated Joint Ventures in 159 Japanese Enterprises.

Industry	Jointly Owned Subsidiaries						Total
	30 or more	29–20	19–10	9–2	1	0	
Fishery, Agriculture, and Forestry	0	0	0	5	0	0	5
Mining	0	0	0	1	0	2	3
Foodstuffs	0	0	0	3	0	2	5
Textiles	1	0	5	7	1	0	14
Pulp and Paper Products	0	0	0	4	1	0	5
Chemicals	0	0	0	7	2	13	22
Rubber Products	0	0	0	1	0	1	2
Stone, Clay, and Glass Products	0	0	0	4	1	1	6
Iron and Steel	0	0	2	5	1	5	13
Nonferrous Metals	0	0	0	4	0	4	8
Fabricated Metal Products	0	0	0	0	0	1	1
Machinery	0	0	0	4	5	5	14
Electric Machinery	0	0	1	6	5	18	30
Precision Instruments	0	0	0	0	2	8	10
Transportation Equipment	0	0	0	6	2	7	15
Miscellaneous Products	0	0	0	3	0	3	6
Total	1	0	8	60	20	70	159

Source: Calculated from Tōyō Keizai-sha, ed., *Kaigai Shinshutsu Kigyō Sōran* (Japanese Multinationals: Facts and Figures) (Tokyo: Tōyō Keizai-sha, 1976).

their own distribution channels and marketing organizations worldwide until the late 1960s. Consequently, when they began to enter foreign markets by direct investment, the general trading companies were excluded. Table 7 shows the number of sogo shosha's joint ventures with 159 international Japanese enterprises, classified by industry.[13] The number of sogo shosha participated joint ventures with electric machinery, precision instruments, transportation equipment, and chemical industries was rather small.

In the case of electronics or electric machinery, these companies had faced a changing environment in the export markets in the 1970s and decided to establish large-scale manufacturing plants

TABLE 8 Ownership of Textile and Electric Machinery Industries.

Industry	Parent Company Ownership				Total
	25–49%	50%	51–94%	95–100%	
Textiles					
Ownership of Parent Company Only					
Number of Subsidiaries	48	10	21	8	87
Percent	55.2	11.5	24.1	9.2	100
Ownership with Other Japanese Partners					
Number of Subsidiaries	28	10	30	19	87
Percent	32.2	11.5	34.5	21.8	100
Electric Machinery					
Ownership of Parent Company Only					
Number of Subisidiaries	60	18	21	51	150
Percent	40	12	14	34	100
Ownership with Other Japanese Partners					
Number of Subsidiaries	52	20	26	52	150
Percent	34.7	13.3	17.3	34.7	100

Note: "Other Japanese Partners" means sogo shosha in the textile industry. However, for electric machinery, "other partner" usually means a manufacturer in the same industry.

Source: Ken'ichi Yasumuro, "Nihon no Sen'i Kigyō no Kaigai Senryaku to Shoyū Seisaku-Denki Kiki Kigyō tono Taihi ni oite" (The Strategy of Foreign Business and Ownership Policies of Japanese Textile and Electric Machinery Industries: A Comparison), *Shōdai Ronshū*, 31, no. 6 (1980), p. 89. The data covered about 50 percent of each industry.

overseas. They moved their production plants into neighboring countries, such as Taiwan, South Korea, Hong Kong and Singapore, and from these offshore subsidiaries, the parent companies exported their products to overcome U.S. import restrictions and took advantage of the preferential tariffs granted to developing countries. Japanese products made in the developing countries with the parent company's trademarks or brands were then exported through the parent company's worldwide distribution network.

These large-scale, export-oriented subsidiaries had very different characteristics from local market-oriented, small-scale import supplementary joint ventures in developing countries. The parent company transferred a high level of technical and manpower resources to the export-oriented subsidiaries and hence needed tight control over these subsidiaries. To keep this tight control, the parent company did not want participation by the general trading companies in the ventures. However, when they could not avoid local government pressure or requests for a joint venture, they reluctantly accepted a local participant and then set up joint ventures. In these cases, the Japanese parent company insisted on a majority ownership and, in return, guaranteed to export the finished products. There is a clear distinction in the ownership policies of the textile and the electric machinery industries (see Table 8). The percentage of wholly owned subsidiaries is only 9.2 percent in textiles, whereas 34 percent of the electric machinery industries are wholly owned by the parent company.

Conclusion

In recent years, a new type of Japanese multinationalization has emerged. Typical examples are the electronics and precision machinery industries. These companies prefer a more integrated global strategy of subsidiaries. These companies transfer a high level of technology and management resources to their subsidiaries, so they must maintain tight control over production, finance, and marketing (see Appendix B). They have recently begun to invest directly in advanced countries such as the U.S. and the E.C. countries. In the coming age of multinationals, the role of sogo shosha participated joint ventures in manufacturing is already obsolete yet is still important in the field of extractive industries. The subsidiaries that are jointly owned by a general trading company and a Japanese industrial enterprise, sometimes with participation by local partners, are connected with the export strategy of the enterprises, and their roles are rather limited in the transitional stage of the multinationalization of Japanese industrial enterprises.

NOTES

1. Sogo shosha include the following nine largest general trading companies in 1981: Mitsubishi Corporation, Mitsui & Co., Ltd., C. Itoh & Co., Marubeni Corporation, Sumitomo Shoji Kaisha, Ltd., Nissho-Iwai Co., Ltd., Toyomenka Kaisha Ltd., Kanematsu Gosho, Ltd., and Nichimen Company, Limited. Ataka & Co., Ltd., went bankrupt and its major business departments were integrated into C. Itoh & Co., in May 1977.

   Sogo shosha have the following attributes: (1) they are large-scale firms; (2) they handle an almost infinite number of products and are highly diversified; (3) their core business is foreign trade, but domestic transactions are considerable (40–50% of total sales); and (4) they have great financial resources to handle trade.

2. M. Y. Yoshino, *Japan's Multinational Enterprises* (Cambridge, Mass., 1976). p. 95.

3. Joint ventures which are wholly owned by two Japanese partners, such as a sogo shosha and an industrial enterprise are called "a three-legged" joint venture. Joint ventures with three kinds of partners, such as a sogo shosha, Japanese industrial enterprise, and local partners are called "four-legged" joint ventures.

4. Koyata Iwasaki, the owner and leader of the Mitsubishi zaibatsu, aggressively promoted foreign direct investment to develop natural resources in China, Saghalien and the South Seas Islands. In spite of his pioneering spirit, these investments were mostly unsuccessful. Divestment continued from 1921 to 1927, and large losses were suffered.

5. Nihon Keieishi Kenkyujo, ed. *Mitsui Bussan Hyaku Nen Shi*, I (One Hundred Years of Mitsui & Co., Ltd.) Nihon Keieishi Kenkyujo, 1978, p. 432.

6. Mitsui & Co., Ltd. established new ventures with foreign partners and by licensing from 1925 to 1931:

   Sanki Kogyo Co., Ltd. (1925)—wholly owned by Mitsui & Co.,

to install U.S. Radiator's products in Japanese plants.

Toyo-Rayon (1925)—wholly owned by Mitsui & Co. and licensed by a German consulting firm, Oskar Korhon.

Toyo-Babcok (1927)—a joint venture with Babcok & Wilcox (U.K.). Mitsui & Co. owned 33.3 percent of the joint venture.

Toyo-Carrior (1930)—a joint venture with Carrior Corporation (U.S.). Ownership by Mitsui & Co. was 45 percent.

Toyo-Otis Elevator (1931)—a joint venture with Otis Elevator (U.S.). Ownership by Mitsui & Co. was 40 percent.

7. William W. Lockwood, *The Economic Development of Japan: Growth and Structural Change, 1868–1938* (Princeton, 1954), p. 65.

8. Lockwood, *op. cit.*, p. 68.

9. After the Sino-Japanese War in 1937, Japanese cotton textile companies established many new cotton spinning mills and expanded productive capacity of subsidiaries which were already established in China. Japanese cotton textile companies owned 2,220 thousand

TABLE I   Japan's Foreign Investment before World War II (millions of dollars).

1914	1919	1930	1936
China 216.2	China 588.8	China 1,283.1	China 463.2
Loans to government 9.4	Loans to government 105.3	Chinese Mainland 556.4	Manchuria 868.5
Loans to private enterprises 17.2	Loans to local governments 30.4	Loans 405.8	South Sea Islands and other regions 86.9
Direct investment 189.6	Loans to private enterprises 75.9	Direct investment 150.6	Hawaii, North and South America 29.0
The Philippines and South Sea Islands 19.7	Direct investment 377.2	Manchuria 726.7	Miscellaneous investment (esp. expatriates) 86.9
Hawaii and the U.S. 24.6	South Sea Islands and other regions 40.5	Loans 114.5	
	Hawaii, North and South America 25.3	Direct investment 612.2	
	Loans to allied power countries 312.9	South Sea Islands and other regions 64.2	
		Hawaii, North and South America 24.9	
Total 260.5	967.5	1,372	1,534.5
(¥100=$49.25)	(¥100=$50.625)	(¥100=$49.367)	(¥100=$28.951)

Source: Yamazawa, Ippei and Yuzou Yamamoto, *Bōeki to Kokusai Shūshi* (Foreign Trade and Balance of Payments—Estimates of Long-Term Economic Statistics of Japan Since 1968) (Tokyo, 1979), p. 56.

spindles and 34 thousand looms in China in 1941.
10. The records of foreign direct investments before World War II are very scarce, and much of the basic data was lost in the war. Consequently, it is very difficult to estimate accurate numbers of Japanese direct investment in this period. However, these tables are adequate for the purpose of this research.
11. This figure was estimated by Gen Numaguchi (1970), who used data from the Bank of Japan.
12. Tables I and II show another estimate of Japanese foreign investment abroad before World War II.

TABLE II   Japan's Investments in Colonial Regions. (millions of dollars)

Country & Year	Governmental loans	Corporate investment	Private investment	Total	Exchange rates
Taiwan					
1924	52.5	581.4	—	633.9	¥ 100 = $46.875
1939	39.8	282.0	—	321.8	¥ 100 = $23.437
1943	39.8	452.3	—	429.1	¥ 100 = $23.437
Korea					
1931	438.9	530.6	70.9	1,040.4	¥ 100 = $48.871
1938	370.4	618.6	41.7	1,030.3	¥ 100 = $28.496
1941	460.8	1,004.7	219.6	1,684.7	¥ 100 = $23.437

Source: Yamazawa, I. and Y. Yamamoto, (1979), *Ibid.*, p. 56.

13. The 159 international Japanese enterprises were selected from Hideki Yoshihara's article "Nihon no Takokuseki Kigyō Ichiran" (A List of Japan's International Enterprises), *Chūo Kōron* (Spring 1973), pp. 270–88. These enterprises had one or more the following of attributes: (1) they had foreign production subsidiaries in five or more countries in 1973; (2) their export ratio was constantly 25 percent or more for the past three years; (3) they had foreign direct investment in four or more countries; (4) their total amount of foreign investment was ¥250 million or more.

REFERENCES

Mitsuru Aihara, "Asia ni okeru Nippon no Tōshi" (Japan's Investment in Asia), *Sekai Keizai Hyōron*, vol. 19, no. 1 (1975), pp. 41–49.
Isao Hatada, *Nihon no Zaibatsu to Mitsubishi* (The Zaibatsu and Mitsubishi) (Tokyo, 1975).

Johannes Hirschmeier and Tsunehiko Yui, *The Development of Japanese Business, 1600–1973* (London, 1975).

Kiyoshi Kojima, "Nihon Gata Takokuseiki Kigyō no Arikata" (Unique Type of Japanese Multinationals) *Sekai Keizai Hyōron*, vol. 19, no. 8 (1975), pp. 43–52.

William W. Lockwood, *The Economic Development of Japan: Growth and Structural Change 1868–1938* (Princeton: Princeton University Press, 1954).

Mataji Miyamoto, Yoshio Togai, and Yasuo Mishima, eds., *Sogo Shosha Keieishi* (The History of Sogo Shosha) (Tokyo, 1976).

Hiroshi Nakano, "Sogo Shosha no Honshitsu to Nihon-gata Takokuseki Kigyō" (The Nature of Sogo Shosha and Japanese-Style Multinationals) *Sekai Keizai Hyōron*, vol. 20, no. 2 (1976), pp. 71–79.

Nihon Kagaku Sen'i Kyokai, ed., *Nihon Kagaku Sen'i Sangyō Shi* (The History of Japan's Chemical Fiber Industry) (Tokyo, 1974).

Gen Numaguchi, "Nihon no Kaigai Jigyō Tōshi" (Japan's Foreign Direct Investment: An Historical Analysis) *Chiba Shōdai Ronsō*, vol. 14-B (1970), pp. 244–68.

Ken'ichi Yasumuro, "Nihon no Sen'i Kigyō no Kaigai Senryaku to Shoyū Seisaku—Denki Kiki Kigyō tono Taihi ni oite" (The Strategy of Foreign Business and Ownership Policies of Japanese Textile and Electric Machinery Industries; A Comparison) *Shōdai Ronshū*, vol. 31, no. 6 (1980), pp. 84–104.

Hideki Yoshihara, "Nihon no Takokuseki Kigyō Ichiran" (The List of International Japanese Enterprises) *Chūo Kōron* (Spring, 1973), pp. 270–88.

"Shosha Sanka no Kaigai Seizō Gōben" (An Analysis of Sogo Shosha Participated Joint Manufacturing Ventures Abroad) in Takokuseki Kigyō Kenkyu Kai, ed., *Nihon-teki Takokuseki Kigyō Ron no Tenkai* (Theoretical Investigations into Japanese Multinational Enterprises) (Tokyo, 1979).

M. Y. Yoshino, "The Multinational Spread of Japanese Manufacturing Investment Since World War II", *Business History Review*, vol. 48, no. 3 (1973), pp. 357–81.

Japan's Multinational Enterprises (Cambridge, Mass., 1976).

Yasuo Mishima, "Sogo Shosha no Shihon Yushutsu Nenpyō" (The Capital Exports of Sogo Shosha), *Konan Keiei Kenkyu*, vol. 12, no. 3 (1971), pp. 143–60.

Tetsuya Kuwabara, "Senzen ni okeru Nihon Bōseki Kigyō no Kaigai Katsudō" (Japanese Cotton Textile Industry Abroad before World War II), *Rokkōdai Ronshū*, vol. 22, no. 1 (1975), pp. 1–30.

APPENDIX

(A)

This paper concentrates on three phases of Japanese investments abroad. First, the number pre-World War II sogo shosha participated joint ventures was small; by 1942 only 18 joint ventures had survived. Second, the number increased in the postwar era, especially between the years 1960 and 1973, in accordance with Japan's double-digit economic growth. Finally, in the third phase, the number of sogo shosha participated joint ventures has declined rapidly.

Figure I shows this in more detail. It shows the number of newly established sogo shosha participated joint ventures, including the extractive and manufacturing industries as well as their service and sales offices. It is important to note that the establishment year has

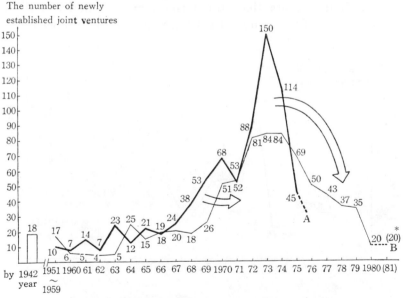

FIG. I   Spread and Decline of Sogo Shosha Participated Joint Ventures.

Note: The line A: Permitted year base (Data available from 1951 to 1975).
The line B: Opening year base.   * The plans for the future.

Source: Toyo Keizai Shinpō-sha, ed., *Kaigai Shinshitsu Kigyō Sōran* (Japanese Multinationals: Facts and Figures), 1976, 1981.

two meanings: (1) the year in which the establishment of the joint
venture was permitted by the local governments, and (2) the year
in which the plant or office started operations. If we wish to know
the year in which the top management decided to invest abroad,
the first of the above-mentioned years is a better representation than
the latter. In Fig. 1, line A is drawn using the former criteria while
line B is drawn using the latter.

From line A, we can see that the peak was reached in 1973. In
that year 150 joint ventures were granted permission while 114 were
granted permission in the following year. Thereafter, the number
has declined sharply; in 1975 only 45 joint ventures were granted
permission. Since 1975 data has not been available; the dotted
part of the line, which is based upon my interviews, indicates the
expected tendency in the decline of sogo shosha participated ventures. The figures are somewhat different for the other line. Although the peaks occurred in the same year, the line shows a much
more gradual increase than the former, and numerically it was
about one half of the former. In short, whereas the number of per-

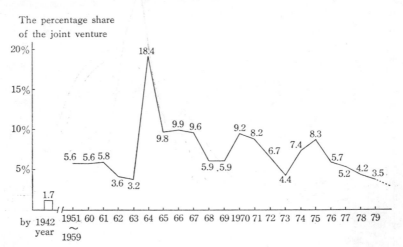

Fig. II   The Percentage Share of Sogo Shosha Participated Joint Ventures in Japan's
Total Foreign Direct Investments.

Note: Data based on the opening year.

Source: Toyo Keizai Shinpō-sha, ed., *Kaigai Shinshitsu Kigyō Sōran* (Japanese Multinationals: Facts and Figures), 1976, 1981.

TABLE I   The Number of Sogo Shosha Foreign Direct Investments by Year.

Opening (the operation) year — The type of sogo shosha's venture	By 1942	1951–1959	60	61	62	63	64	65	66	67	68	69	1970
I Sogo shosha participated joint ventures													
i) In extractive industries	18	2							1	4	2	2	7
ii) In manufacturing		8	6	5	4	4	20	13	15	15	12	18	34
iii) In commercial & service	N.A.	7				1	5	2	3	1	4	6	10
Subtotal (A)	18	17	6	5	4	5	25	15	19	20	18	26	51
II Directly affiliated ventures by sogo shosha (exclude I)													
i) In extractive industries	N.A.			1	1		1	1				2	7
ii) In manufacturing	N.A.	2	1	1	1	1	2	4	2	1	3	2	3
iii) In commercial & service	N.A.	7		3		3	2		2	1		3	8
iv) Branch	N.A.	36	3	2	3	4	2	3	2	7	2	3	11
Subtotal (B)		45	5	7	5	8	7	8	6	9	5	10	29
Total (A+B)		62	11	12	9	13	32	23	25	29	23	36	80
Total number of Japan's foreign direct investments (C)	1,041	305	104	86	112	155	136	153	191	209	304	439	556
Share of sogo shosha participated joint venture (A/C×100) (%)	1.7	5.6	5.6	5.8	3.6	3.2	18.4	9.8	9.9	9.6	5.9	5.9	9.2
Share of sogo shosha's investments ((A+B)/C×100) (%)	—	20.3	10.6	14.0	3.0	8.4	23.5	15.0	13.1	13.9	7.6	8.2	14.4

Note: Sogo shosha means the nine largest general trading companies.   * Plans for the future.

Continued . . .

TABLE I Continued.

Opening (the operation) year												Un-
The type of sogo shosha's venture	1971	72	73	74	75	76	77	78	79	1980	81*	known
I Sogo shosha participated joint ventures												
i) In extractive industries	7	5	6	3	2	2	2	5	5	3	8	4
ii) In manufacturing	30	38	51	53	57	27	28	13	22	14	10	16
iii) In commercial & service	16	38	27	28	10	21	13	19	8	3	2	4
Subtotal (A)	53	81	84	84	69	50	43	37	35	70	20	24
II Directly affiliated ventures by sogo shosha (exclude I)												
i) In extractive industries	9	5	9	5	3	3	1	1	1	1	1	8
ii) In manufacturing	5	10	11	9	9	5	5	2	5	1	1	14
iii) In commercial & service	13	19	33	39	13	12	13	21	16	9		21
iv) Branch	5	7	8	8	9	2	4	1	2	1		31
Subtotal (B)	32	41	61	61	34	22	23	25	24	12	2	74
Total (A+B)	85	122	145	145	103	72	66	62	59	32	22	98
Total number of Japan's foreign direct investments (C)	648	1,206	1,926	1,137	833	882	830	889	990	N.A.	N.A.	—
Share of sogo shosha participated joint venture (A/C×100) (%)	8.2	6.7	4.4	7.4	8.3	5.7	5.2	4.2	3.5	N.A.	N.A.	—
Share of sogo shosha's investments ((A+B)/C×100) (%)	13.1	10.1	7.5	12.8	12.4	8.2	8.0	7.0	6.0	N.A.	N.A.	—

Source: A, B: *Kaigai Shinshitsu Kigyō Sōran* (1981), C: MITI, *Shihon Jiyūka to Kaigai Shinshitsu Kigyō* (1969) and MITI, *Waga Kuni Kigyō no Kaigai Jigyō Katsudō* (1980).

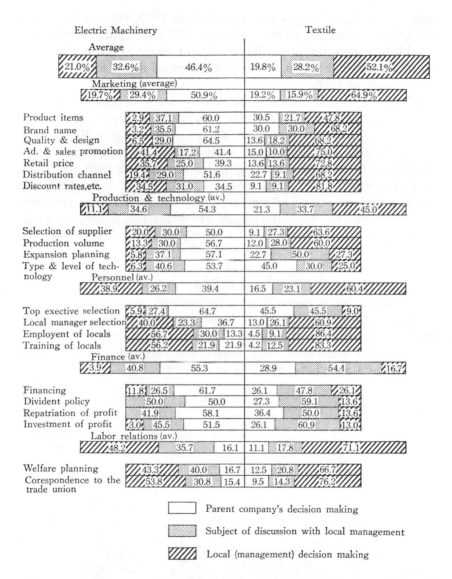

Fig. III   Degree of Centralization of Decision Making in Textile Firms and Electric Machinery Firms.

Data Available: Electronics, 35 firms; Textile, 24 firms.

Source: Ken'ichi Yasumuro, *op. cit.*, pp. 99, 100.

* Local management includes partner and expatriates.

mits to establish joint ventures peaked in 1973, the joint ventures did not start their operations until after 1975. The number of newly established sogo shosha participated joint ventures did not increase to its former high when the second boom of direct foreign investment came in 1978.

Figure II, which shows the percentage share of sogo shosha participated joint ventures compared with the total number of ventures abroad, has a similar tendency. The peak occurred in 1964, not in 1973 or 1974. The thirty-four newly opened sogo shosha ventures amounted to 18.4 percent. Highs also occurred in 1970 and 1975, but at a much lower level than in 1964. This clearly shows the decline in importance of sogo shosha participated joint ventures. Table I shows the basic data from which the two figures were calculated.

(B)

Figure III shows the differences in the degree of centralization of decision making between the textile industry and the electric machinery industry. Every item of decision making is more centralized in the latter than in the former. High precision industries wish to have stricter control of their investments abroad than industries such as the textile industry.

COMMENTS

Masaru Udagawa
Hosei University

Professor Yasumuro has traced the history of the multinationalization of Japanese industrial enterprises. His study denies well-known views and contains several important conclusions. General trading companies did not play large roles in past multinationalization, except on limited terms, and their role will decrease more with the future multinationalization of Japanese industries. He analyzed the process of multinationalization of Japanese industrial enterprises based mainly on product life-cycle models or trade-cycle theory. It is already known that to explain multinationalization, these frameworks for analysis are very useful. But, we also know that under the same circumstances, behavior is very different among enterprises. When the export conditions for a particular industry degenerate, there is room for variation in the behavior of companies belonging to that industry. It is a matter of the choice of strategy. Business historians are interested in the decision-making process: whether or not and for what reasons a company decides to go into direct investment instead of exporting. Therefore, if possible, Professor Yasumuro should have shown an actual example in a particular industry —why, how, and under what conditions a particular company decided to invest or not to invest abroad.

My second point concerns the relationship between private business and government, since government plays such an important part in overseas business activities. As is well known in Japan, this relationship has been extremely close. Also, the government has consistently followed a policy to limit foreign investment in Japan. What policy did the government take on the direct investment of Japanese companies abroad? And how did that policy change over time, for example, prior to 1937 compared with after World War II? Moreover, I would like to ask Professor Yasumuro how government policy influenced the strategy and decision-making process of companies in their overseas activities, and how overseas business activities influenced the process of government policy making.

As Professor Yasumuro shows, new postwar industries such as electronics and precision machinery were established in Japan. Most companies in these industries moved into the world market in the 1960s and founded large-scale manufacturing and marketing subsidiaries in foreign countries during the 1970s without the assistance of general trading companies. Their success definitely depended on techniques and systems of marketing. The commercial organization then existing was not set up to deal in these commodities. Therefore, these companies themselves had to import marketing techniques and systems from the United States. They modified them to suit the Japanese economy and social conditions and then developed what has been called the Japanese style of marketing.

Although beyond the scope of Professor Yasumuro's paper, another important question is did these companies export Japanese-style marketing when they moved into the world market and became multinational, and if they did, how was it modified? Moreover, to what degree can Japanese-style management be transferred to foreign countries? As Japanese companies moved directly into foreign marketing, how did general trading companies react to this further decline in their contribution to multinationalization of Japanese industries?

Multinational Growth of Japanese Manufacturing Enterprises in the Postwar Period*

Hideki Yoshihara
Kobe University

Introduction

The present paper is an investigation into the multinational growth of Japanese manufacturing enterprises in the postwar period. More specifically, this paper examines the strategy, foreign operations and ownership policies of Japanese multinational enterprises, and compares them with multinationals based in the United States and Europe. The purpose of this comparative analysis is to reveal the Japanese style of multinational growth. The primary research method is statistical analysis of quantitative data (including information from questionnaire surveys).

I. Japanese Multinational Enterprises

In order to identify the Japanese multinational enterprises, we need to define what multinational enterprises are. No unanimous definition exists at present (Aharoni, 1972). This paper adopts the definition of the Harvard Multinational Enterprise Project for two reasons. Firstly, the Harvard definition has gained a wide acceptance among researchers and so seems to represent common understanding in the field. Secondly, it is suitable for comparative analysis, since the Harvard Project has already attempted a study of American and European multinational enterprises.

In the Harvard Project, multinational enterprises are defined as firms having the following attributes (Vernon, 1971, pp. 4–11):

1. They are large firms. Specifically, they appear in the list of *Fortune*'s 500 largest U.S. industrial firms.
2. They are engaged in manufacturing or extractive operations abroad.
3. Their foreign subsidiaries are widely scattered all over the world. Specifically, they have foreign manufacturing subsidiaries in six or more countries.
4. A parent company and its foreign subsidiaries make up a multinational enterprise system, which has access to a common pool of resources and is responsive to a common strategy.

Let us adapt this definition to the Japanese setting. In this paper Japanese multinational enterprises are defined as follows:

1. They appear in *President*'s list of the 500 largest industrial firms (September 1975 special issue).
2. They have manufacturing subsidiaries in five or more foreign countries.
3. They themselves are not subsidiaries of other companies.

Overseas manufacturing subsidiaries are identified according to the following three attributes. Firstly, they are engaged in manufacturing or extractive operations abroad. Secondly, management commitment of parent companies is substantial. Operationally, this means that at least one of the following three conditions must be met: (1) the parent company's ownership is 25 percent or more; (2) the parent company's ownership is 15 percent or more, and largest among Japanese investors whose total ownership is 25 percent or more; and (3) the full-time uppermost management is sent from parent companies. Thirdly, the date of investment of parent companies is prior to January 1, 1974, and in operation at the time of research (first half of 1976).

The data were obtained from two sources: the published data book *Kaigaishinshutsu-Kigyo-Sōran* (Japanese Multinationals Facts and Figures, 1975 edition) and mail questionnaires sent to prospective multinational enterprises.

The 37 companies represented in Table 1 are the Japanese multinational enterprises. For each, the table shows: (1) size ranking in terms of sales (1974); (2) name of the company; (3) number of foreign manufacturing subsidiaries and the number of foreign countries; (4) respective figures of foreign sales subsidiaries; and (5) the

Table 1 Japanese Multinational Enterprises (Manufacturing).

Serial number	Size (sales) ranking	Company name	Overseas manufacturing subsidiary		Overseas sales subsidiary		Export ratio (%)
			Country	Number	Country	Number	
1	25	Asahi Chemical Industry	6	6	0	0	15.96
2	51	Ajinomoto	8	9	4	5	7.16
3	97	Kao Soap	5	6	1	1	1.70
4	30	Kanebo	8	12	1	1	15.98
5	10	Kawasaki Steel	5	5	0	0	27.63
6	182	Kyokuyo	6	7	1	1	5.76
7	31	Kubota	5	5	1	3	4.08
8	33	Sanyo Electric	14	16	5	5	30.00
9	237	Shikishima Spinning	5	7	0	0	21.65
10	35	Showa Denko	5	6	1	1	7.86
11	1	Nippon Steel	5	6	0	0	27.73
12	80	Sekisui Chemical	5	6	3	3	4.40
13	74	Dai Nippon Ink and Chemicals	6	6	2	2	4.93
14	54	Dai Nippon Printing	5	5	2	2	1.88
15	28	Taiyo Fishery	9	11	5	6	12.36
16	50	Takeda Chemical Industries	6	6	5	5	4.88
17	161	Omron Tateishi Electronics	5	5	2	2	14.20
18	37	Teijin	12	16	2	2	31.41
19	3	Toyota Motor	6	6	3	3	27.96
20	11	Tokyo Shibaura Electric	9	11	6	8	13.63
21	428	Toko	8	9	2	2	19.53
22	41	Toyobo	7	10	2	2	23.48
23	34	Toray Industries	11	20	1	3	34.83
24	66	Toppan Printing	5	5	0	0	—
25	99	Nichiro Gyogyo Kaisha	8	9	2	2	11.06
26	4	Nissan Motor	6	6	3	3	32.30
27	79	Nippon Suisan Kaisha	5	6	0	0	7.61
28	32	Nippon Electric	6	6	4	5	20.43
29	241	Nippon Paint	5	5	1	1	1.46
30	7	Hitachi	9	12	10	12	14.28
31	46	Bridgestone Tire	5	5	5	5	18.41

Continued . . .

TABLE 1   Continued.

Serial number	Size (sales) ranking	Company name	Overseas manufacturing subsidiary		Overseas sales subsidiary		Export ratio (%)
			Country	Number	Country	Number	
32	6	Matsushita Electric Industrial	21	25	14	17	20.48
33	65	Mitsui Mining and Smelting	5	7	0	0	5.45
34	8	Mitsubishi Heavy Industrial	5	6	1	1	26.53
35	87	Mitsubishi Rayon	5	7	1	1	19.58
36	56	Unitika	8	10	0	0	17.56
37	390	Riken	5	5	1	1	7.18

Note: Export ratio: average for the past three years (1972–74).
Source: Author's Multinational Enterprise Data Base.

average export ratio (export-to-sales) for the three-year period 1972–74.

II.   Japanese Pattern of Multinational Growth

1.   Profiles of Parent Companies

Data on the size, strategy, and performance are available for the 118 largest manufacturing firms including 30 multinational enterprises. In Table 2 these 30 multinational enterprises are compared with the remaining 88 non-multinational companies. The 30 multinational enterprises described in Table 2 represent a main sample of the Japanese multinational enterprises.

Size

Table 2 shows that the average size (in terms of sales) of the 30 multinational enterprises is 2.3 times as large as the 88 non-multinational corporations. Large size is clearly a feature of the Japanese multinational enterprises.

In the United States the average size (in terms of sales) of the 187 multinational enterprises is 3.3 times as large as the 304 non-multinational enterprises (Vernon, 1971, p. 8). The feature of large size is also found in the European multinational enterprises. All but three of the 85 largest manufacturing enterprises based in Continental European countries have at least one foreign manufactur-

TABLE 2   Comparison between Multinational and Non-multinational Enterprises.

	Multinational enterprises (30 companies)	Non-multinational enterprises (88 companies)	Difference
Size			
Sales (1973)	347,336 million yen	148,593 million yen	S
Strategy			
R & D expenditures	0.489%	0.625%	NS
Advertising expenditures	1.026%	1.097%	NS
Product concentration	0.536	0.615	NS
Performance			
Return on equity	11.803%	10.733%	NS
Sales growth	12.860%	13.099%	NS

Notes: 1. R & D expenditures: Average ratio of research and development expenses over sales for 1968–73.
2. Advertising expenditures: Average ratio of advertising expenses over sales for 1968–73.
3. Product concentration: Herfindahl index of the company's sales in 1973.
4. Return on equity: (net income after tax)/(net worth), average for 1969–73.
5. Sales growth: measured by a time-series log-linear regression for 1969–73.
6. The samples for the R & D expenditures and the advertising expenditures are the 30 multinational and the 87 non-multinational enterprises.
7. S: Significant, NS: Not significant.

Source: Data Base of Corporate Resources Project.

ing subsidiary. No fewer than 64 of these 85 enterprises own manufacturing subsidiaries in six or more foreign countries (Franko, 1976, p. 3).[1]

Thus, multinational enterprises based in Japan, the U.S. and Europe have the same feature of large size.

Strategy

The 187 American multinational enterprises are distinct with respect to their strategic behavior: (1) high R & D intensity; (2) relatively heavy expenditure on advertising; and (3) high product diversity (Vernon, 1971, p. 12).

The average R & D expenditures as a percentage of sales for the 38 European multinational enterprises (R & D data are available for these companies only) is 3.2 percent. The corresponding figure for the U.S. multinational enterprises is 2.4 percent (Franko, 1976,

p. 19). Therefore, "Continental multinational enterprises fit the high-technology image that had long been associated with the American multinationals" (Franko, 1976, p. 18).

With respect to product diversity, the European enterprises are more prone to diversify than are the U.S. multinationals. There are very few European equivalents of the American enterprises (for example, IBM, Caterpillar, or Kellogg) that cover the world with one product line. Some European multinationals are even more diversified in their foreign production than they are at home. The data on advertising expenditures of the European multinational enterprises are very scarce due to "a logical consequence of the lesser importance of advertising and marketing expenditures in the industries and products of Continental enterprise activity" (Franko, 1976, p. 22, footnote 40).

As for the Japanese multinational enterprises in Table 2, R & D expenditures as a percentage of sales, advertising expenditures as a percentage of sales, and the product concentration index are compared between the 30 multinational enterprises and the 88 non-multinational firms. With respect to these three strategy variables, no significant (5% significance level) differences exist between these two kinds of enterprises. Thus, with respect to marketing strategy, R & D strategy and diversification strategy, the Japanese multinational enterprises are not so different from the largest non-multinational enterprises. In this respect the Japanese multinational enterprises are rather different from those of the U.S. and Europe.

Exports and foreign manufacturing are the two main routes for a company to expand abroad. Regarding exports, the Japanese and European multinationals share a common feature and are rather distinct from the American multinationals. The 187 American multinational enterprises play a central role in exporting manufactured goods from the United States, but their exporting propensity is not very strong. The average export ratio (export as a percentage of sales) of the 187 American multinational enterprises was 6.9 percent in 1963. The 85 largest European firms on the average exported 26 percent of their sales in 1970. The corresponding data for the Japanese multinational enterprises are 14.6% (1968), 14.8% (1969), 15.1% (1970), 17.1% (1971), and 16.3% (1972).[2]

Performance

The profitability data suggest that the 187 U.S. multinational enterprises are better performers than the 304 non-multinational firms. But, the difference may not be so significant (Vernon, 1971, p. 12). No performance data are available for the European multinational enterprises. The performance data for the 30 Japanese multinational enterprises are shown in Table 2. No significant (5% significance level) differences exist with respect to both profitability and growth between the 30 multinational enterprises and the 88 non-multinational enterprises.

The above examination shows that on the whole, the American and the European multinationals are distinct from the non-multinational enterprises. On the other hand, in the case of the Japanese multinationals, such distinctions are not so clear. Large size is the only characteristic that differentiates multinationals from non-multinationals.

2. Multinational Expansion of Foreign Subsidiaries

History

The 37 Japanese multinational enterprises have 310 foreign manufacturing subsidiaries. As shown in Table 3, 157 subsidiaries (50.6 percent) were established or acquired in the 1970's. The overseas manufacturing subsidiaries mostly have short histories, hence their parent companies also have short histories as multinational enterprises. Of the 37 enterprises, 27 (73.0 percent) companies have become multinationals in the 1970's. Thus, in the case of the Japanese manufacturing enterprises, the multinationalization process gained momentum in the 1970's.

TABLE 3. Foreign Manufacturing Subsidiaries Established in Various Periods by Japanese Multinational Enterprises.

Period	Number of subsidiaries
1955–59	13 (4.2%)
1960–64	36 (11.6%)
1965–69	104 (33.5%)
1970–73	157 (50.6%)
Total	310 (100.0%)

Source: Author's Multinational Enterprise Data Base.

The postwar history of Japanese foreign direct investment may be divided into two phases. The first phase covers the first twenty-one years (1951–71) and represents a rather long infant stage. Annual foreign direct investment during this first phase showed a steady increase, but never reached one billion dollars (approval basis). The investment in 1971 was 858 million dollars, and in 1972 jumped to 2.338 billion dollars. After this year the annual investment never decreased from this level. Therefore, 1972 represents a watershed, and after this year Japanese foreign direct investment entered a new stage of full development. The short history of the Japanese multinational enterprises is a reflection of this postwar history of Japanese foreign direct investment.

The comparable data for American and European multinational enterprises are shown in Table 4. These certainly have a longer history of foreign production than do the Japanese multinationals. The manufacturing subsidiaries established prior to the end of World War II range from 9 percent (France) to 34 percent (Switzerland) of the total foreign manufacturing subsidiaries. The corresponding figure for the U.S. multinational enterprises is 22 percent.

TABLE 4 Foreign Manufacturing Subsidiaries in Various Periods by Large American, British and Continental European Companies.

Country of parent companies	Period						Total number of subsidiaries established (100%)
	Before 1914	1914–1929	1930–1945	1946–1955	1956–1964	1965–1970	
United States	3%	8%	11%	14%	46%	18%	9,127
United Kingdom	2	6	5	10	30	47	2,530
Germany	6	9	3	8	21	53	1,024
France	2	3	4	7	18	67	457
Italy	2	4	5	18	34	37	123
Belg. & Lux.	8	15	4	8	12	53	311
Netherlands*	3	11	4	6	21	55	455
Sweden	3	19	10	11	16	41	209
Switzerland	12	13	9	9	19	38	458

Notes: 1. *Excludes Unilever.
2. Total percentages may not equal 100 due to rounding.
3. U.S. data as of January 1, 1968; all other data as of January 1, 1971.
Source: Comparative Multinational Enterprise Project; Lawrence G. Franko, *The European Multinationals* (Harper & Row, 1976) p. 94.

These figures are substantial. Still, a major spurt in the movement of foreign production has taken place rather recently. More than half of the total manufacturing subsidiaries were established during the most recent fifteen years (1956–70) for any one of the nine countries represented in this table. Thus, the multinational spread of foreign manufacturing subsidiaries is also a recent movement in the case of the U.S. and the European multinational enterprises.

Geographical pattern

The geographical distribution of the 310 foreign manufacturing subsidiaries of the 37 Japanese multinational enterprises is shown in Table 5. The table shows that the overseas production of the Japanese multinational enterprises is concentrated in the less developed countries, especially in Asia. Of the 310 subsidiaries, 166 (53.5 percent) subsidiaries are located in Asia, and 64 (20.6 percent) are in Latin America. Only 47 (15.2 percent) subsidiaries operate in the developed countries. On a country basis, Indonesia ranks first with 32 subsidiaries. Twelve countries have 10 or more subsidiaries (the figures in parenthesis show the number of subsidiaries): Indonesia (32), Republic of China (26), Thailand (25), Brazil (25), Malaysia (21), Singapore (17), U.S.A. (16), Korea (14), Philippines (11), Mexico (11), Australia (11), and Hong Kong (10). Of these twelve countries eight are in Asia and two in Latin

TABLE 5   Geographical Distribution of Foreign Manufacturing Subsidiaries.

Area	Numbers of subsidiaries (%)	
Asia	166	(53.5)
The Middle and Near East	8	(2.6)
Africa	20	(6.5)
Europe	12	(3.9)
North America	23	(7.4)
Latin America	64	(20.6)
Oceania	17	(5.5)
Developed area	47	(15.2)
Less developed area	263	(84.8)
Total	310	(100.0)

Note: The developed areas cover Europe, North America, Australia and New Zealand. The other countries are in the less developed areas.

Source: Author's Multinational Enterprise Data Base.

TABLE 6 Foreign Manufacturing Subsidiaries of Large American, British, Japanese, and Continental Enterprises Located in Various Less Developed Regions.

National base of parent enterprise	Region of Subsidiary Location:						Total:	
	Latin America	British Africa* & Mid-east	French Africa; Africa	Less devel-oped Asia	Less devel-oped Europe	Devel-oped coun-tries**	%	Number
United States	27%	6%	1%	6%	6%	54%	100	4,246
United Kingdom	6	27	2	10	4	51	100	2,269
Japan	18	9	2	63	2	6	100	483
France	18	6	15	4	13	44	100	429
Germany	18	10	1	8	11	51	100	792
Italy	34	10	6	6	18	26	100	133
Bel & Lux	5	7	5	2	9	72	100	276
Netherlands	9	5	3	8	3	72	100	429
Sweden	15	4	1	6	3	71	100	171
Switzerland	14	5	—	6	7	68	100	397

Notes: 1. * Includes South Africa.
2. ** Countries with 1970 *per capita* GNP exceeding US$1,200.
3. January 1, 1971; U.S. data as of January 1, 1968.
Source: Comparative Multinational Enterprise Project; Lawrence G. Franko, *The European Multinationals* (Harper & Row, 1976) p. 108.

America. Only two developed countries, the United States and Australia, have 10 or more subsidiaries.

This geographical pattern of Japanese overseas production is in sharp contrast with that of the U.S. and Europe. As shown in Table 6, the American multinational enterprises have more sub-sidiaries in developed countries than in less developed countries. Except for the French and the Italian multinational enterprises, the European multinational enterprises have more subsidiaries in de-veloped countries than in less developed countries. When the less developed European countries are included in the category of de-veloped countries (this writer treats all the European countries as developed countries), then more than half of the foreign manu-facturing subsidiaries are located in developed countries. Conse-quently, except for the Italian multinationals, the main portion of the foreign manufacturing subsidiaries of the American and Euro-pean multinational enterprises is located in the developed areas.

With respect to the less developed countries, Latin America and Africa are more important than Asia.

Industry Characteristics

The industrial distribution of foreign manufacturing subsidiaries of the Japanese, American, and European multinational enterprises is presented in Table 7. In the Japanese multinational enterprises (column of Japan (2)), 85 subsidiaries are in the textile industry and 84 in electric machinery. These two leading industries are followed by foodstuffs including fisheries (45 subsidiaries), chemicals (33), transportation equipment (18), and machinery (10).

In textiles the synthetic fibers industry occupies the central position. Of the 85 textile subsidiaries, 69 are in the synthetic fibers industry. They are classified by their major manufacturing process as follows (the figures in parenthesis show the number of subsidiaries): fiber making (15), textile manufacturing (52), and apparel making (2). Toray and Teijin are the leading companies in promoting the multinational extension of synthetic fiber production. Toray has 20 manufacturing subsidiaries in 11 countries, and Teijin 16 subsidiaries in 12 countries.

In the electric machinery industry, of the 84 subsidiaries, 53 produce electrical home appliances. Most assemble and sell a variety of home appliances such as radio and TV sets, refrigerators, air conditioners, fans, and dry cell batteries. Matsushita and Sanyo are the leading companies in promoting the multinationalization of their production bases. Twenty subsidiaries manufacture components. Recently, the electric components companies have become active in foreign production following the overseas assembling movement of the major electrical home appliances companies. Overseas production is still limited in the case of industrial electric machinery, as well as communications equipment and computers.

When we compare the industrial distribution of the Japanese multinational enterprises with that of the U.S. and European multinationals, we see both similarities and differences. Electric machinery occupies a considerable proportion of the foreign production activity by the Japanese, American and European multinationals. The Japanese proportion (27.1 percent or 17 percent) is the second largest, and is twice as large as that of the U.S. and British multinational enterprises. Still, electric machinery occupies an important

TABLE 7　Foreign Manufacturing Subsidiaries of U.S., British, Japanese, and Continental European Multinational Enterprises Active in Various Industries.

Industry Group	National Base of Parent Enterprises:										
	U.S.	U.K.	Japan	Japan (2)	Germany	France	Italy	Belg. & Lux.	Holland	Sweden	Switz-erland
Food and tobacco	14%	25%	5%	14.5%	—%	—%	—%	2%	—%**	—%	21%
Textiles and apparel	3	4	38	27.4	—	2	5	—	3	3	—
Wood, paper and furniture	5	6	3	0.0	2	—	—	7	—	13	—
Chemicals and drugs	29	21	8	10.6	46	24	20	25	32	14	40
Petroleum refining	6	3***	—	0.0	—	10	12	6	10***	—	—
Rubber and tires	3	2	3	1.6	2	4	10	—	—	6	4
Primary metals	3	8	9	4.8	7	11	3	15	2	1	7
Fabricated metals	5	4	8	0.3	8	5	8	12	3	—	11
Non-electrical machinery	10	4	6	3.2	4	2	3	4	3	26	12
Electrical†	10	11	17	27.1	18	10	21	9	34	25	—
Transport	6	5	8	5.8	6	9	17	—	3	8	2
Instruments	2	—	—	0.0	3	—	—	2	8	—	—
Other	6	5	4	3.2	2	21	2	17	8	6	—
Total Percent*	100%	100%	100%	100%	100%	100%	100%	100%	100%	100%	100%
Total Number	3,756	2,160	438	310	666	376	101	253	410	157	371

Notes: 1.　* Column totals may not equal 100 due to rounding.
2.　** Unilever is counted in the U.K. column, reallocation to 'company-parent' Holland would increase this number significantly.
3.　*** Royal Dutch-Shell is counted as Dutch in this tabulation.
4.　— Indicates 1% or less.
5.　† Includes office equipment and computers.
6.　January 1, 1971; U.S. as of January 1, 1968 and Japan (2) as of December 31, 1973.

Source: Comparative Multinational Enterprise Project; Lawrence G. Franko, *The European Multinationals* (Harper & Row, 1976) p. 78; Japan (2) is from the author's Multinational Enterprise Data Base.

position in the American and British multinationals. On the whole, this is a leading industry which has promoted foreign manufacturing activity in the countries represented in Table 7.

On the other hand, textiles is not a leading industry in foreign production in the case of the U.S. and European multinationals. The proportion of textile subsidiaries is just 5 percent in the Italian multinational enterprises, and is less than 5 percent in the others. Thus, the fact that textiles occupy a central position in the overseas production of Japanese multinationals is clearly a distinctive feature. The position of chemicals is also different between the Japanese and other multinational enterprises. Chemical subsidiaries occupy 20 percent or more of the total subsidiaries in all but the Swedish multinationals. Among the Japanese multinationals chemical subsidiaries occupy only 10.6 or 8 percent.

3. Ownership Pattern
Minority-owned Joint Ventures
The data shown in Table 8 compare the ownership pattern of the Japanese, American and the European multinational enterprises. Of the Japanese multinationals, approximately two-thirds of the total 310 subsidiaries are minority and 50–50 joint ventures. More accurately, there are 165 (53.2 percent) minority-owned joint ventures and 28 (9.0 percent) 50–50 joint ventures. Only 50 (16.1 percent) are wholly-owned subsidiaries. The preponderance of minority-owned joint ventures is more evident in the subsidiaries located in the less developed areas than in the developed countries. There are 269 subsidiaries in the less developed areas, of which minority-owned joint ventures total 149 (55.4 percent). On the other hand, of the 47 subsidiaries located in the developed areas, 16 (34.0 percent) are minority-owned joint ventures.

A contrasting ownership pattern is found in the U.S. multinational enterprises. Nearly two-thirds of all subsidiaries are wholly-owned, and the proportion of minority and 50–50 joint ventures is only 22 percent. This marked preference for 100 percent ownership is almost equally observed in the subsidiaries located in the less developed areas.

The data in Table 8 indicates that the ownership pattern of the European multinational enterprises is somewhere between the two

TABLE 8 Foreign Manufacturing Subsidiaries of Large Enterprises Based in Various Parent Countries.

National base of parent enterprise	Ownership Position:			Total %	Total number of subsidiaries known
	Wholly owned subsidiaries*	Majority-owned joint ventures**	Minority & 50–50 joint ventures***		
In All Countries					
United States	63%	15%	22%	100%	3,720
United Kingdom	61	19	20	100	2,236
Japan	9	9	82	100	445
Japan (2)	16.1	21.6	62.3	100	310
France	24	29	47	100	333
Germany	42	28	30	100	753
Italy	42	24	35	100	106
Belg. & Lux.	37	34	29	100	184
Netherlands	61	18	20	100	401
Sweden	64	17	19	100	155
Switzerland	59	29	19	100	292
In Less Developed Countries†					
United States	57%	19%	24%	100%	1,583
France	11	37	52	100	157
Germany	44	31	25	100	323
Italy	33	25	45	100	67
Belg. & Lux.	21	51	28	100	39
Netherlands	33	28	39	100	82
Sweden	39	32	29	100	44
Switzerland	54	33	26	100	84
Japan (2)	13.7	22.1	64.3	100	169

Notes: 1. * Owned 95% or more by a foreign parent.
2. ** Owned more than 50% but less than 95% by a foreign parent.
3. *** Owned more than 5% but less than 50.01% by a foreign parent.
4. † 1970 *per capita* GNP under US $1,200.
5. January 1, 1971; U.S. data as of January 1, 1968 and Japan (2) as of December 31, 1973.

Source: Comparative Multinational Enterprise Project; Lawrence G. Franko, *The European Multinationals* (Harper & Row, 1976) p. 121; Japan (2) is from the author's Multinational Enterprise Data Base.

extremes of the Japanese and American patterns. The multinational enterprises from the U.K., Netherlands, Sweden, and Switzerland are nearer to the U.S. pattern of 100 percent ownership. On the other hand, the multinational enterprises based in France, Germany, Italy, Belgium, and Luxemburg are more likely to be joint ventures. Among the European multinationals, however, the proportion of minority and 50–50 joint ventures is smaller than in the Japanese multinational enterprises.

Joint Ventures with Trading Companies

Table 9 shows that more than half of the 310 subsidiaries, 157 (50.6 percent) have one or more Japanese partners in addition to their parent companies. Of these 157 subsidiaries, trading companies are partners in 150 subsidiaries, industrial enterprises are partners in 27, and a bank is a partner in one subsidiary. Of the

TABLE 9 Breakdown of Japanese Partners of Foreign Manufacturing Subsidiaries.

	Number of subsidiaries
Subsidiaries having no Japanese partners other than parent companies	153 (49.4%)
Subsidiaries having other Japanese partners in addition to parent companies	157 (50.6%)
Industrial companies	27 (8.7%)
Trading companies	150 (48.4%)
Others	1 (0.3%)

Source: Author's Multinational Enterprise Data Base.

TABLE 10 Breakdown of Investing Companies.

National base of parent company	Investing Companies		Total
	Parent company only	With other companies	
Japan	941 (65.6%)	493 (34.4%)	1,434 (100.0%)
U.S.A.	333 (97.4%)	9 (2.6%)	342 (100.0%)
Great Britain	221 (97.8%)	5 (2.2%)	226 (100.0%)
West Germany	85 (91.4%)	8 (8.6%)	93 (100.0%)
Europe (including other countries)	449 (96.1%)	18 (3.9%)	467 (100.0%)

Notes: 1. The number in the table shows the number of the manufacturing subsidiaries located in Asian countries.
2. Local partners are not included in the investing companies.

Source: Kayoko Kitamura, ed., *The List of Investments in Asian Countries Made by the Companies of the Developed Countries* (Institute of Developing Economies, 1979).

trading companies, the general trading companies (sogo shosha) are most important and participate in 126 subsidiaries. The sogo shosha have played an indispensable role in the multinational growth of Japanese industrial enterprises.

The data in Table 10 compare investing companies. For the Japanese companies, approximately one-third of the total 1,434 manufacturing subsidiaries located in Asian countries have one or more Japanese partners in addition to their parent companies. On the other hand, such joint ventures are very rare among the U.S. and European companies. The investing parent companies indicated in Table 10 are not necessarily multinational enterprises. Some may have only one foreign manufacturing subsidiary, and others may be small-to-medium sized companies. The data also cover only the Asian countries. Still, Table 10 clearly shows another Japanese pattern of ownership, that is, joint ventures with multi-Japanese partners, especially joint ventures with sogo shosha.

III. Logic of the Japanese Ownership Pattern

1. Ownership and Management Commitment
Total Japanese Ownership
As seen in the last section, more than half of the total foreign manufacturing subsidiaries of the Japanese multinational enterprises are minority-owned subsidiaries, and this proportion is much higher than in the case of the U.S. and European multinational enterprises. Why is the Japanese ownership pattern different?

The investigation into the ownership data has already shown that approximately half of the subsidiaries have one or more Japanese partners in addition to their parent companies. Based on this writer's interview research, it may well be for the reason that Japanese partners (parent companies and the other Japanese partners such as sogo shosha) share common interests and cooperate to safeguard their common interests against local partners. Thus, the total ownership of Japanese partners is equally as important as the ownership of parent companies. Table 11 shows both the ownership pattern of parent companies and the ownership pattern of all Japanese partners. The average ownership of all Japanese partners is 65.3 percent and 11.6 percent higher than that of parent companies.

TABLE 11   Japanese Parent Ownership and All Japanese Ownership.

	Developed area Number of subsidiaries (%)		Less developed area Number of subsidiaries (%)		Total Number of subsidiaries (%)	
Wholly-owned (95–100%)	14 (29.8)	20 (42.6)	36 (13.7)	54 (20.5)	50 (16.1)	74 (23.9)
Majority-owned (51–94%)	9 (19.1)	9 (19.1)	58 (22.1)	82 (31.2)	67 (21.6)	91 (29.4)
Co-owned (50%)	8 (17.0)	10 (21.3)	20 (7.6)	35 (13.3)	28 (9.0)	45 (14.5)
Minority-owned (10–49%)	16 (34.0)	8 (17.0)	149 (56.7)	92 (35.0)	165 (53.2)	100 (32.3)
Total (Average ownership)	47 (64.3)	47 (74.3)	263 (51.9)	263 (63.7)	310 (53.7)	310 (65.3)

Note: Left figures represent parent ownership and right figures show all Japanese ownership.

Source: Author's Multinational Enterprise Data Base.

Minority-owned subsidiaries decrease to 100 (32.3 percent) from 165 (53.2 percent), and wholly-owned subsidiaries increase to 74 (23.9 percent) from 50 (16.1 percent). The proportion of minority and 50–50 joint ventures in the less developed countries becomes 48.3 percent. This proportion is twice as high as that of the U.S. multinational enterprises. But the difference is not so large when compared with the European multinational enterprises (see Table 8). The Japanese proportion is lower than the proportion of the French multinational enterprises and almost equal to that of the Italian multinationals.

Relationship between Management and Ownership

Through interviewing, it has become clear that management commitment of Japanese parent companies is quite different between the wholly-owned or the majority-owned subsidiaries and those which are minority-owned. In the majority-or-wholly-owned firms, Japanese parent companies place their managers in the top positions and assume managerial responsibility. In a real sense, the subsidiaries are managed by Japanese parent companies. On the other hand, in the minority-owned subsidiaries, the management commitment of Japanese parent companies is usually limited and weak. The top managerial positions are held by local partners, and managerial responsibility is also assumed by local partners. The

TABLE 12 Management Commitment and Ownership in the Less Developed
Countries.

Ownership category (%)	General Magagement				Total
	Parent company	Other Japanese companies	Local partners	Other partners	
1—9	0	8	26	0	34
10—24	2	9	31	1	43
25—49	27	5	72	1	105
50	11	0	12	1	24
51—94	59	4	2	0	65
95—100	77	2	1	0	80
Total	176	28	144	3	351

Notes: 1. The number in the table shows the number of foreign manufacturing subsidiaries.
2. When the parent company's ownership is largest among the Japanese
investors, the ownership of other Japanese companies is added to the
parent company's ownership.

Source: Author's questionnaire survey of the 48 enterprises (most of them are multinational), October and November 1980.

role of Japanese parent companies is usually confined to some particular aspect of operations such as technical assistance, material
procurement, or production management. Most of the minority-
owned subsidiaries are not managed by Japanese parent companies.

As shown in Table 12, there are 351 subsidiaries in the less developed countries, and of this total 176 are managed by Japanese
parent companies. Of these 176 subsidiaries, wholly-owned and majority-owned subsidiaries amount to 136 (77 percent), and only 29
(16 percent) are minority-owned. The latter total 182, and of these
153 (84 percent) are not managed by Japanese parent companies.
Thus, Table 12 affirms the correlation between management commitment and ownership indicated in the interview research.

2. Ownership and Strategy
Export of Intermediate Materials and Parts
Japanese parent companies usually leave management of minority-owned joint ventures to local partners. Japanese companies play
only a limited and passive role in the management of minority-

owned joint ventures. Then, why do Japanese firms hold a minority ownership in the subsidiaries?

It is now widely recognized that one of the popular motives of foreign manufacturing investment is to defend the export market (Yoshino, 1976, p. 143). Faced with the import substitution type of industrialization policy of local governments of less developed countries, Japanese companies have to make a choice between losing the export market or local manufacturing. In making the manufacturing investment, some companies concentrate their attention on the export of intermediate materials and parts to subsidiaries. The basic motive for investment in these companies is to establish a steady flow of intermediate materials and parts to the subsidiaries. The exported goods are now no longer finished goods but semifinished goods. Therefore, management of the subsidiaries is not their major concern. Japanese companies hold a minority ownership in the subsidiaries in order to strengthen their position as exclusive exporter of intermediate materials and parts to their subsidiaries.

Export of technology and plants is sometimes accompanied by minority ownership. Japanese companies are urged to hold a small proportion of ownership in the companies to which they export technology and plants. Local companies prefer to have Japanese minority ownership to strengthen the relationship and secure continued technological service. In this case the role of Japanese companies is limited to the technical aspects of the operation, and general management of the subsidiaries is assumed by local partners.

Local Strategy and Global Strategy

As for the American multinational enterprises, the studies of the Harvard Multinational Enterprise Project have revealed that ownership policy is basically determined by strategy. Louis T. Wells, Jr. has pointed out the following four strategies as those strongly correlated with 100 percent ownership: (1) strategies that concentrate on standardized marketing techniques; (2) strategies involving international rationalization of production; (3) strategies based on control of raw materials; and (4) strategies that emphasize product innovation (Stopford and Wells, Jr., 1972, Chapter 8). Lawrence G. Franko (1971), in analysing ownership changes in overseas manufacturing subsidiaries, has observed that strategy is a major variable explaining ownership change. For American multinational

enterprises, one of the most basic strategic choices is between product diversification or product concentration. As for the connection
with ownership policy, the strategy of product concentration is
strongly correlated with 100 percent ownership. On the other hand,
multinational enterprises pursuing the product diversification strategy have shown a high degree of tolerance for joint ventures.

The European multinational enterprises have shown a stronger
preference for joint ventures than the American multinationals (see
Table 8). This relative preference for joint ventures may be explained by the following factors: (1) relatively small size of the
enterprises; (2) relatively short history of foreign manufacturing;
(3) diversified product lines; (4) rarity of operations in consumer
products; (5) experience of joint ventures at home; and (6) production for local markets (Franko, 1976, pp. 122–24).

Is a similar relationship between strategy and ownership observed
in the Japanese multinational enterprises? In analysing the strategy
of Japanese multinationals, the distinction between a local market
oriented strategy (local strategy) and that for the global market
(global strategy) is especially important. Overseas manufacturing
subsidiaries which are managed according to local strategy sell their
products only in the local markets. They produce many lines of
goods such as TV sets, stereo sets, electric fans, refrigerators, and air
conditioners. Each product line is manufactured in small quantities
with small-scale assembling facilities, and therefore productivity is
not high. Yet, the subsidiaries are competitive and profitable since
the market is usually small and protected against imported goods.
Subsidiaries are largely independent of each other and are usually
given considerable decision autonomy by the parent companies.
Thus, the parent companies tend to be tolerant of local partner
participation in these overseas subsidiaries.

On the other hand, global strategy subsidiaries have different
characteristics. Their products are not only sold in local markets
but also exported to Japan and third countries. In order to be
internationally competitive and fit for exporting, they have to meet
international standards of cost, quality, and delivery. To realize
economy of scale, they concentrate on a single product or a few
lines and produce them in large quantities using up-to-date large-
scale manufacturing plants. Overseas subsidiaries are also treated

as an indispensable element in a global logistic system of purchasing, production and marketing. The parent companies need to have the power to change the plans for production and marketing of overseas subsidiaries from the viewpoint of the total profitability of the multinational enterprise system. For that purpose, the parent companies reject participation of local partners in these overseas subsidiaries.

The above argument leads to the following relationship between strategy and ownership: (1) local strategy=high degree of decision autonomy given to overseas subsidiaries=joint venture subsidiaries; and (2) global strategy=lower degree of decision autonomy given to overseas subsidiaries=wholly-owned subsidiaries.

The following is an attempt to test this hypothesis for the electric machinery industry. Of the 37 Japanese multinational industrial enterprises, 7 are in the electric machinery industry. These 7 companies have a total of 84 overseas manufacturing subsidiaries. The following method is used to judge whether these 84 are local-strategy or global-strategy subsidiaries. When a subsidiary not only sells its products in its local market but also exports them to Japan or third countries, this subsidiary is identified as a global-strategy subsidiary. In short, a subsidiary's export behavior is the standard of judgment for global-strategy. Those subsidiaries not exporting are considered local-strategy subsidiaries.

Strictly speaking, all exporting subsidiaries are not necessarily global-strategy subsidiaries. Some exporting subsidiaries sell most of their products in local markets and export the residual. These subsidiaries are not managed according to a global strategy and should be treated as local-strategy subsidiaries. The global-strategy subsidiaries are those which either export all their products or regard exporting as their main business. Thus, the above-mentioned method of identification is not without problems, but seems appropriate given the degree of precision of the data base.[3]

The 84 subsidiaries are divided into 47 local-strategy and 37 global-strategy subsidiaries. In order to analyze the relationship between strategy and ownership for these 84 companies, the method of multiple regression analysis was applied. The result is shown in Table 13.

Indicated in Table 13, the regression coefficient of the dummy variable of strategy is 21.46. This means that the parent companies'

TABLE 13   Regressions with Strategy Dummy.

Independent variables	Dependent variable (t-values) Ownership of parent companies (%)
Constant	45.51
Strategy (dummy)	
export	21.46 (3.63)a
Location of subsidiaries (dummy)	
The Middle and Near East	−24.37 (1.90)c
Africa	−3.83 (0.29)
Europe	7.25 (0.55)
North America	31.56 (2.06)b
Latin America	25.73 (3.63)a
Oceania	38.75 (2.18)b
Year of establishment	1.25 (0.30)
R^2	0.314
$\bar{R}^2$	0.241
Samples	84 subsidiaries

Notes: 1. Independent variables of strategy and location subsidiaries are dummy variables.
2. Significance levels—a: 1%, b: 5%, c: 10%.
3. The sample includes all 84 overseas manufacturing subsidiaries of 7 multinational enterprises in the electric machinery industry.

Source: Author's Multinational Enterprise Data Base.

ownership of global-strategy subsidiaries is 21.46 percent higher than that of local-strategy subsidiaries, after allowing for the influence of the regions where subsidiaries are located and the year of their establishment. This difference of ownership between the two types of subsidiaries is significant at the 1 percent level. When we examine the average ownership after allowing for the influence of the two non-strategic variables, the average for all subsidiaries is 66.98 percent, that of global-strategy subsidiaries 78.81 percent, and local-strategy 57.67 percent. Thus, the relationship in the hypothesis of local strategy—lower ownership, and global strategy—higher ownership, is confirmed in this analysis.

Ownership Follows Strategy

The above examination supports the proposition that ownership policy is basically determined by multinational business strategy. Three sets of relationships between strategy and ownership are identified in the Japanese multinational enterprises:

(1)   strategy of exporting intermediate materials and parts=minority-owned subsidiaries

(2)   local market oriented strategy=majority-owned subsidiaries

(3)   global strategy=wholly-owned or majority-owned subsidiaries

IV.   Recent Development

As already noted, large-scale development of Japanese foreign direct investment has a short history of ten years beginning in 1972. Because of the limitation of this writer's multinational enterprise data base, the examination so far has been mostly confined to the

TABLE 14   Textile and Electric Machinery Investment, and Investment to Asia and U.S.A.

	1965	1970	1975	1980
Textile				
Number	154	259	648	838
Value	62	190	1,016	1,457
Electric machinery				
Number	70	206	652	1,056
Value	9	71	522	1,270
Textile/Electric				
Number	0.45	0.80	1.01	1.26
Value	0.15	0.37	0.51	0.82
Manufacturing investment to				
Asia				
Number	627	1,013	2,768	3,946
Value	177	334	2,038	3,847
North America				
Number	60	67	461	991
Value	95	239	832	2,030
Asia/North America				
Number	0.10	0.07	0.17	0.25
Value	0.54	0.72	0.41	0.53

Note: Number and value: number and money value (million yen) of the manu-facturing investment, accumulated at the end of the respective years.

Source: *Keizai Kyoryoku no Genjo to Mondaiten*, Ministry of International Trade and Industry, respective editions.

earlier infant stage of multinational growth of Japanese enterprises. This last section will briefly look at the more recent development.

Compared with the American and European multinational enterprises, the preponderance of textile investments in Asian countries is clearly a marked feature of the Japanese multinational enterprises. Recently this distinction has tended to weaken.

Shown in Table 14, in 1975 textile investment was surpassed by electric machinery investment (in terms of the number of investments). Recently electric machinery investment has increased more rapidly than textile investment and gained first position among manufacturing investments. The data in Table 14 show, although less clearly, another recent development, that is, the relatively more rapid increase of manufacturing investment in the United States rather than in Asian countries. In fact, Japan's electric machinery investment in the U.S. has shown a marked increase since the latter half of 1970, representing a new trend for the multinational growth of Japanese manufacturing firms. All the major electric machinery companies have established their color TV set assembling plants in the United States (the figure in parenthesis shows the year of initial operation): Sony (1972), Matsushita (1974), Sanyo (1977), Mitsubishi (1978), Toshiba (1978), Sharp (1979), and Hitachi (1979). The total capacity of these plants amounts to over three million sets per annum (as of the end of 1979).

Recently established or acquired manufacturing subsidiaries in the United States also reveal a new trend with respect to ownership pattern. Firstly, most of the subsidiaries are wholly-owned, and the proportion of minority-owned subsidiaries is exceptionally low. Secondly, joint ventures with trading companies have become very rare. Most subsidiaries are wholly-owned by the parent companies only.

Thus, it may be said that Japanese multinationals recently have tended to lose their unique style of multinationalization, and have begun to resemble the American and European multinational enterprises.

V. Conclusion

Basic findings of the present paper may be summarized in the following three propositions.

(1)   Prior to the first half of the 1970's, the Japanese multinational enterprises were rather distinct from the American and European multinationals.

(2)   The Japanese multinational enterprises may be unique, but are not irrational. They have a particular logic, and therefore are rational.

(3)   Since the latter half of the 1970's, the Japanese multinational enterprises have become more similar to multinationals based in the United States and Europe.

Notes

* The present paper is a development of this writer's earlier works written mostly in Japanese. The Japanese references are not included in this paper. Most of them are shown in his Japanese book, *Takokuseki-Keieiron* (Managing the Multinationals) (Hakuto shobō) 1979.

1. These 64 enterprises are the Continental European multinational enterprises which correspond to the 187 U.S. and the 37 Japanese multinational enterprises.

2. The figures represent the average export ratio (export to sales) in percentage form for the 35 Japanese multinational enterprises. The export ratio of Dai Nippon Printing is 1.88 percent, and that of Toppan Printing seems to be at a similar level (data are not available). So, if we include these two companies in the sample, the average export ratio would decrease about one percent.

3. The data are obtained from two sources: (1) this writer's questionnaire survey; and (2) for those companies not responding to the survey, *Kaigaishinshutsu-Kigyo-Sōran* (Japanese Multinationals Facts and Figures, 1975 edition).

References

1.   Yair Aharoni, "On the Definition of a Multinational Corporation," in A. Kappor and Phillip D. Grub, eds., *The Multinational Enterprise in Transition* (Darwin Press, 1972), pp. 3–20.

2.   Lawrence G. Franko, *Joint Venture Survival in Multinational Corporations* (Praeger, 1971).

3.   ——, *The European Multinationals* (Harper & Row, 1976), p. 3.

4. John M. Stopford and Louis T. Wells, Jr., *Managing the Multinational Enterprise* (Basic Books, 1972), Chapter 8.
5. Raymond Vernon, *Sovereignty at Bay* (Basic Books, 1971), pp. 4–11.
6. M. Y. Yoshino, *Japan's Multinational Enterprises* (Harvard University Press, 1976), p. 143.

COMMENTS

Matao Miyamoto
Osaka University

Professor Yoshihara pointed out various unique features in Japanese multinational growth before 1971 from the viewpoint of international comparison. I would like to raise a couple of questions regarding the uniqueness of Japanese multinational enterprises.

I.

Professor Yoshihara discovered that both in geographical and industrial distributions the Japanese subsidiaries abroad had distinctive characteristics: 84.8 percent of Japanese subsidiaries were located in less developed countries and 54.5 percent belonged to the textile and the electrical machinery industries. What were the reasons for these distributions? Why did or why could Japanese textile and electrical machinery companies begin foreign direct investment ahead of companies in other industries?

II.

According to Professor Yoshihara, the preponderance of minority-owned joint ventures was another important characteristic of Japanese multinational enterprises. He argues that the ownership pattern was connected with strategy—namely, "ownership follows strategy"—and proposes a hypothesis based on the relationship between strategy and ownership. His hypothesis is very interesting and attractive, and I agree with him in recognizing the importance of strategy variables. I do not think, however, that the ownership pattern of Japanese multinational enterprises—namely, minority-owned joint ventures—can be attributed solely to the strategy variables that he mentioned. Other variables should be added to account for this pattern. The following variables also seem to be important:

(A)   In the period before 1971, in which most of Professor Yoshihara's study is focused, Japan's international balance of payment was not always favorable and the value of yen to the dollar was underestimated. These conditions were unfavorable for foreign direct investment. Moreover, it does not seem to me that most Japanese firms had sufficient funds and manegerial resources to have wholly owned subsidiaries abroad. Did not these considerations also affect the ownership pattern of Japanese multinational enterprises?

(B) Professor Yoshihara mentioned that Japanese foreign investment tended to concentrate on the developing countries. As is well known, the inflow of foreign capital is often regulated by various means in these countries. Did local government policy on foreign capital affect the Japanese ownership pattern?

(C) What is called country risk is, I think, another element to be considered. I found it interesting that among the coefficients of "location dummies" in Table 13, the signs of the coefficients of North and Latin America and Oceania are positive and high value. Do these facts not suggest that country risk is also important in determining ownership policy?

(D) Other types of risk must also be considered. If risk involved in foreign direct investment is supposed to come from the shortage of information about foreign countries, it may well be said that this type of risk is the diminishing function of experience in foreign direct investment. In this sense, it is quite natural that in the infant phase of multinational growth manufacturing companies are reluctant to invest much money in foreign subsidiaries and are inclined to join with trading companies which have more information about foreign countries.

(E) Finally, I would like to ask Professor Yoshihara about the relationship between product characteristics and ownership, a point also mentioned by Professor Kinugasa.

III.

According to Professor Yoshihara, Japanese multinational activity was in an infant stage prior to 1971 and exhibited unique characteristics. I would like to know if multinational activity by the U.S. and European countries also went through a similar infant stage. If this stage was not present in other countries, perhaps the pre-1971 style of Japanese multinational activity was unique to Japan. In other words, can a generally applicable "infant stage" be identified, or was there a unique pre-1971 "Japanese type" of multinational activity?

The Expansion of British Multinational Manufacturing, 1890–1939

Geoffrey Jones
London School of Economics

I.

The decision by a number of British manufacturing companies in the late nineteenth century to establish factories in foreign countries did not herald a fundamental new departure in British business organization. If the term multinational enterprise is defined broadly, as an enterprise possessing a controlling interest in income-generating assets or productive activities outside its national boundaries, then the phenomenon has a long ancestry. By the middle of the last century many British investments in foreign railways, public utilities and raw materials carried some degree of managerial control.[1] This control was exercised in a variety of ways and, with the rather fluid structures of business organizations in this period, any attempt to categorize these early ventures in international business as either multinational or non-multinational raises complex conceptual problems. Any reasonable definition of a multinational would include the engineering contracting firm S. Pearson & Son which built, managed and often owned railways, tunnels and harbors in several countries (including Britain); after 1900 this company developed a large integrated oil business and managed the whole venture from London. Other cases, however, such as the many investments carrying managerial responsibilities by British capitalists in Argentine railways, are more problematic.

These problems of definition help to make it difficult to quantify British multinational activity, especially before 1914. Many writers take foreign direct investment as the measure of multinational activity, but the two concepts are not identical. Although multina-

TABLE 1   Estimates of British Foreign Direct Investment before 1939.

Source	Year	£ million	Percentage of total foreign investment
H. Feis	1914	300	7.4
Economist	1937	500	12.5
J. Stopford	1914	406	10
	1927	780	20
	1939	1,480	40

tional enterprises use the medium of foreign direct investment, such investment need not be multinational. Moreover, the significance of multinational investment, both to the enterprise and to the host country, is not fully captured by measuring capital flows.[2] Many British companies before 1914 invested management and technology rather than capital in their foreign subsidiaries, and during the interwar years it was common for British companies to sell off minority shareholdings, often for political reasons, in their foreign companies. At best, foreign direct investment can be used as a proxy to indicate the general level, timing and direction of multinational activity. Table 1 gives some estimates of British foreign direct investment before 1939.[3]

This data is most unreliable. The estimates for total foreign investment in 1914 are dubious and probably overestimate the amount of British capital placed abroad.[4] The Feis and *Economist* estimates define foreign direct investment as merely that investment which did not leave a trace in the securities market. It is, therefore, hardly surprising that portfolio lending seems to loom so large in British foreign investment. Recent studies, using current definitions of foreign direct investment that stress the importance of managerial control, suggest that as much as 50 percent of British foreign investment by 1914 was direct.[5] The Stopford estimates are an attempt to reclassify contemporary data, but the resulting statistics are no more than crude guesses. Moreover, additional complexities are introduced by Stopford's threefold division of foreign investment into direct, portfolio and "expatriate" categories.[6] Nevertheless, these various estimates do lend some statistical support to the following propositions. First, investments that carried control were a well-established form of British foreign investment before this strategy was adopted in the manufacturing sector. Second, this type of investment grew substantially between 1918 and 1939. Various regional studies suggest this growth was greatest in the 1920s.[7] Third, British foreign direct investment grew in relative importance to portfolio investment, particularly during the 1930s when British foreign portfolio lending dried up with the collapse of international credit, diminishing investment opportunities and the weakness of the balance of payments.[8]

The significance of the manufacturing sector in British foreign direct investment is not clearly established. It was during the 1890s that British manufacturing companies started to undertake the market-oriented foreign direct investments (investments designed to reach foreign markets) that are the primary concern of this paper. The pioneer companies included Lever Brothers (soap), J. and P. Coats (cotton thread), Nobel's Explosives (dynamite), and Dunlop (tires). Vickers, Courtaulds, Pilkingtons and dozens of other firms had adopted this strategy by 1914, and some of their foreign investments were substantial. J. and P. Coats and Lever Brothers, for example, owned factories in the United States, Canada, South Africa, Australia, Russia, Germany, Switzerland, France and Japan. Vickers had at least £2 million invested in factories in nine countries by 1914.[9] In addition, some of these companies had made direct investments abroad that were designed to establish sources of supply.[10] Although British firms began foreign manufacture about three or four decades after the first instances of American multinational manufacture, it is probable that by 1914 British firms had almost as great a stake in foreign manufacture as American ones, while total British foreign direct investment exceeded that of the United States.[11]

The 1920s saw a considerable growth in British foreign manufacturing investment. An analysis of the 200 largest British manufacturing firms revealed the growth pattern in Table 2.[12]

By 1930 many British firms, some of them small by United States

TABLE 2   The Multinational Spread of British Business, 1919–1948.

	1919	1930	1948
Number and Percentage (%) of top 200 firms with overseas subsidiaries	21 (10.5)	62 (31)	73 (36.5)

standards, were heavily committed abroad; there is no evidence of significant disinvestment during the following decade. Ten of the largest twelve British corporations in 1930 had foreign manufacturing activities.[13] Unilever, formed by a merger between Lever Brothers and Dutch interests, had numerous foreign factories. Imperial Tobacco was the joint owner with American interests of British American Tobacco, a large multinational company. ICI, the giant chemicals group formed in 1926, had £8.4 million, or 12 percent of capital employed, invested in manufacturing companies in Canada, South Africa, Australia and South America by the mid-1930s. J. and P. Coats by 1939 had thirty-four overseas subsidiaries with a capital value of £29 million and seventeen manufacturing plants in European countries, five in the Americas and three in Asia. Distillers, the Scotch whisky producer, acquired distilleries and other manufacturing interests in Canada and Australia during the 1920s. The Ford Motor Company was the British subsidiary of the American multinational, and in 1928 it assumed control of the Continental manufacturing and selling operations of US Ford. GKN, the metal manufacturing company, built or acquired factories in Australia, India, Sweden and Holland during the interwar years. Vickers had manufacturing interests in twelve countries in the early 1930s.[14] The foreign activities of Dunlop and Courtaulds will be surveyed later, but suffice it to say that their stake in foreign manufacture by 1930 was considerable.

Nevertheless, British multinational manufacturing does not seem to have kept pace with the rapid growth of American-based multinational enterprises during the 1920s.[15] The annual estimates of British foreign investment produced during the 1930s by Sir Robert Kindersley paid increasing attention to foreign manufacture by British firms. In 1939 Kindersley reported that such investments had "attained important dimensions," yet he noted that their overall level fell "far short of similar American foreign investment of this type."[16]

II.

In the following sections the performance of Courtaulds, Dunlop and the Gramophone Company will be examined to elucidate the dynamics behind the expansion of British multinational manufacturing before 1939. A number of basic questions need to be asked. Why did British companies begin multinational manufacturing in the 1890s? In what circumstances did companies first consider foreign manufacture? Why was foreign manufacture preferred to other forms of resource allocation such as export or licensing? Why did companies choose to operate in particular countries? What effect did the First World War have on multinational activity? Why did British multinational investment grow in the 1920s? Why did this growth apparently slacken in the following decade? The evidence of the three case studies will be supplemented by comparisons with the experience of other pre-1939 British multinationals.

The firm of Samuel Courtauld and Co. had existed as a small private domestic manufacturer of silk since the early nineteenth century. Its position was transformed by the purchase in 1904 of certain patents for the manufacture of artificial silk or rayon. Following a period of rapid expansion in Britain, the company purchased a factory and American artificial silk patents in the United States in 1910. By 1920 the American subsidiary was the largest rayon producer in the world and a source of remarkably large profits to its British parent. Between 1924 and 1927 large investments in manufacturing ventures were made in France and, with a German company, Germany and Italy. Smaller plants were also established during the 1920s in Canada, India, Denmark and Spain. By 1930 the American company was valued in Courtaulds balance sheets at £18 million, and its earnings represented 63 percent of Courtaulds' gross income.[17]

Dunlop Rubber had it origins in the Pneumatic Tyre and Cycle Agency Company, which was formed in Dublin in 1889 to acquire and develop the Dunlop pneumatic tire patent. Over the next couple of years, other important patents concerned with methods of attaching the tire to bicycle rims were acquired. Until 1900 the company did not manufacture cycle tires itself but purchased the component parts of the tire from already established manufacturers. In 1892 the board of directors decided to establish factories in France and Germany and took minority interests in local companies in return for licensing them to use the patents. In 1893, local manufacture was begun in the United States, but five years later the company sold its rights to trade in the United States to local interests. The use of Dunlop patents and trademarks was also licensed to locally owned companies in Canada and Australia in the 1890s. Further expansion came in the 1900s. A factory in Japan at Kobe was established and it began production in 1909. In the same year a policy of backward vertical integration was adopted with the acquisition of rubber plantations in Malaya and Ceylon. The company acquired full ownership of the French and German companies in 1911 and made arrangements during the First World War to reacquire its trading rights in the United States and start manufacturing there. In 1920 land was acquired at Buffalo for a factory; production there began two years later. During the 1920s Dunlop diversified from tires to a range of other rubber products, and the Canadian, Australian and Japanese companies were effectively merged with the rest of the Dunlop group. New factories opened in Ireland and South Africa in 1935 and India in 1936.[18]

The third company, the Gramophone Company, was smaller than Courtaulds and Dunlop. It was formed in London in 1899. Its activities rested on the ownership of the British Empire and certain other foreign rights (in some cases for selling and in others for manufacturing) of various patents taken out during the 1880s and 1890s in the United States for flat disc records, gramophones, gramophone motors and recording processes. The capital of the company was British, but its management was a mixture of British and expatriate American. Strong connections were retained with the United States. Until 1911 the company imported gramophones from its associated American company. The records sold in Britain and elsewhere were originally pressed in Hanover, Germany, at a plant in which the Gramophone Company held a third share. This peculiar arrangement stemmed from the fact that the brother of Emile Berliner, the inventor of the flat disc record and the gramophone, owned a telephone factory in Hanover.

The Gramophone Company was international from the beginning. During the first year of its existence, it had formed selling companies in Germany, France and Italy, and the following decade saw remarkable expansion. In 1901 London purchased complete control of the Hanover factory, but a British factory was not established until 1908. By 1914 the Gramophone Company had factories in Britain, Germany, France, Austria-Hungary, Russia, Spain and India as well as numerous selling companies. New factories were built in Australia in 1926 and Turkey in 1930. In 1931 the Gramophone Company merged with its major British rival, the Columbia Graphophone Company, to form Electrical and Musical Industries Ltd., or EMI. After the merger EMI owned some fifty factories in nineteen countries.[19]

Explanations of the circumstances in which manufacturing companies such as Courtaulds, Dunlop and EMI consider market-oriented foreign direct investment often stress the situation of firms in an oligopolistic home market as a major determinant. A school of American economists, in particular, suggested a model of a process whereby firms in an oligopolistic position at home seek to appropriate quasimonopoly returns in other markets by manufacturing in foreign countries. It is often assumed that such firms are large-scale, or at least that there is a critical size below which a firm does not envisage overseas expansion.[20] Although this model was originally formulated to explain the post-1945 United States experience, variants have been used to explain the pre-1939 growth of both British and Continental multinationals.[21]

This kind of approach is only partially helpful in explaining the early British experience. On the one hand, if foreign manufacture is a function of a firm's size and oligopoly, the fact that British multinational manufacturing began later than that of the United States and may have reached a lower level by 1914 could be conveniently ascribed to the lower degree of industrial concentration in the British economy.[22] On the other hand, the relationships between internationalization, oligopoly and a firm's size are uncertain.

It is undeniable that the characteristics of an oligopolistic home market, especially patented inventions and differentiated products, were present in all three companies before they began their multinational expansion. However, only Courtaulds felt secure in its market position. Courtaulds' purchase of the viscose patents gave it a virtual legal monopoly in Britain before the First World War. In contrast, the initial multinational expansion of Dunlop and the Gramophone Company was conditioned less by a desire to maximize monopolistic returns than by a sense of insecurity about protecting their patents. The Gramophone Company's early expansion

took place against a background of disputes over patent infringe-
ments and uncertainties about the validity of patents. In the late
1890s the American who was sent to market the gramophone in
Europe was advised that his policy must be "to over-run the market everywhere with our machine and records . . . and use the
patents to frighten off others with or without law suits because . . .
it would take as long as the patents have to run yet to finally win
a law suit."[23] The Pneumatic Tyre Company during the early
1890s was similarly faced by disputes in Britain and abroad over
its patents. The decision to begin manufacture in France and Germany was conditioned by the belief that the patents could only be
protected if local manufacture was undertaken.[24] Many other British companies did not hold secure oligopolistic home market positions when they began to establish factories abroad.[25] The concept
of "advantage" rather than oligopoly provides a more accurate
description of the preconditions for the initial foreign investments
of many British companies.

The relationship between multinational activity and a firm's size
is also not clear. Both the Gramophone Company and Dunlop were
small (by any standard) when they undertook their initial foreign
investments. Even the rapid growth of Courtaulds came after the
American investment and was partly a result of the large profits
earned in the United States. The threshold size below which a firm
did not invest abroad seems to have been very low in the 1890s.
Research on the more recent experience of Swedish multinationals
suggests that many small manufacturing firms continue to make
multinational investments.[26]

The structure of the home market can only provide a precondition for market-oriented foreign investments. By itself, it can explain neither why some British oligopolistic firms stayed firmly at
home before 1914 nor why firms opted for foreign manufacture
rather than export or licensing. Some "trigger mechanism" is usually referred to, and the most often observed "trigger" is tariffs. The
imposition of tariffs by governments in Continental Europe and the
United States on imported manufactured goods in the late nineteenth century was the single most important factor behind many
British firms' initial decisions to begin foreign manufacture. Almost
none of the companies were enthusiastic about starting factories

overseas. The risks seem high and, moreover, British businessmen were firmly attached to free trade principles and looked with disdain on artificial obstacles to trade. Tariffs, however, had to be accepted as faits accomplis to which a response had to be made if a market was to be preserved. "The question of erecting works in another country is dependent upon the tariff or duty," explained William Lever in 1902, "When the duty exceeds the cost of separate managers and a separate plant, then it will be an economy to erect works in the country so that our customers can be more cheaply supplied from them."[27] The same pattern was repeated frequently. A company would find its export market threatened by a tariff, and the painful decision to manufacture abroad was taken. Courtaulds' decision to invest in the United States stemmed from fears that the company's expanding export trade to that country would be wrecked by a tariff increase.[28] An increase in the Spanish duties on imported records in 1906 prompted the Gramophone Company to establish a local pressing plant.[29] Similarly, Dunlop's decision to undertake local manufacture in Japan was based on information that the Japanese government intended "the imposition of heavy import duties for the protection of native manufacture."[30]

Despite their great importance, however, tariffs were not the only influence behind the expansion of British multinational manufacture before 1914. Foreign manufacture was only one possible response to tariffs. A market could also simply be abandoned[31] or sometimes a portfolio investment would suffice. When the specter of American tariffs threatened Brunner, Mond—whose largest market for alkali in the 1880s was the United States—the firm deftly made a portfolio investment in a small American alkali firm. Brunner, Mond's American export trade was run down over the following decade, but the firm received a growing income from its investment in the American company.[32] A range of considerations other than tariffs prompted some firms to manufacture abroad and others to stay in Britain. After the initial foreign investment decisions had been made, Lever Brothers discovered that local tastes in soap could be better catered to by local manufacture.[33] The sales of some products depended on a fast response to changing consumer tastes. The Gramophone Company found that the establishment of local pressing plants reduced the delays in bringing out new lists of locally recorded music. The foreign markets for some products, such as metal containers which are very bulky in relation to their value, could only be profitably exploited by local manufacture and not export.[34] Occasionally, supply-oriented investments led to foreign manufacture. During the late 1930s Bowaters' search for timber in Newfoundland led on to the manufacture of sulphite pulp and newsprint.[35] At least before 1914, lower manufacturing costs rarely figured in the reasons of British firms for manufacturing abroad.

But why experience the costs of foreign manufacture when a local company could be licensed to produce one's goods? The recent theoretical literature which suggests that the growth of multinational enterprise stems from the desire of firms to overcome high transaction costs by "internalizing" market functions is relevant here.[36] British manufacturers discovered what investors in foreign railways, for example, had learned earlier in the century: although doing business in a foreign country always involved risks, these risks could be partly reduced if operations were kept under one's control. British companies were reluctant, or learned to become reluctant, to allow carefully preserved trade secrets or brand names to pass into unreliable hands.

Dunlop's history illustrates some of the problems a business could face in this connection. By the end of the first year of its establishment, the company had developed an export trade of cycles fitted with tires to the Continent and the United States. When fears about establishing the legality of patents led the company to consider local manufacture, which was arranged in France and Germany by taking a minority interest in companies formed by the Pneumatic Tyre Company's former selling agents. The British company contributed patents and experience rather than finance. The company did establish a factory in the United States, but this was sold in 1898, mainly because the parent company needed extra finance to make the transition from an assembler of tire components to a full rubber manufacturer before its main tire patents expired in 1902.

During the 1900s Dunlop began to regret its former policies. The French and German companies were inefficiently managed, thus Dunlop products were "absolutely discredited" in those countries.[37] Yet Dunlop had both insufficient control over the foreign companies to remedy the situation and was prohibited from directly exporting to markets controlled by "sister companies." In 1911 Dunlop bought out the local interests and assumed full control. The company's predicament in the United States was even less fortunate. In 1898 the company had sold its American rights to sell Dunlop tires "for use on cycles and other vehicles."[38] This regrettable phrase meant than when the rapid growth of the American automobile industry began after the turn of the century, Dunlop found itself excluded from the largest market in the world for motor tires. From 1909 the company sought with increasing urgency to reacquire the right to manufacture and trade in America under the name Dunlop. Dunlop's experience suggested that it cost less, in the long run, to manufacture directly than rely on licenses or agents of various kinds.

A number of reasons, therefore, can be assembled to explain why certain British companies began multinational manufacture before 1914. These include advantages of various kinds in the home market, the response to "market failures" and especially tariffs, the need to cater to local tastes or sentiments, transport costs, and the desire to internalize transaction costs. One important remaining reason why some firms were more interested than others in foreign expansion is the particular entrepreneurial inclinations and abilities found within companies which, especially before 1914, could exercise the predominant influence on corporate decision making. An entrepreneur such as William Lever saw the world as his market and was prepared to adopt any strategy to capture that market. Other firms contained foreigners in senior management who were unlikely to take a parochial view of potential markets, such as B. Zaharoff at Vickers and O. Philippi at J. and P. Coats. The management of the Gramophone Company from the very beginning planned an international market for the company. By the end of 1899 the firm had dispatched recording experts to Italy, Hungary, Austria, France, Germany, Russia, Spain, Portugal, Sweden and Poland; by the beginning of 1903 these experts had reached Japan. Despite a total ignorance of Japanese music, and an initial discovery that it sounded "simply too horrible," over the next three months they made some 270 records, "selections from everything Japanese."[39] Perhaps the greatest "advantage" of early British multinationals lay in the visions and abilities of their entrepreneurs rather than in patented technology or differentiated products.

What of the geographical destination of pre-1914 British multi-national investment by manufacturing companies? The early companies displayed no strong preference for any single region or cultural area. The Gramophone Company's factories were, with the exception of India, all in Continental Europe. Courtaulds' only manufacturing subsidiary was in the United States. Dunlop had plants in France, Germany and Japan. J. and P. Coats and Lever Brothers had factories in the United States, the Continent and some of the white Dominions. The primary common denominator was that these makers of soap, tires, cotton thread, man-made fabric, records and gramophones sought high income markets. The exceptions were the investments in Russia, India and Japan which were designed to meet the demand of the higher income members of these low average per capita income economies.

Trading agreements with foreign companies played a major role in influencing the direction of the international expansion of British companies. The geographical direction of the Gramophone Company's expansion, for example, was determined by its close relationship with the Victor Talking Machine Company of the United States. The 1899 agreement effectively gave the Gramophone Company the European and Empire rights to the processes owned by the Victor Company. Subsequently, the two companies worked in the closest harmony, although before 1920 neither company held an equity shareholding in the other. The Gramophone Company contributed 50 percent of the cost of Victor's experimental laboratory in the United States and, moreover, the two companies had a matrix exchange agreement.[40] In 1907 the geographical sphere of influence of the two companies was put on a formal basis. At a meeting in 1907 of representatives of the two companies, two lines were drawn on an outspread map of the world. One ran down latitude 30° west with a bend in the top to take in the whole of Greenland. The other ran down latitude 170° west with a large loop to take in China, Japan and the Philippines. The territory within these two lines was colored red and "given" to Victor. The area to the east of latitude 30° west and west of latitude 170° west was colored green and "given" to the Gramophone Company. Such magisterial divisions of the world occurred in several other industries, including dynamite and alkali.[41] Similarly, Courtaulds involvement in two consortia of European viscose producers between 1906 and 1914 meant that the company did not consider manufacture in Continental countries. The only exception was a small and largely portfolio investment in a Belgian artificial silk company taken as a joint action by all the major consortium members.[42]

The early British multinationals were particularly drawn to the United States, one of the few high income markets outside Western Europe and also a source of new technology in many sectors. Moreover, the U.S. government was increasingly protectionist. William Lever was fascinated by the country from the 1880s, although he failed to turn his American subsidiary into a commercial success before 1914.[43] By 1900 English Sewing Cotton, manufacturers of cotton thread, had thirteen manufacturing plants in the United States and controlled over 50 percent of the thread industry; in the decade before 1914 the greater part of the firm's profits originated with their American Thread Company. Courtaulds' American subsidiary, which monopolized the American artificial silk industry because of its patents and the large protective tariff, also found the country an enormously profitable market. Other British companies were attracted to the United States but were unable to overcome the various obstacles to entry. Vickers failed to establish a direct investment in the United States but partly compensated by securing American submarine technology through a licensing agreement with the Electric Boat Company.[44] Dunlop tried with increasing urgency before and during the First World War to reverse the error that had excluded it from the American market.

III.

The First World War, as the British Secretary of the Nobel Dynamite Trust wrote to the United States in 1914, caused "unfortunate international complications" to multinational business,[45] although business survived surprisingly well. Until 1917 the American multinationals in Europe comfortably straddled both sides of the trenches. British companies with American subsidiaries generally prospered. Courtaulds' American company earned even higher profits,[46] and during the war Lever Brothers' American company ceased to incur losses and started to make large profits.[47]

British companies with subsidiaries on the Continent, however, learned the risks of international investment in the twentieth century. The £55 million of British capital invested in Russian industries and banks was simply expropriated by the new Soviet regime. J. and P. Coats, Vickers and the Shell Group were among the companies that suffered heavy losses. British companies with investments in Germany found themselves stripped of their assets. Thereafter, the experiences of individual companies varied. Dunlop's German company—valued at just under £300,000—was sequestrated and sold to local interests. However, throughout the duration of the war, London continued to correspond through a Dutch subsidiary with its former management in Germany. Meetings were arranged immediately after the end of the war in Switzerland between the British and Germans, and by 1921 Dunlop was back in full possession of its German company. The experience of the Gramophone Company was a complete contrast. Before the war the sales of the German, Austria-Hungarian and Russian companies had contributed 66 percent of the Gramophone Company's total annual turnover of £600,000.[48] The disruption caused by the loss of this business, therefore, was considerable. Moreover, the German management of the Gramophone Company harbored none of the benevolent feeling toward their former British owners displayed at Dunlop; indeed, their main concern was to overthrow British control once and for all. The wartime sale of the company to local interests meant not only the loss of the Hanover factory but also the loss of a great number of historical matrices and the rights to the invaluable "Dog" trademark in Germany. After the armistice, the Gramophone Company not only failed to recover its property but was faced by the galling prospect of watching its markets in third countries being flooded with low cost records made by the German company from the Gramophone Company's matrices. The British Company was forced to begin legal actions in a string of countries. By the end of the 1920s the Gramophone Company had been involved in more than fifty actions in foreign countries.

The experience of requisition does not seem to have led to a dampening of many British firms' interest in foreign manufacture. On the other hand, it may have strengthened the feeling in some companies that investments in Continental Europe were more risky than in North America or the Empire.

IV.

The 1920s saw the expansion of foreign manufacture by British industrial companies. Courtaulds, Dunlop and the Gramophone Company and many of the other pre-1914 multinationals extended and deepened their foreign investments. Moreover, a new generation of companies, such as GKN and Babcock and Wilcox in engineering, Cadbury and Rowntree in food products, and Metal Box in metal cans, established their first foreign factories. This section looks at some of the reasons behind the new spate of multinational activity in the 1920s and concentrates once again on the experience of Courtaulds, Dunlop and the Gramophone Company.

The original stimuli behind multinational investment continued to function and most of them increased in intensity. There were more tariffs after the First World War than before 1914, tariffs were higher, and they prompted even more foreign manufacture. The experience of Distillers, which was obliged to undertake local manufacture to protect valuable export markets threatened by Canadian and Australian tariffs, was typical of many British companies.[49] Tariffs also continued to prompt further foreign investments by established multinationals. By the end of the 1920s, when the world tire industry was suffering from considerable surplus capacity, Dunlop's management felt no more foreign investments should be undertaken unless "tariff walls or national sentiment make it impossible to supplement the manufacture in a particular market by exports from other countries."[50] Tariffs were not, however, an arbitrary phenomenon to which companies merely responded but rather were often the subject of intense bargaining between companies and governments determined to expand the industrial sector of their economies. Dunlop was attracted to Ireland in the 1930s by a government promise to "restrict imports in such a way that when our factory is in full operation, imports of tyres will only be allowed in those types, sizes or classes which we do not manufacture in the Irish Free State."[51]

Professor Chandler's view that virtually all the increased British multinational activity in the 1920s was a response to tariff increases is an oversimplification, however.[52] There were a number of important new elements in the situation. Returning to Britain's industrial structure and to the theory of oligopoly, it has been argued that the British firms which invested abroad in the 1890s and 1900s were not always either large scale or oligopolistic when they initiated foreign manufacture. In the interwar years, however, the contemporary explanations of multinational motivation which derive from the theory of oligopoly are more relevant. The British economy experienced a surge of industrial concentration between 1916 and 1930.[53] Although multinational activity is not invariably a function of the size of a firm, there are obvious reasons why large firms are in better positions to invest abroad than small ones. The positive correlation in the 1920s between the growth of large firms and the increase in British multinational manufacture needs no further comment. By the 1920s Dunlop, Courtaulds and the Gramophone Company were all large organizations operating in oligopolistic home market structures. Dunlop and Courtaulds dominated their respective industries in the United Kingdom, while the Gramophone Company shared the British market with Columbia. All three companies faced increased competition, however, from large foreign companies. The result was that the British companies began to manifest the kind of behavior characteristic of oligopolistic competition or "reaction."[54]

During the 1920s investment decisions were taken against the background of the oligopolistic interaction between large international companies. It is no longer possible to consider the reasons which led a firm to invest in a particular country in isolation from that firm's overall international business strategy. Thus, superficially market-oriented investments could in reality be designed as moves in oligopolistic games. The British government's decision to impose duties on imported artificial silk in 1925 prompted fears at Courtaulds that their French competitors would seek to jump the tariff barrier and manufacture in Britain. Consequently, a decision was taken to establish a manufacturing company in France. This was intended, as the chairman later put it, "not . . . as a money-making venture, but rather as a piece of artillery in the enemy's country . . .

it was considered essential to have interests abroad in case foreign yarns became a nuisance in England."[55] Similarly, although Dunlop's French company lost over £750,000 between 1909 and 1924, the company was supported and expanded by its British parent as part of a strategy to combat a powerful French rival. The French company was regarded as a form of "assurance for the Company's general business throughout the World."[56] "Were we not in a position to exploit the French market as we are," Dunlop's Board was told in 1924, "our principal competitor, having no serious competition, would be enabled to increase his prices on the French market and make corresponding decreases on the English market, and this would have a most serious effect on this Company's business as a whole."[57]

Foreign investment decisions were sometimes made as a means of pre-empting moves, or suspected moves, of competitors. In May 1935 Dunlop decided to proceed with the construction of a factory in India because "unless we do something within the next six months we are convinced that one of our competitors—and probably Goodyear—will decide to establish such a factory."[58] Foreign companies also served an intelligence-gathering function on competitors. Pilkington's French company seems to have been regarded in this light.[59] During the First World War it was hoped that Dunlop's projected American company might provide "constant and regular technical information upon manufacturing processes in America" and "a new field for the training of suitable men."[60]

The growing complexity of international business meant that decisions to invest in a foreign country could be based on the requirements of various markets. Dunlop's determination to reestablish itself as a manufacturer in the United States stemmed from a desire to overcome a major problem faced by the firm in British and third country markets. The automobile markets of the world, including that of the United Kingdom, were dominated by American manufacturers such as Ford and General Motors. These companies almost invariably gave their first equipment tire business to American tire companies. Dunlop hoped that if it had an American manufacturing subsidiary this would encourage the American carmakers to fit Dunlop tires on their exported cars. This would have given the company a reasonable chance of securing the replacement business when the original tires wore out.[61] Courtaulds' decision to buy £2.5 million worth of shares in the Italian rayon producer Snia Viscosa in 1927 was similarly not based on interest in the domestic Italian market. Snia's exports of cheap rayon to the United States during the 1920s threatened the price levels which kept Courtaulds' American company extremely profitable. Courtaulds responded by seeking control of the Italian company in order to force it to adopt a policy of "no increase in production; no further lowering of prices anywhere; immediate restriction of imports to the U.S.A. and raising of prices there."[62]

If the process of international investment decision making became more complex during the 1920s, so did the political context in which those decisions had to be made. Governments began deliberately to encourage firms to manufacture in, rather than export to, their territories. The phenomenon of "government-initiated investment"[63] had already appeared in the very specialized business of armaments before the First World War. In 1905 Nobel's Explosives, Armstrong Whitworth and the British subsidiary of a German explosives group established a cordite factory in Japan at the request of the Japanese government.[64] After 1918 governments became interested in industries such as chemicals and tires as well as armaments, and even firms such as Courtaulds and J. and P. Coats received several invitations to build plants, especially from the new Central and Eastern European countries. Dunlop, when faced by governmental pressure to manufacture locally, always tried to sign an exclusive agreement with a country, whereby Dunlop secured tariff protection for its products and usually other assistance as well. When the company was asked to manufacture in New Zealand in 1937, its reply was: "against an Industry as . . . New Zealand would be better served if it continued to import. If, however, there is to be an Industry, we believe several manufacturing units to be uneconomic and would recommend an exclusive manufacturing and selling concession."[65] British companies also found themselves under pressure from governments to expand the capacity of their foreign factories. This kind of pressure was exercised on Dunlop in Germany during the Nazi rearmament program. In December 1936 Dunlop decided that the manufacturing capacity of their German company should be expanded by 35 percent because "friendly relations with the Government depend upon our willingness to contribute at least as much relatively as other Companies to the motorisation of Germany."[66] Once a sufficiently large investment has been made, the power of a multinational against a determined sovereign state is very small.

By the 1920s and 1930s the need to cater to "local feeling" was widely recognized by British multinational companies. This meant not only locally manufactured goods but also subsidiary companies with as much local appearance as possible. Dunlop had once encouraged local shareholding in its subsidiaries in order to save money. By the 1930s it was doing the same thing out of urgent political expediency. "It is most desirable to have a local capital interest in the company," a paper on the new Irish Dunlop company, explained to Dunlop's board of directors in 1934, "owing to the pronounced nationalistic feeling that has developed in all countries."[67] In the totalitarian countries the pressures were much greater. From 1931 Dunlop tried to sell first a 49 percent and then a majority shareholding in its Japanese company to local interests to be "accepted by the Japanese authorities as a really local Company."[68]

A combination of governmental and political pressures exercised a significant influence in the growth of British multinational activity in India. During the interwar years a number of leading British companies—including Dunlop, Courtaulds and ICI—established first sales subsidiaries and then manufacturing companies in India.[69] A number of factors lay behind this policy. Changes in government purchasing policy favoring local manufacture and tariff protection were the most significant reasons in several cases.[70] Other companies were attracted by the large potential market.[71] Lever Brothers' interest in Indian manufacture during the 1920s and 1930s varied inversely with the threat to its export trade from the nationalistic *swadeshi* movement.[72] Dunlop was influenced by all three reasons. As the company relied for a high percentage of its turnover on central and municipal government business, it keenly felt the pressures for local manufacture. In 1924 it decided to abandon its former policy of selling through agents and form an Indian registered selling company that would "have a much greater chance of securing Government business."[73] Ten years later the company decided to build a factory. By the early 1930s the attractions of the Indian market were paramount,[74] although the form of the investment showed that Dunlop felt a growing need to respond to local political pressures. Although Dunlop was to control the company, 55 percent of the capital was allocated to outside interests in India and was alloted "so as to favour small investors."[75]

A final prompter of interwar multinational activity—especially in the 1930s—can be termed "enforced investment."[76] During the 1930s British companies with investments in Germany, Italy and Japan began to experience increasing difficulty in remitting profits, dividends or original capital. These "blocked funds" had to either be left on deposit at local banks, invested in local securities, or reinvested in the business. The problem was particularly galling for companies such as Dunlop and Courtaulds whose German subsidiaries had incurred heavy losses during the late 1920s and early 1930s but which began to make profits during the years of rearmament-led economic recovery after 1933. The dominant view at Courtaulds was "in favour of getting as much money as possible out of [Germany] even at a discount of 80 percent,"[77] yet the company did undertake considerable capital expenditure on its German factory between 1937 and 1939.[78] Similarly, Dunlop expanded the capacity of its German factory and it also employed its growing profits to write down the firm's assets.[79]

V.

The 1930s saw two overall trends in British multinational manufacturing activity. First, the general rate of growth of British multinational investment slackened compared with the 1920s, although the experience of different companies varied considerably. Dunlop continued its international expansion during the 1930s. EMI concentrated on rationalizing the duplicated foreign manufacturing plants it had inherited from the Gramophone Company and Columbia Graphophone. Courtaulds undertook no further foreign investment and closed down its small factories in Denmark, Spain and Italy. Second, British companies displayed a growing trend toward investment in the Empire, particularly Australia, South Africa and India. There were important exceptions to this trend in the interwar years. Courtaulds made large investments in France, Germany and Italy during the 1920s, and firms such as GKN, Metal Box and even ICI did not restrict their investments to British territory. Yet the Empire-clustered investments of Dunlop, Cadbury, Rowntree and Distillers seem more typical.

It has been suggested that the preference of British multinationals for the Empire stemmed from their lack of international competitiveness. British companies took "the path of least resistance."[80] It is more satisfactory, however, to regard the Empire preference as simply a preference for making profits. The Dunlop archives provide some insight into the profitability of various geographical regions in which British companies invested. A calculation of the rates of return on capital invested by Dunlop during 1936 reveals that the company's poorest investments, which yielded negative rates of return, were in the United States and Canada. Dunlop had faced this problem for a considerable time. Between 1923 and 1936 Dunlop America made a profit only in 1926 and over the whole period accumulated losses of £5.5 million. Dunlop's French and German companies yielded small returns of 3.9 percent and 4.6 percent, respectively, representing a recovery from the losses sustained earlier in the decade. The Japanese company earned 9.2 percent. The new South African company delivered a handsome 12.6 percent during its second year of operation. The highest returns on capital employed were in Dunlop's United Kingdom investments. In the early 1930s the return on capital employed at the Fort Dunlop tire division was over 35 percent.[81] These statistics, however, must be used with great caution. Current rates of return say nothing about the motivation behind the initial investment decision. There were very special reasons behind some of Dunlop's results, especially the disastrous American investment. Yet the general picture indicated by the Dunlop evidence seems to have been experienced by other British multinationals in the 1930s. Investments at home yielded the highest profits, followed by the white Dominions and India, followed sometimes by South America and Japan. Continental subsidiaries yielded low returns which were often positive in France and Germany and negative in the smaller economies. Profitability in the United States was less predictable. Dunlop and the Shell Group did badly in the 1930s, but Unilever earned good profits. Courtaulds' American subsidiary became less profitable and incurred a loss in 1937.[82]

There were several reasons why the Empire was usually more profitable than other regions. British companies understood the Dominions; there were established commercial links, ties of culture and language; and the countries offered a stable political framework in an increasingly unstable world. These reasons both attracted investment and tended to make it profitable. Conditions in Europe were very different. The early years of Continental subsidiaries of British companies were often disastrous, frequently because of ill-conceived initial strategies and poor local management.[83] During the 1930s political instability in many European countries and the rise of fascism also created many problems for British companies. British businessmen tried their best to accommodate themselves to local political circumstances. EMI deleted all "Jewish" records from its German catalogue at the German government's request.[84] Courtaulds assured the German government that its subsidiary would "adhere rigidly to whatever tendency is ordained by the German people."[85] Such flexibility was rewarded with profits, although the exchange control regulations and similar measures often meant that these could not be remitted to the parent company after the mid-1930s.

A second significant reason was the income level of markets. Many Continental economies offered falling or depressed markets for products during the 1930s. Dunlop's tire sales in most Continental countries had fallen to a very low level by the middle of the decade.[86] United States markets were rarely as profitable in the 1930s as in the 1920s, and certain products such as oil and tires suffered from massive surplus capacity. In contrast, the South African GNP grew 70 percent between 1932 and 1937, while the Australian and Indian markets for some products were made profitable by tariff protection. The fact that British firms found it easier to negotiate tariff concessions and other special protective measures with Dominion governments than with, for example, Continental countries encouraged firms to look to the Empire.

In many instances, however, the most significant factor determining market profitability was the presence or absence of cartel agreements. This has been isolated as a major reason in explaining the regional differences in ICI's profitability,[87] and it seems true of other British companies. British companies prospered where market sharing or other cartel arrangements were in existence and experienced difficulties where they were not. Dunlop America faced continual competition from the four large American tire producers and was quite unable to generate a sufficient turnover to match its large overheads. Dunlop's more profitable investments were located where competition had been reduced. In 1934 Dunlop and Goodyear reached an agreement on reciprocal manufacturing. Goodyear would manufacture Dunlop tires in Argentina, and Dunlop would manufacture Goodyear tires in South Africa. The French and German markets became extensively cartelized during the 1930s, and this was a significant reason for the growing profitability of British companies. Yet British companies were rarely able to secure a sufficiently large percentage of the market under these agreements to earn high profits. Courtaulds' German company was never allocated more than 13 percent of total sales.[88] The fact that international trading agreements with Continental and American firms usually allocated the Empire to British companies largely explains both the greater interest in, and better performance of, British companies in that region.

This last point is a reminder of the importance of incorporating restraint of trade agreements into an understanding of multinational enterprise. The presence of such agreements plays an important part in explaining the slackening of British multinational activities during the 1930s, as well as their geographical destination. In the market conditions found in many countries in the 1930s, foreign direct investment was not necessarily the most profitable means of exploiting a market, except when it was in the form of joint manufacturing and marketing arrangements with major competitors. This was the case with Dunlop and Goodyear in South Africa and du Pont and ICI in South America. Alternative strategies were often more profitable. While some British companies with manufacturing investments in the United States lost large sums of money, other companies with licensing agreements with American firms, such as ICI and Metal Box, benefited considerably from American technology at comparatively little cost.[89] The series of reciprocal marketing agreements and exchange of matrix arrangements with American companies contributed significantly to the Gramophone Company's and later to EMI's profitability. As late as 1950, 57 percent of EMI's total record sales came from American matrices acquired for a mere 1.5 percent pressing fee plus artiste royalties. The banking sector provides another example of this general point. During the 1920s, four out of five of the large British clearing banks established branches on the Continent, and all of them incurred large losses. The fifth bank, the Midland Bank, restricted itself to correspondent relations with Continental banks and made a large profit on business.[90] The slackening in British multinational activity in the 1930s compared with the 1920s needs to be regarded, at least in part, as the result of the adoption by British companies of alternative strategies to foreign direct investment to protect, defend or acquire foreign markets. The mirror image of the decline of multinational activity was the increased participation by British companies in international cartels. Products covered by international agreements amounted to about 16 percent of the output of United Kingdom factory trades by 1935.[91] It is hardly evidence of the international weakness of British companies if they, unencumbered by the antitrust restrictions which occasionally circumscribed the actions of American companies, opted for alternative and more profitable strategies to foreign direct investment during the 1930s.[92]

NOTES

1. C. Wilson, "The Multinational in Historical Perspective," in K. Nakagawa, *Strategy and Structure of Big Business* (Tokyo, 1977), pp. 267–73.
2. M. Wilkins, "Modern European Economic History and the Multinationals," *Journal of European Economic History* (1977), p. 576.
3. H. Feis, *Europe: The World's Banker* (Yale, 1930), p. 24; *Economist*, 20 November 1937; J. M. Stopford, "The Origins of British-based Multinational Manufacturing Enterprises," *Business History Review* (1974), p. 310.
4. D.C.M. Platt, "British Portfolio Investment Overseas before 1870: Some Doubts," *Economic History Review* (1980), pp. 14–16.
5. P. Svedberg, "The Portfolio-Direct Composition of Private Foreign Investment in 1914 Revisited," *Economic Journal* (1978). I. Stone, "British Direct and Portfolio Investment in Latin America before 1914," *Journal of Economic History* (1977), considered over 40 percent

of British investment in Latin America "direct" by 1914. In contrast, research on Canada has indicated the continuing predominance of British portfolio lending, and a poor performance of British foreign direct investment in that country, especially in manufacturing. See also D. G. Paterson, *British Direct Investment in Canada 1890–1914* (Toronto, 1976).

6. J. M. Stopford, *op. cit.*, p. 305. Stopford's "expatriate" category is probably best considered as a special form of foreign direct investment. Also see M. Wilkins, *op. cit.*, p. 586.

7. B. R. Tomlinson, "Foreign Private Investment in India 1920–1950," *Modern Asian Studies* (1978). The Department of Commerce, *Foreign Investments in the U.S.* (Washington, 1937), p. 17, estimated that by 1934 British firms had acquired investments in American manufacturing alone valued at $305 million, or over £60 million, most of it during the 1920s.

8. Royal Institute of International Affairs, *The Problem of International Investment* (London, 1937), pp. 20–40.

9. C. Trebilcock, *The Vickers Brothers* (London, 1977) and further information supplied by Trebilcock.

10. It is not possible in this paper to consider British supply-oriented foreign direct investment, which was considerable before 1914, and a great deal more than that of the United States. Differences in domestic resource availability undoubtedly explain some of this pattern. See M. Wilkins, "Multinational Enterprises," in H. Daems and H. van der Wee, *The Rise of Managerial Capitalism* (The Hague, 1974), p. 217–18.

11. American foreign investment had reached $2.6 billion direct and $0.9 billion portfolio by 1914. M. Wilkins, *The Emergence of Multinational Enterprise* (Cambridge, Mass., 1970), p. 201. J. M. Stopford, *op. cit.*, p. 326, argued that American investment in foreign manufacturing in 1914 was much greater than British, but this conclusion is based on an incomplete data base limited to those pre-1939 British multinationals which were amongst the 100 largest manufacturing firms in 1970. Moreover, Stopford relied on secondary sources, some of which are highly inaccurate.

12. L. Hannah, "Visible and Invisible Hands in Great Britain," in A. D. Chandler and H. Daems, eds., *Managerial Hierarchies* (Cambridge, Mass., 1980), p. 57–58. Hannah considers that these figures understate the amount of British foreign direct investment in manufacturing.

13. A list of the largest companies in 1930 is given in L. Hannah, *Rise*

of the Corporate Economy (London, 1979), pp. 120–21. The two companies without foreign investments were Guinness and Allied Newspapers.

14. C. Wilson, *Unilever*, vol. 1 (London, 1954); B. Alford, *W. D. and H. O. Wills and the Development of the United Kingdom Tobacco Industry 1786–1965* (London, 1973), pp. 159–60; W. J. Reader, *Imperial Chemical Industries*, vol. 2 (London, 1975), p. 149; J. D. Gribbin, ed., *Survey of International Cartels* (London, 1975), pp. 140–42; R. Wilson, *Scotch: The Formative Years* (London, 1970), pp. 337–42; M. Wilkins and F. Hill, *American Business Abroad: Ford on Six Continents* (Detroit, 1964), pp. 193–97; information supplied by GKN; Royal Commission on the Private Manufacture of and Trading in Arms (1935–36) Report, cmd 5292, p. 58.

15. M. Wilkins, "Multinational Enterprise," *op. cit.*, p. 225.

16. R. Kindersley, "British Overseas Investments, 1938," *Economic Journal* (1939), p. 683.

17. D. C. Coleman's excellent study of Courtaulds in the first half of the twentieth century, *Courtaulds*, vol. 2 (Oxford, 1969) gives a detailed account of the American investment, but pays less attention to the other foreign investments.

18. Information from documents in Dunlop Archives, hereafter referred to as D.A.

19. Information from documents in EMI Music Archives hereafter referred to as EMI.

20. This is a very bald summary of the kind of approach adopted in, for example, R. E. Caves, "International Corporations: the industrial economics of foreign investment," *Economica* (1971); S. Hymer, *The International Operations of National Firms* (Cambridge, Mass., 1975).

21. J. M. Stopford, *op. cit.*, L. M. Franko, *The European Multinationals* (Stanford, Conn., 1976). This approach has also been found useful by P. Hertner, "Fallstudien zu deutschen multinationalen Unternehmen vor dem Ersten Weltkrieg," in N. Horn and J. Kocka, *Law and the Formation of the Big Enterprises in the 19th and Early 20th Centuries* (Gottingen, 1979).

22. For comparisons of levels of concentration in the two economies, see the essays in A. D. Chandler and H. Daems, *Managerial Hierarchies* (Cambridge, Mass., 1980).

23. E. Berliner to B. Owen, 4 May 1898, EMI.

24. Board Meeting, 1 April 1891 and 5 April 1892, D.A.; Pneumatic Tyre Company Minutes.

25. C. Wilson, "The Multinational in Historical Perspective," *op. cit.*, p. 296.
26. The Swedish case is well documented. For example, see J. Johanson and F. Wiedersheim-Paul, "The Internationalization of the Firm —Four Swedish Cases," *Journal of Management Studies* (1974–75), pp. 305–322.
27. C. Wilson, *Unilever*, vol. 1, *op. cit.*, p. 99.
28. D. C. Coleman, *Courtaulds*, vol. 2, *op. cit.*, p. 107.
29. Foreign Branch Reports 1906, EMI.
30. Board Meeting, 13 November 1906, D.A.; Dunlop Rubber Company, Minute Book, No. 2.
31. T. C. Barker, *Pilkingtons* (London, 1977), pp. 156–57.
32. W. J. Reader, *Imperial Chemical Industries*, vol. 1 (London, 1970), pp. 64, 98–100.
33. C. Wilson, *Unilever*, vol. 1 (*op. cit.*), pp. 99–100.
34. W. J. Reader, *Metal Box: A History* (London, 1976), p. 97.
35. W. J. Reader, *Bowater: A History* (Cambridge, 1981), pp. 129–48.
36. A good introduction to this approach is P. J. Buckley and M. Casson, *The Future of the Multinational Enterprise* (London, 1976).
37. A. Dutreux, Report on the French Business, November 1912, D.A.: File French Income Stock.
38. Evidence of Harvey du Cros, 64th Day. Vol. 18 Dunlop Investigation Evidence 1922, D.A.
39. Diary of Fred Gaisberg quoted in L. Petts, *The Great Far Eastern Recording Expedition 1902–1903*, Paper to City of London Phonograph Society, 17 November 1981.
40. B. L. Aldridge, *The Victor Talking Machine Company* (unpublished ms.), pp. 45–46, copy in EMI.
41. W. J. Reader, *ICI*, vol. 1, pp. 97–98, 159–60.
42. D. C. Coleman, *Courtaulds*, vol. 2, pp. 76–103.
43. C. Wilson, *Unilever*, vol. 1, p. 90.
44. C. Trebilcock, *Vickers Brothers*, pp. 136–38. The licensing agreement was cemented by the acquisition by Vickers of £130,000 equity holding in the Electric Boat Company.
45. W. J. Reader, *ICI*, vol. 1, p. 300.
46. D. C. Coleman, *Courtaulds*, vol. 2, pp. 137–47.
47. C. Wilson, *Unilever*, vol. 1, pp. 224–25.
48. Memorandum on General Conditions in Europe, 7 February 1921, EMI.
49. R. Wilson, *Scotch*, pp. 339–41.
50. Board Paper, No. 1424, July 1929, D.A.

51. *Ibid.*, Board Paper 2540, 27 July 1934.
52. A. D. Chandler, "The Growth of the Transnational Industrial Firm in the United States and the United Kingdom," *Economic History Review* (1980), p. 401.
53. L. Hannah, *Rise of the Corporate Economy*, pp. 101–15.
54. F. T. Knickerbocker, *Oligopolistic Reaction and the Multinational Enterprise* (Boston, 1973).
55. Foreign Relations Committee, 13 November 1935, Courtaulds Archives, hereafter referred to as C.A.
56. Board Paper 1369, 26 April 1929, D.A.
57. *Ibid.*, Board Paper 322, 13 June 1924. A similar strategy motivated the Shell Group's expansion into the United States before 1914.
58. Board Paper 2724, 3 May 1935, D.A.
59. T. C. Barker, *Pilkingtons*, p. 162.
60. Board Meeting, 11 July 1916, D.A.: Dunlop Rubber Company, Minute Book 3.
61. Evidence of Mr. Szarvasy, 18th Day. Vol. 5, Dunlop Investigation, D.A.
62. D. C. Coleman, *Courtaulds*, vol. 2, p. 282.
63. For an analysis of this phenomenon in the contemporary world, see G. L. Reuber, *Private Foreign Investment in Development* (Oxford, 1973), pp. 77–80.
64. W. J. Reader, *ICI*, vol. 1, p. 148.
65. Board Paper 3326, 23 July 1937, D.A.
66. *Ibid.*, Board Paper 3147, 18 December 1936.
67. *Ibid.*, Board Paper 2563, 28 September 1934.
68. *Ibid.*, Board Paper 1765, 23 January 1931.
69. B. R. Tomlinson, "Foreign Private Investment in India 1920–1950"; Rajat R. Ray, *Industrialisation in India* (Delhi, 1979), pp. 271–76.
70. This was the case with the Swedish Match company. See Hans Modig, *Swedish Match Interests in British India during the Inter War Years* (Stockholm, 1979).
71. W. J. Reader, *Metal Box*, pp. 101–102.
72. D. K. Fieldhouse, *Unilever Overseas* (London, 1978), pp. 148–74.
73. Board Paper 378, 3 October 1924, D.A.
74. *Ibid.*, Board Paper 2724, 3 May 1935.
75. *Ibid.*, Board Paper 3030, 24 July 1936.
76. Royal Institute of International Affairs, *The Problem of International Investment*, pp. 43–44.
77. Foreign Relations Committee, 17 September 1936, C.A.

78. J. P. Koppel, An account of the Cologne Company from its formation until the present day, 1947, C.A.: File GCC 74.

79. For the similar experience of American companies in Nazi Germany, see M. Wilkins, *The Maturing of Multinational Enterprise* (Cambridge, Mass., 1974).

80. J. M. Stopford, *op. cit.*, p. 333.

81. Results for the year 1936 for various countries, Board Papers 1937, D.A.

82. K. Beaton, *Enterprise in Oil* (New York, 1957), pp. 361–73, C. Wilson, *Unilever*, vol. 2, pp. 352–57.

83. British investments in the Continent continued to suffer from such problems in the 1950s and 1960s. See, for example, W. J. Reader, *Metal Box*, pp. 194–98; W. J. Reader, *Bowater*, pp. 275–76.

84. Memorandum on Germany, 25 May 1939, EMI: File Territorial Germany.

85. Points for Visit to Herr Schmitt, early 1934, C.A.: GCC 73.

86. Board Paper 3035, 24 July 1936, D.A.

87. W. J. Reader, *ICI*, vol. 2, pp. 229–30.

88. Report by J. P. Koppel, 1947, GCC 74 C.A.

89. W. J. Reader, *ICI*, vol. 2, *passim*; W. J. Reader, *Metal Box*, pp. 54–55.

90. Geoffrey Jones, "Lombard Street on the Riviera: The British Clearing Banks and Europe 1900–1960," *Business History* (1982).

91. J. D. Gribbin, ed., *International Cartels*, p. 8.

92. Antitrust sentiments in the United States were quiescent during the 1920s but became powerful in the late 1930s. See M. Wilkins, *Maturing of Multinational Enterprise*, p. 204; W. J. Reader, *ICI*, vol. 2, pp. 419–22.

COMMENTS

Masami Kita
Soka University

Professor Jones's paper on the behavior of British multinational manufacturing in overseas countries since the late nineteenth century clearly outlines and describes British big business activities through the three case studies of Courtaulds, Dunlop, and Gramophone Company.

I wish to raise some questions to test his assertions. First, during the 1920s, why did British multinational companies not instantly respond to America's aggressive policy rather than wait to try to catch up with the Americans in the 1930s? Besides the business leaders at that time, I wonder why the British government and trade unions were not able to anticipate the future problems and relative decline of British industries. Why did they not react to the problem posed by the Americans, and were they to have reacted, what reaction would they have shown?

Second, when British multinational enterprises began establishing direct branches in foreign lands, how did they succeed in recruiting local staff and organizing work forces there? Was it always possible to find suitable persons in foreign countries where the languages, cultures, and training necessary to understand sophisticated manufacturing activities varied so widely?

Third, I am interested in learning more about the Japanese branches of Dunlop and Gramophone in the early twentieth century. Did not these British companies encounter difficulties because Japan is so removed from the Anglo-Saxon world? And what of the branches of British companies in Russia or Spain?

Fourth, referring to the Dunlop branch in America, why was it unprofitable? The highest return on capital for the company was in Britain. This seems rather paradoxical. Were the foreign direct investments of Dunlop just speculative?

Fifth, concerning British banking overseas in the 1920s, all the major British clearing banks except Midland Bank incurred heavy losses in the Continent. What kinds of business were they engaged in and why were they not able to avoid such disasterous results? What was their relationship with American businesses at that time?

The Evolution of United States
Multinational Enterprises

M. Yotaro Yoshino
Harvard University

One of the most significant business developments in recent decades has been the rapid growth of multinational enterprises. Although a number of United States and European firms, such as Ford Motor Company, Singer Sewing Machines, Unilever, and Philips established manufacturing and marketing subsidiaries in a number of foreign countries prior to World War II,[1] the total magnitude of their investments was quite limited. In the early 1950s, the pace began to accelerate. Initially the field was dominated by American multinationals, but they were soon followed by European and Japanese enterprises. Since the multinational enterprise is a rather new phenomenon, so is systematic academic inquiry into this fascinating subject. This paper is a modest attempt to present a synthesis of the patterns of evolution of the strategy organization and management systems of U.S.-based multinational enterprises and is based on a combination of my observations of U.S.-based multinational companies and the results of recent studies undertaken by colleagues at the Harvard Business School.

There is no universally accepted definition of a multinational enterprise, although some scholars make rather subtle distinctions among international firms, multinational enterprises, and transnational corporations. For the purposes of this paper, I shall define as multinational any enterprise that owns and manages production and marketing operations in at least two countries and in which the affiliates are managed and controlled by the corporate headquarters.

I. Expansion

Historical studies of the development of multinational enterprises reveal that few companies consciously set out to become multinationals. Most companies in the United States began their overseas operations by exports or licensing or both. Typically, they responded to unsolicited inquiries from abroad about their products or technologies. Vernon's product cycle theory provides a persuasive explanation of how U.S. companies began their international operations.[2] Vernon postulates that historically the United States economy possessed three characteristics that encouraged the introduction of innovative products: (1) a high per capita income, (2) a relative scarcity of labor with the consequent result of high wages, and (3) the presence of a mass market. The combination of these elements provided a hospitable climate for the commercialization of technical innovations, particularly of labor-saving innovations. Vernon suggests that innovative products were initially manufactured in the United States because it was advantageous to locate production plants close to R & D centers in the early stage of product development; at an early stage, the possibility of gaining access to low-cost production was not an important consideration. Furthermore, the characteristics noted earlier about the U.S. market provided fertile soil for the development of modern marketing concepts and techniques. The U.S. companies that were successfully established in the domestic market began to receive inquiries from foreign businessmen who perceived profitable opportunities in their home markets for these products.

Typically, at this stage, American companies did not mount a systematic search for export markets. No central corporate policy was developed; exports were an easy way to obtain extra revenue. It is also at this stage that American companies began to receive inquiries about the possibility of licensing their technology—that is, granting the right to use their technology or knowledge to produce a given product in return for royalties and to market the product usually under the licensor's brand for a limited duration. Typically a company's response to such an inquiry was no more systematic than its initial approach to exporting. Licensing too was viewed simply as an attractive extra source of revenue. Licensing required virtually no additional commitment of financial and managerial resources; therefore, it was perceived as a risk-free and easy way to obtain additional return from a given technology. Thus, many firms discovered foreign market opportunities quite accidentally. From such modest beginnings, a number of U.S. companies made rather rapid inroads into foreign markets in the 1950s and 1960s, because their technological and organizational superiority was often supported by the aggressive efforts of local entrepreneurs.

The initial gains achieved through exporting were often short lived. The success of imported products invited active entries by local firms. Local competitors were often able to overcome the technological barriers through the simple process of imitation or through obtaining alternate technology by licensing from another foreign source. Local manufacturers generally enjoy substantial cost advantages over the foreign firm exporting to that market, since the latter must incur the costs of transportation and tariffs and must pay a share of the high corporate overhead typically associated with the bureaucracy of large companies. Moreover, the local firm may be able to obtain special privileges, such as low-cost loans and subsidies, from the government.

To remain competitive in an overseas market, the exporting company has to establish local manufacturing operations to avoid the tariffs and transportation costs and to capitalize on lower local wages and various privileges accorded to local firms. In some cases, the limitations on export are even more immediate if the host country, eager to promote local production, imposes severe import restrictions. The exporting company faces the choice of giving up the export market or establishing local manufacturing operations if it wishes to continue to serve the market. Given the usual reluctance of a company to give up an existing market, the response is usually quite obvious.

Investment strategy at this stage has two main characteristics: it is defensive—its goal is to defend the position held by the firm in the previous export market—and it aims to minimize risks. Top management is not willing to make a large commitment in an unfamiliar market. Information is costly to obtain, and the perceived risk is high. Because investment is viewed as a defensive action in a less-than-familiar market, a company is eager to minimize its commitment. United States multinationals have tended to invest first in those countries that are geographical or cultural neighbors; thus, Canada and Mexico were among the first targets for investment.[3]

The aversion to take risks often leads to tolerance of or even preference for joint ventures, unless there is a strong concern by the management about leakage of proprietary technology to local partners. Joint ownership enables the foreign parent company to tap its knowledge of the local market and the financial resources of a local partner. Also, joint ventures are an excellent way to gain quick access to local managerial talents and the local labor force. The local partner can also be helpful in providing local government contracts who, in turn, reduce risks by lowering the level of resources to be committed and speeding up the timing of policies regarding expansion, dividends, and exports.

Concerning internal commitment to foreign projects, the management of many U.S. companies is usually willing to cooperate in establishing one or two subsidiaries for a variety of reasons. First, a subsidiary is a novelty. The new subsidiary also enjoys a degree of high organizational visibility and top management attention disproportunate to its size and importance, thereby facilitating the participation of domestic groups. After the first one or two projects, however, the parent company quickly discovers that the continued goodwill of its subsidiary is not forthcoming and that the export department is inadequate to support the establishment, let alone the management, of the new struggling foreign affiliate. Responding to this need, the company establishes a small dedicated unit that is the beginning of the international division.

The construction of a plant requires a feasibility study and the choice of a location, equipment, machinery, and technology. Technology and manufacturing knowledge must be transferred. Quality control programs must be established. Personnel must be trained. Production methods and even products may need to be adopted. Many of the skills required are company specific and must be transferred from the product division to facilitate the development.

After the initial visibility of the first projects fades, domestic product groups typically come to believe that foreign opportunities are neither significant nor attractive enough to justify the regular commitment of their resources, particularly their key personnel. In this rather hostile environment, the international division must struggle to mobilize corporate resources for international projects. Lacking legitimacy and credibility, the division must engage in active lobbying efforts to persuade domestic groups or corporate staff to allocate some of their scarcest resources.

At the expansion stage, the international division does not actively seek to manage the foreign affiliates. The country manager typically enjoys considerable autonomy for several reasons. First, the principal strategy during this phase is to establish the company's market position in a particular country as rapidly as possible. These activities are principally entrepreneurial in character. The country manager is in the best position to decide what actions should be taken to expand the subsidiary's market position. Another vital task of the country manager is building local management by recruiting and training local nationals and by developing an organization. This important yet difficult task requires consistent and constant attention. The autonomy of the country manager is also assured by the lack of expertise and resources at the international division. At this stage, foreign affiliates are also likely to be quite small and their performance is not likely to have a major impact on total corporate performance. In effect, therefore, the autonomy enjoyed by a country manager is partly a reflection of neglect by the corporate headquarters. The parent company allows almost total autonomy as long as dividends are repatriated on a regular basis. Control imposed on the country organization is characteristically straightforward. Simple targets in sales and profits are most commonly employed. Control imposed on the country organization is also simple. Beyond routine control, intervention by the international division is infrequent, particularly if the country manager's performance is deemed satisfactory by standard measures.

A critical task of the international division is to build its own management cadre to meet the rapidly growing demand for well-qualified and experienced personnel by recruiting capable—but often reluctant—domestic staff to accept temporary assignments either in the growing foreign affiliates or in the international division. Much of the recruitment must be done internally, since growing and struggling foreign subsidiaries need the expertise of corporate staff groups as well as of domestic product divisions. An international assignment for a domestic manager can offer interesting professional and personal opportunities for growth. At this stage of international business development, such assignments tend to give far greater responsibilities to those willing to go abroad than they can expect in large, well-established domestic operations. Nevertheless, there are some difficulties in recruiting well-qualified personnel. Potential candidates for foreign assignments may see considerable risk in going abroad because of the high level of uncertainty. Personal considerations, such as the hardships of relocation and the heavy travel commitment, may also be hindrances. The candidate may have difficulty in predicting his ability to succeed in a position in a foreign subsidiary or, even more seriously, may be uncertain about reentry into the mainstream of his career path in the domestic organization. There is considerable evidence to suggest that company organization during the period of expansion does not give a high premium to international experience; an overseas manager may even run the risk of being forgotten.

To summarize, the strategy in the early stages can be characterized as a defensive ad hoc response to a specific threat. The strategy is to achieve growth in certain markets, and the company has yet to formulate a comprehensive international strategy. The management control system is simple and uncertain, and organization and career paths are not yet well established.

II. Consolidation and Centralization

Even without much conscious strategic direction and support, the foreign subsidiaries of U.S. companies achieved rapid growth, particularly during the 1960s when U.S. companies still enjoyed technological dominance in a number of industries. Europe had regained economic strength, and the emergence of the EEC further contributed to the development of a demand for the products of American multinationals. Of course, the aggressive entrepreneurial drive of country managers no doubt contributed to the successful exploitation of market opportunities.

The early successes of foreign subsidiaries were often quite dramatic, and requests for allocation of capital and qualified personnel became frequent and substantial. These developments led to increasing interest by corporate management in international operations. This new interest manifested itself in a variety of ways, such as a gradual recognition that the past strategy of incremental defensive commitment was no longer adequate. Recognition of growth opportunities, coupled with increasing demand for major financial commitments, forced corporate management to adopt a strategy of proactive but selective commitment.

Opportunities and risks are now carefully assessed, and return on investment becomes a dominant concern. Capital investment has become substantial. This rapid growth has two important implications. First, international businesses have become an increasingly important part of total corporate sales and profit. The parent company can no longer treat the performance of its foreign affiliates with neglect. This adjustment of priorities often coincides with the time when the foreign affiliate begins to exhaust its initial competitive advantages and to face serious competitive pressures as new companies enter the field. Second, in response to these pressures, the international division typically tightens its control. The lines of monitoring and controls become increasingly sophisticated and go considerably beyond the simple measures used in the expansion stage.

With a substantial commitment of corporate resources abroad, the international division is now charged with a clear responsibility for the profitability of the foreign affiliates, so it keeps a watchful eye on the performance of subsidiaries. The international division also becomes more active in suggesting ways that the foreign affiliate could strengthen its market position, particularly if the performance of a subsidiary fails to meet a predetermined target. At the stage of consolidation, interventions by the international division in the management of foreign affiliates are direct and frequent; the affiliates also look to the parent company for assistance and begin to recognize that technology, knowledge, and skills from the corporate headquarters can become major competitive advantages. The international division will be likely to encourage the introduction of new products, suggest new marketing approaches, and urge the subsidiary to initiate a rigorous cost control program.

The need for greater control and coordination of the activities of various subsidiaries will also arise from the conflicts regarding export operations that are likely to arise among some of the subsidiaries. Some subsidiaries, purely on an ad hoc basis, will begin to export part of their output to neighboring markets as they expand their capacities. Such exports in capital-intensive industries are characterized by large lumpy investments which will, from time to time, result in temporary excess capacity. Without central coordination, this state of affairs fequently leads to several subsidiaries competing for the same export markets.

Another kind of conflict can occur in export markets in which a company supplies certain products to the subsidiaries of another multinational company. If the sales activities of the major subsidiaries are not coordinated, the low prices offered by a particular subsidiary may be quickly disseminated within the worldwide network of customers, thereby adversely affecting the profitability of other subsidiaries. Clearly, as the subsidiaries begin to export on a regular basis, coordination among the subsidiaries in this area becomes necessary and most likely leads to the need for coordination of manufacturing activities and future capacity planning.

These forces will result not only in tighter control over foreign affiliates but also in greater coordination among the foreign affiliates. The first step takes the form of coordination among subsidiaries. The newly emerging strategy of selective commitment of substantial resources in key subsidiaries and the desire to minimize low performance will lead to a changing role of the international division. There is also a growing recognition by foreign affiliates that to obtain maximum access to the substantial resources and assistance of the parent company, they must establish close links with the international division, which can lobby on their behalf at corporate headquarters.

During the period of consolidation and centralization, rapid growth and outstanding overall performance will lead to the emergence of a strong international division that is quite autonomous from the corporate headquarters. At this stage, the international division will be likely to develop a regional structure and a functional staff. In effect, by this time, the international division probably will have developed parallel structures and positions to those found at the corporate headquarters. The newly emerging strategy will have several features. First, there will be a corporatewide direction and priorities that should be stressed for the markets. There will also be proactive search for new market opportunities. A second element of the new strategy will be the management and coordination of the activities of the principal foreign affiliates to minimize unnecessary duplications. Still another aspect will be a conscious effort to formalize the planning and control systems in the key subsidiaries, thereby enabling the international division to influence—if not dictate—the goals, policies, and strategies of the subsidiaries.

Of course, implementation of the new strategies will not be without tension. There will be a familiar power struggle between the international division and subsidiaries. The subsidiary, buoyed by its success and its achievements, will not readily concede its much-cherished autonomy and independence. The older and better established subsidiary by now will have become a substantial size and will have a full staff. Indeed, the country manager of such a subsidiary runs the company almost as a fiefdom and, understandably, he will tend to resist any form of intervention by the international division. The tension is further aggravated because, particularly in the early phase of this stage, the intervention is poorly orchestrated. The international division, anxious to exert its power, may choose an insignificant set of issues as an excuse to intervene. It may attempt to impose a standardized system in an arbitrary manner. The new control system and the detailed data generated by such a system often invite frequent intervention.

Many of the staff members of the international division have been recently recruited and often lack international experience, as compared with those who have spent many years in the country organization and have played important roles in its success. Real and perceived gaps in the knowledge and experience of the staff members as seen by the country managers are also sources of considerable tension. In contrast to the first stage, the pendulum will tend to swing almost completely from an informal and decentralized approach to the development of a highly formal system.

Despite these organizational tensions, the trend toward centralization will continue, particularly in finance. Country managers generally lack technical expertise in international finance. American accounting standards require that the balance sheet and profit and loss statements of the foreign subsidiaries be translated in a certain prescribed manner. The rules of translation tend to result in changes in the movement of foreign exchange rates, which are reflected directly in total corporate earnings. Thus, once the relative importance of the foreign affiliates to the whole corporation becomes substantial, the financial staff at the international division must watch over the overall finances of each subsidiary quite carefully. Foreign exchange management is seen by the international division staff as an area that lends itself to effective centralization.

As the international division begins to exert greater control over foreign affiliates and attempts to coordinate their activities, inevitably differences in views and expectations emerge between the partners, leading to a high incidence of breakups in joint ventures. This trend is augmented by the decreased need for local partners as the subsidiary gains experience and knowledge about foreign markets.

The new strategy can be summarized as having the following aims: (1) proactive search for market opportunities through large selective investments, (2) a better return on capital through active management and control over the subsidiaries, and (3) an attempt at coordination among the subsidiaries in export markets and capacity planning.

As the company enters the stage of consolidation and capitalization, different skills are required for the country managers than in the first stage when entrepreneurial skills were most important. By this time at least some of the subsidiaries have become multiproduct and multifunctional operations. A critical task of the country manager is to achieve balanced growth and to obtain the optimum return on investment. No longer is growth alone the primary concern; the country manager must also be prepared to manage his subsidiary as a part of an integrated multinational system. He also faces the challenge of building a strong local management team and organization to cope with the growing size and complexity of the enterprise. The country manager, at this stage, will find that he must interact much more frequently with the international division and even with the corporate headquarters. He must be able to compete for corporate resources: a process that may well involve a series of negotiations with other country managers as well as with the staff of the international division. Particularly in diversified companies, the product groups begin to exercise increasing influence over the international operations as they become aware of the potential importance of international business. As the product lines expand, the country manager needs the support of the product divisions, but he must balance the interests of the total country operation with that of any specific product division. The balancing of the interests of product and area is particularly difficult in the early stage, since the relationship has not yet become formalized. These emerging needs put new requirements on country managers, as the critical skills shift from those centering on entrepreneurial activities to more general management activities.

By this time, the international division will have attained full legitimacy and maturity. It has gained the status of being the focal point for the company's international business and has gained considerable experience in managing the international business.

Moreover, the first generation of country managers will have been replaced by those appointed by the international division. The credibility of the international division will also increase, since a substantial number of the staff of the international division will have had an assignment or two in foreign subsidiaries. The international division is now responsible for an increasingly important and growing part of total corporate activities. By this time it has also established credible career paths at least within international business. However, the corporate headquarters staff and domestic product divisions have not yet acquired the full expertise and competence to enable them to take over the management of international business. The international division still must formulate policy, set goals and performance objectives, and monitor the performance of each subsidiary.

III. Strategic Divergence

It is not uncommon for many multinational enterprises to remain in the second stage, but some will find it necessary to reexamine their strategies as they face a new set of opportunities and threats. The most serious challenge that generates the need for a new strategy is competitive pressure. A notable feature of this stage is that, unlike the two previous situations, the responses begin to diverge, depending to a large extent on the particular industry and the political environment in which it operates.

1. Emphasizing an Integration Strategy

One response is to work toward a strategy built around the integration of manufacturing activities—that is, to move away from a country-specific strategy in which manufacturing capacities are geared to serve a specific market to that of an integrated system which can profit from the economies of scale in manufacturing.

A classic example of such a strategy is in the automobile industry.[4] In recent years a certain segment of the industry—namely, small fuel-efficient passenger cars—is increasingly becoming global in nature. Product preferences have become quite homogeneous. Other factors are the rise of Japan as a major producer and exporter and the formation of the EEC, which has contributed to global marketing.

By the early 1970s, because of these developments, the industry had become quite mature and extremely competitive in most countries, particularly in Western Europe. For mass-produced economy cars, price had become the primary competition. Though the area was quickly developing as an integrated regional market, European industry has a large number of national producers as well as subsidiaries of the Big Three automakers in the United States.

The automobile industry is extremely sensitive to scale, yet manufacturers could not ignore market needs; to gain a market share, they had to offer differentiated and cost-efficient products. Thus, the manufacturers had to strike a delicate balance between the need to obtain maximum economies of scale in production and marketing on the one hand and the equally demanding need to offer differentiated models and product lines on the other.

As the European market became increasingly competitive in the early 1970s, Ford and GM were among the first to suffer from the intense competition. In the key national markets such as the United Kingdom, Germany, and France, there were strong local producers. The leading local firms were larger than the subsidiaries of the two U.S. automakers; moreover, they enjoyed the distinct advantages of being national firms in their respective markets. Ford responded to this competitive situation in a rather imaginative way by attempting to exploit the potential benefits of integration through linking its various subsidiaries in Europe into an integrated manufacturing network. Ford's strategy of integration was quite straightforward and consisted of the following elements: (1) development of common product lines for Europe, (2) specialization of engineering design and function by country, and (3) streamlining production.

Ford's strategy was simple, but implementation posed a major challenge. It took almost a decade to bring about integration between the two large existing country organizations in Germany and the United Kingdom. As a part of its new strategy, Ford built new plants in France and Spain to manufacture transmissions and certain engines. The Spanish plant also handled assembly. Both France and Spain offered lower labor costs than Germany and better productivity than the United Kingdom. Ford also sought to achieve a greater degree of specialization in its German and British plants. Thus by the end of the decade of the 1970s, Ford's European manufacturing activities had been streamlined. A program to achieve plant-by-plant specialization and the cross shipment of parts and components had been established, and the company had achieved considerable flexibility in the use of common components. Furthermore, Ford used this integrated system to launch a new car called Fiesta. Significantly, Fiesta was conceived, designed, engineered, and introduced first in Europe and only later in the United States. Ford's example illustrates the strategy of regional integration. A number of companies such as IBM and Texas Instruments have attempted to go even a step further by seeking to achieve global integration.

The transition from a country-specific strategy to one built around regional or global integration is not an easy task. Considerable adjustment must be made in organizational structures and management systems. Looking at the structural changes alone, the response pattern that is required varies considerably and depends on such elements as product diversity, market heterogeneity, and requirements for marketing products.

A common structural approach is to abandon the international division in favor of a global product division. The international division's previous sole purpose has been to manage the company's far-flung subsidiaries which the domestic market has organized

along product lines. Stopford notes that as international business
gains relative importance it contributes to the breaking up of the
international division, particularly among firms with wide product
diversity.[5] According to Stopford, with the rapid growth of international business, there is an ever-increasing need for a smooth
technological flow from the domestic product division to foreign
affiliates. Basic technology as well as other knowledge are found in
the domestic product divisions, and a growing interest in international business by the product division will eliminate the need for
the international division. In fact, Stopford goes as far as to assert
that the international division often becomes a barrier for effective
communication between the product division and foreign affiliates.

The international division is also dissolved when its size becomes
politically unacceptable to the other divisions. The rapid growth of
international business in many companies propels the international
division into becoming the largest division in the company and this
drives the domestic divisions into a coalition against the international division, which will eventually lead to its dissolution. Company commitment to a regional or global strategy tends to speed up
the process of dissolution.

The pursuit of an integration strategy, however, does not always
lead to the dissolution of the international division in favor of the
adoption of global product divisions. A recent study by Bartlett[6]
suggests the presence of considerable adaptability on the part of
the international division, enabling it to change its functions and
orientation to meet a changing environment and thereby assure its
continued viability. Bartlett suggests that domestic product divisions are not always effective or capable when managing international business. For one thing, it is often not practical for a company
to give dominance to the product groups in such an unambiguous
manner, since the product divisions sometimes lack the competence
and experience to manage their businesses on a global basis. This is
evidenced in a recent study that shows when such restructuring
takes place, contrary to the initial expectation, the rate of new
product introduction in foreign subsidiaries slows down considerably.

Another reason cited for the continued viability of the international division is that it is not practical to totally ignore the area

organization. Certain tasks must be performed in a country organization and they include relations with unions and the government: two key external forces that multinational enterprises must be sensitive to. Each country operation, regardless of how it is internally organized, is expected to present a consistent posture on matters relating to public and external relations. Some products require extensive local adaptation in product features, manufacturing processes, and marketing activities, and these adaptions can be managed more effectively at a country level.

In addition to creating pressure for change in the organizational structure, the strategy that seeks regional or global integration imposes a series of new managerial challenges. One complication is that the desired level of integration differs according to function. For example, research and development usually must be more closely integrated than marketing or distribution.[7] Considerable economies of scale can be gained by undertaking large-scale research centrally, but except for certain limited activities, marketing still must be carried out on a national basis.

Integration strategy also requires a new management system. No longer can each subsidiary be considered an independent and autonomous entity whose performance can be easily measured. During the stage of consolidation and centralization, an elaborate evaluation system was installed that centered only on each national unit. The country manager was evaluated on the performance of his country organization because the integrity of country operations was still maintained.

As the company pursues a strategy of integration, however, the power of the country manager is particularly affected in the key areas of engineering and product development, and manufacturing. Both of these activities will tend to be centralized, and the country manager's authority over the decisions affecting these areas will be reduced substantially. The primary tasks of the country manager are to coordinate local sales efforts and to represent the company abroad. A smooth flow of goods and services is an essential ingredient of this strategy and requires the establishment of a proper system of transfer prices. The internal accounting and measurement systems must be consistent so that they may serve as an equitable base for performance evaluation.

The system of transfer pricing must also be scrutinized by the host government. The host government is often suspicious of intra-company transactions within a multinational enterprise and fears that the transfer pricing system may be used as a disquieting means to repatriate profit from a particular country to the corporate head-quarters overseas without paying taxes to the host government. The strategy of integration also raises another set of thorny problems vis-á-vis the host government and labor unions. A common fear felt by the host country is that multinationals have the ability to shift their production bases at will among several countries and that they do so with little consideration for national welfare. Whether or not multinationals truly enjoy such flexibility is questionable; neverthe-less, this concern by host countries is quite prevalent. For under-standable reasons, the fear is particularly serious for a company that is pursuing an integrated strategy. Therefore, the country manager has an important responsibility to provide ongoing advice and in-formation about the local political climate and the union situation and he also must assume much of the responsibility for representing the company to the host government on a number of sensitive mat-ters. While these are important duties for country managers under any circumstances, they are particularly important when a multi-national enterprise commits itself to the pursuit of an integrated strategy. To complicate matters further for the country manager, many of the decisions which will affect him, including those relating to manufacturing as mentioned earlier, are not under his direct control.

2. Emphasizing a Country Specific Strategy

Not every multinational enterprise responds to competitive pres-sure in the same way. In fact, some enterprises seek to gain com-petitive leverage by pursuing a strategy particularly geared to satis-fying local requirements. In this category there are two major types of companies. Companies of the first type are characterized by (1) individual markets which are quite heterogeneous, (2) low tech-nology content, (3) few economies of scale in manufacturing and marketing, and (4) effective marketing and distribution as their keys to success. The packaged food industry is an excellent example. The packaged food industry in the United States made major inroads into the foreign markets in the 1950s and 1960s. Packaged food companies developed highly standardized products with a strong convenience appeal supported by aggressive marketing to meet the particular demands of the U.S. market.

After active initial expansion, which almost always combined acquisitions of small family-owned local manufacturers and newly established affiliates, each of these companies typically went through a process of consolidation and received additional resources and new management talents.

As a part of this consolidation, regional headquarters were established to implement tighter control and to obtain the benefits of integration in manufacturing and marketing among the subsidiaries. As a part of this effort, a detailed and sophisticated information system was established, and the staff group, both at regional headquarters and in the international division, became closely involved in the strategic and tactical decisions of individual foreign subsidiaries. In many cases, these efforts failed to produce the expected results; on the contrary, the problems associated with centralization and integration became increasingly apparent. The inherent characteristics of the industry did not lend themselves to such a centralized strategy. For most products in the packaged food industry, economies of scale in production are not important, and aside from packaging and brand names, there are few benefits associated with economies of scale in marketing.

The critical task in the packaged food industry is marketing. The successful introduction of American marketing skills or new products developed in the United States market are no doubt important; however, such skills and products are reasonably easy to adopt, so there is little need for close and frequent communication. Because the basic technology neither is complicated nor subject to frequent changes, there is no compelling need for the subsidiaries to maintain strong ties with the corporate headquarters. Similarly, marketing expertise, once it is internalized by foreign affiliates, is not so complex that it requires constant guidance from headquarters. Fundamental to the success of such an operation is the development of an effective blend of American and local marketing approaches. Much individual discretion and judgment are required to customize such a blend since arbitrarily imposed standardization is neither workable nor effective. Recognition of the disadvantages associated with centralization has resulted in a gradual shift of power back to the local managers, who in turn are encouraged to design and pursue a strategy that addresses the needs of a specific country.

It is important to recognize that the new autonomy enjoyed by the country managers emphasizing a country specific strategy is quite different from the first stage of expansion. In contrast to the earlier stage, autonomy represents an explicit decision on the part of corporate headquarters to decentralize key decisions to the country level while making sure that the management of subsidiaries is familiar not only with the fundamental policies, strategies, and practices of the parent company but also with the resources available at the headquarters. By now even the acquired companies have become acculturated into the norms of the corporate system. Because of this acculturation, country management knows how and when to tap corporate resources and is in a position to design an effective blend of American and local approaches.

Bartlett characterizes the strategy, structure, and managerial system followed by this particular group of multinational enterprises as a federal system that is comparable to a federal system of government in which each state—in national enterprises, each country organization—maintains its autonomy and retains the basic rights and responsibilities of government.[8] Each local unit, however, is tied to a common parent that assumes responsibilities for those areas which affect the entire system. Structurally, such a system may organize itself by area or may retain the traditional international division. An earlier study by Stopford indicated that under these conditions the area organization will eventually replace the international division, particularly when international business becomes very important. In such an organization, the world is divided into five or six regions, including the United States, and the head of each region reports directly to corporate management. A recent study by Bartlett, however, challenges this conclusion by noting that the demise of the international division does not necessarily follow as the company emerges into the third stage and depends to a large degree on the effectiveness with which the international division can respond to the changing strategy.

The second type of industry which pursue country specific—or what Doz calls "nationally responsive"—strategies have characteristics that are fundamentally different from those of the previous example.

These industries show one common characteristic: they are "politically salient"—that is, they are those industries in which the host government has the most vital interest. These industries are important to the national economy because of their political sensitivity. The telecommunications equipment industry provides an excellent example. In most countries its major customers are heavily controlled, if not owned outright, by the government. The telecommunications equipment industry has several important characteristics that make multinational integration impractical, despite the possibility of economic benefits associated with such a move. For example, long-term contracts with a very small number of suppliers are preferred over competitive bidding; the useful life of equipment is rather long; and customers place high premium on reliability in quality, delivery, and services. Thus, once a supplier for a certain part of a telecommunication equipment network is selected, that supplier can expect to have a substantial contract with the telecommunications industry which will continue for a long time.

Because of its high political visibility, a host country is eager to exert maximum control over technology and local production. In return, the government is usually quite willing to offer protection, subsidies, and incentives. Under these circumstances the integration strategy noted earlier is hardly viable in economic terms, and multinationals, for competitive reasons, are required to conform to the national policies of the host country. Thus, multinationals in these industries must trade off the benefits derived from integration for other advantages.

Another example of a politically sensitive industry in which some companies choose to pursue a country-specific strategy is the computer industry. Virtually every advanced nation in the world is anxious to develop its own computer industry, but few have been successful. A small number of multinational enterprises, most notably I.B.M., have established enormous barriers to entry. In the computer industry, economic imperatives favor large well-established multinational corporations. The economies of scale in R & D, manufacturing, marketing, and service are indeed formidable.

The so-called switching cost a customer may be prepared to incur in changing its computer system can be very high. Moreover, the market for data processing equipment is homogeneous. These barriers to entry must be overcome by national champions to achieve successful entry into the computer industry, and national governments face a serious dilemma between these economic realities and their compelling political imperatives.

At the same time, small multinationals also find it difficult to prosper in this environment. Obviously, they cannot beat I.B.M. at its own game, which is based on effective global integration. One viable strategy enabling weaker multinational companies to compete against I.B.M. is for them to enter joint ventures with national champions faced with similar competitive disadvantages. This strategy will give the small multinational a national company status, which is a major advantage over the subsidiary of I.B.M. in that country. The small multinational will also be given preferential if not exclusive access to certain segments of the market, particularly the government-related customers, and can most likely benefit from various government incentives and subsidies. In return, the multinational pursuing this strategy must give up a certain amount of strategic freedom, namely, ownership and management control. An outstanding example of this situation is the alliance between Honeywell, a U.S. multinational, and C–2I, the national champion in France, to form a joint venture in France.[9] Honeywell promised to provide C–2I with R & D support for its parent and economic efficiency to be achieved from the integration of its affiliates in other European countries. Honeywell also committed itself to be responsive to French policy and French national interests.

The strategy of Honeywell presents a considerable challenge to management, since there is a constant danger of fragmentation and duplication, particularly in the areas of research and development and manufacturing. To achieve the benefits of integration and coordination to the maximum degree tolerated by the political imperatives becomes a real challenge for the national management. This effort is particularly important in the sharing of technology and relevant managerial practices among the subsidiaries.

Top management must also make certain that the country manager makes the optimum decision after weighing both economic and political imperatives. The measurement system must be such that it encourages the country manager to take political advantage into full consideration. It would be self-defeating indeed if the manager opted for short-term economic gains at the expense of ignoring long-term opportunities.

In joint ventures with state-owned enterprises, management faces even more direct challenges, since the interests of the partners do not always coincide. The U.S. multinational must carefully weigh its own interests against those of its partner. This is a delicate process under any circumstances, particularly so when the national champion is represented directly by a voice within management. It is indeed at the national management level that conflicts of interest are likely to manifest themselves in a concerted manner and, more importantly, that is where they must be dealt with.

The country manager's responsibilities are considerable. He must understand both the economic and the political realities and must be able to respond effectively to demands made by the government officials of the host country as well as by the local partner. These demands are frequently inconsistent with the interests of the multinational company. The ultimate responsibility for striking a proper balance rests with the country manager. For these reasons, the country manager tends to be a native of that country. Because of the great power and responsibility he wields, in contrast to the rather small and limited power of the corporate staff, the country manager is less likely to aspire to a position at the regional or even the corporate headquarters. Unlike the situation in integrated multinationals, career paths in subsidiaries tend to be highly localized.

3. A Balanced Approach

The pursuit of a clear-cut strategy focusing on either a product or area is not always feasible nor is it always desirable. Multinationals in a number of industries face constant pressure from host governments seeking to promote their own national goals and to maximize the local value added. Nevertheless, the economic advantages derived from integration can be substantial.

In the drug industry, for example, R & D can be best carried out at the corporate headquarters, since there are considerable economies of scale. Similarly, maintainance of volume is very important in bulk production; thus, bulk production operations should preferably be located in a few centers that supply a network of subsidiaries. Decisions concerning marketing and most aspects of government relations can best be implemented locally. However, even government relations, which are so vital in this industry, cannot be totally left to the national management. For example, the pressure by one government to reduce the prices of popular drugs can have a major international impact. Moreover, the industry is highly visible politically. The subsidiaries of multinational companies are closely watched and regulated, and the local government can affect the well-being of a subsidiary in a number of important ways. In such cases, top management must carefully balance the economic advantages gained from integration against the political demands made to the foreign affiliates by host governments.

Organizational strategy requires reconciling the often conflicting views expressed by those representing the product and area points of view. Reconciliation is particularly challenging for several reasons. One reason is that the relationship between product and area must be left deliberately ambiguous in order to maximize flexibility. This is particularly difficult for U.S. managers, who seek clearly defined assignments and responsibilities. Another reason is that much of the burden of conflict resolution falls on the middle managers who each represent a particular point of view of either the area or the product. Of course, conflicts in critical areas can be brought to the attention of top management, but there is no way for top management to deal with each conflict. The implicit strategy requires that resolution of less important tensions is up to middle management representing in the area or product. This puts an extra strain on the system.

The task of resolving tensions within the system is further complicated by the geographic dispersion of those who are or must be involved in the decision-making process. Conflict resolution is difficult enough even under ideal circumstances. The absence of frequent opportunities for personal interactions and language and cultural differences are likely to exaggerate the problems of communication.

In a recent study, Doz, Bartlett, and Prahalad[10] shed considerable light on various ways that a business can be managed. The first way is what the authors call substantive decision management. In this approach, top management makes certain that the differing views representing the points of view of products, area, or functions are put forth for their consideration and they in turn make the decisions in each case. The authors cite simplicity as the main advantage of this approach. There are, however, several disadvantages. One disadvantage is the heavy concentration of decision making at the top, which may result in delay or, even worse, in poor decisions. This system of advocacy is likely to encourage the presentation of only those selected facts that favor a particular point of view. Moreover, only very extreme positions may be presented. Pushing a decision up to top management often results in a hardening of the respective positions and may impede effective implementation after the decision is finally made.

The second approach is what the authors call substantive decision arbitration, in which top management deliberately delegates critical balancing responsibilities to a specially designated and trusted group. This approach overcomes the problem of top management overload and avoids frequent direct intervention by top management. However, it can be quite time consuming and devisive. The authors note that this approach can be most effective in a stable industry in which the need to make strategic decisions is infrequent. They note that for companies in an environment fraught with frequent changes and instability and characterized by great tensions between national and global demands, top management must retreat from direct involvement. A way to resolve the tensions in these circumstances is through what they call temporary coalition management which involves task forces, project teams, and other forms of temporary structure to give top management considerable flexibility in managing the composition of these temporary coalitions. The success of this third approach, note the authors, rests on two important variables. First, top management must ensure that there are informal interactions among the managers so those with different perspectives are willing to express their views. Second, top management must be able to move key personnel with different backgrounds in and out of temporary groups.

The fourth approach the authors suggest is the most subtle of all, that is, to manage the decision-making process so that key executives initiate discussions on their own. The authors call this approach decision context management. This approach has two major advantages: top management does not have to intervene formally on every occasion, and the need for necessary interaction and integration are recognized at the level closest to the problem and result in a quick response. This approach, though highly effective once in place, is quite time consuming to build. The authors note that such an approach depends on the two key variables of the existance of a strong sense of a shared value system and many informal administrative structures that are legitimized along with the formal structure, systems, and procedures.

In this paper, I have attempted to put forth a proposition of how multinational enterprises evolve from an early to a mature stage. As is the case with any effort to categorize so many different and seemingly isolated events, I have had to be somewhat arbitrary. Obviously, there are many cases which do not fit a neat pattern, and my observations are based only on the experiences of U.S. multinationals. Nevertheless, by drawing on past and current research on multinational enterprises, I have suggested a generalized proposal of how the strategy of multinationals change and how the structural responses to such strategic changes take place.

NOTES

1. For an excellent treatment of this subject, see Mira Wilkins, *The Emergence of Multinational Enterprises* (Cambridge, Mass., 1970).
2. Raymond Vernon, *Sovereignty at Bay* (New York, 1972), pp. 65–106.
3. William H. Davidson, "Corporate Experience Factor in International Investment and Licensing Activity" (Harvard Business School, 1979), pp. 24–77.
4. For an excellent treatment of this subject, see Y. Doz, "Multinational Strategic Management: Economic and Political Imperatives," manuscript, chapter 5.
5. John M. Stopford and Louis T. Wells, Jr., *Managing the Multinational Enterprise: Organization of the Firm and Ownership of Subsidiaries* (New York,), chapters 1, 2, and 3.
6. Christopher A. Bartlett, "Multinational Structural Evolution: The

Changing Decision Environment in International Divisions" (Harvard Business School, 1979).

7. Y. Doz, *op. cit.*, chapter 7.
8. Christopher A. Bartlett, *op. cit.*, p. 171.
9. Y. Doz, *op. cit.*, chapter 7, pp. 31–38.
10. Y. Doz, C. A. Bartlett, and Prahalad, "Global Competitive Presence and Host Country Demands," *California Management Review* (Spring 1981), pp. 63–74.

COMMENTS

Terushi Hara
Waseda University

I was very unhappy when I heard that Professor Yoshino could not attend the conference because of his illness.

Professor Yoshino's paper is important because it shows very clearly that in the first stage of the evolution of the American multinational enterprises there were many aspects of development that were irrational or unsystematic. One of the new points raised in the paper is that American enterprises also developed without any precise and formally established projects.

Professor Yoshino also discusses strategic divergence not only in relation to integration strategy but also in relation to country specific strategy. This point seems to have considerable merit.

But, in my opinion, the paper lacks a historical approach. Professor Udagawa stressed the importance of the approach taken by business historians and noted that business historians are interested in the decision-making process. Professor Yoshino, in contrast, does not pay much attention to this approach.

The paper also lacks case studies. It cites several individual companies by name, but citation is not a case study in the proper sense. The paper would be more interesting if it had more analyses of management evolution within companies.

The History of Multinational Factories in Australia

Geoffrey Blainey
University of Melbourne

The first British settlement in Australia was at Sydney in 1788. Most of the early settlers had been convicted of crimes in courts in the British Isles and sentenced to be "transported" to Australia for terms of seven or fourteen years or for the remainder of their lives. About 160,000 convicts were shipped to Australia during the following eighty years. Free settlers also came—mostly from the British Isles—and by the 1830s the annual arrival of free settlers far exceeded those who came in the convict ships. The economy expanded as flocks of sheep moved to the inland grasslands of eastern Australia. Wool became the main source of export income but was supplanted temporarily by gold in the 1850s and 1860s, when southeastern Australian gold mines vied with those in California as the largest producers of gold in the world. The population passed one million during the gold rushes of the mid-1850s, passed three million in 1891, and today is close to fourteen million; less than one quarter of a million of the population are descendants of the black aboriginal Australians.

Australia was not a united nation in the late nineteenth century. It consisted of six British colonies, five of which were self-governing. These colonies were defended until 1870 by a few regiments of the British army and ships of the British navy and their own small warships. With few exceptions, the colonies accepted Britain's policy in international issues. The colonies from the 1850s began to impose import duties against each other as well as against Britain but in 1901 they federated to form the Commonwealth of Australia—a common market and defense alliance embracing the entire Australian continent and the island of Tasmania. Australia slowly de-

veloped its own foreign policy, though generally it followed the
leadership of Britain. After the beginning of the Second World War
in 1941, Australia's economic and military links with Britain began
to weaken; today only the cultural, ceremonial, and emotional links
with Britain remain strong. Australia now depends largely on the
United States for defense and capital, on Japan for commerce, and
on non-British lands for most of its immigrants.

Most of the interior of Australia receives so little rain that the
population is concentrated on favored parts of the coast, especially
in the southeast corner. Nearly all the large towns and cities are
ports; Sydney and Melbourne are the biggest cities and together
account for about four of every ten people in the nation. These two
cities have also been the main centers of manufacturing; even in
1890 they held about half of the factory workers in Australia, and
their share continued to increase.[1] In the 1890s the typical factories
or workshops were small and were owned by an individual, family,
or small syndicate rather than by a public company; most or all
of the products were sold in the neighboring districts. Most of the
factory work force produced food, drink, building materials, clothes,
footwear, and printed matter. Early industries used cheap raw materials that were available locally, and imports could not compete
against their products because of the time delays or shipping costs.
Several strong industries, especially clothing and footwear, also
relied on the customs duties imposed on imports from Britain, the
United States, and Germany. The typical Australian factory of a
century ago was not very productive and relied on labor more than
on capital and on physical dexterity and strong muscles more than
on machines.

I. Overseas Ventures in Manufacturing to 1920

British capital poured into Australia in the nineteenth century
and sometimes arrived in greater volume than the continent could
efficiently use. Some of this capital went indirectly into manufacturing through the loans made by British-owned banks, capital
brought to Australia by British emigrants who later set up factories
in Australia, and British merchant houses that operated in Australia and supplied long-term loans or short-term credit to Aus-

tralian factories whose products they sold. But few overseas companies—and most of these were British—actually set up and supervised factories in Australia in the nineteenth century.

A few overseas ventures preceded the gold rushes of the 1850s. In 1838 "Indian capital," which probably signified an investment by British citizens living in India, financed a large sawmill, driven by steam and water, south of Sydney at Kiama. This sawmill was probably the first in Australia to use a circular saw. In 1839 two London men began to set up a sugar refinery in Sydney but soon sold out their interest. In the late 1840s the Patent Copper Company, a firm in Wales, erected a costly copper smelter near the rich copper mine at Burra in South Australia; these smelters were later purchased by the English & Australian Copper Company, which was launched in Britain in 1851. The new company eventually erected large copper smelters at Newcastle in New South Wales that were close to the coal fields but far from the copper mines. The company's fortunes went up and down, in sympathy with those of the copper mines. Between 1883 and 1899 it paid no dividends, but eventually it entered a period of mild prosperity early in this century. Throughout its vicissitudes English & Australian Copper remained a London company. Another English company, formed in 1873, bought pig iron works at Mittagong, New South Wales, and worked a blast furnace there in 1876. The cost of producing the pig iron was too dear, and the company collapsed.[2]

Smelting enterprises were the main target for British capital in Australian manufacturing in the nineteenth century, but investment in smelters was usually the outcome of a prior investment in a mine. In short, the prospects of mining rather than of manufacturing were more attractive to British companies that looked in the direction of Australia. From the mid-1880s the British invested heavily in risky Australian mining ventures.

It is not easy to learn why British manufacturers decided to set up factories in Australia in the late nineteenth century. Most of the early Australian factories have vanished, their main business records have vanished, and some of the reasons for their decisions to set up factories in Australia were possibly never put down on paper. Moreover, the reasons for deciding to build a factory in Australia might well have been personal as well as economic, such as a quarrel in the family, a recommendation from a friend or relative already living in Australia, or the need to provide useful work for a relative whose health was poor and who had been advised to migrate to a warmer climate.

Tobacco was possibly the main manufacturing industry which attracted heavy overseas attention before 1900. Cameron Brothers of the United States sent a representative several times to investigate the strong Australian market for pipe tobacco before spending about $500,000 to erect a large factory in Sydney in 1873. A member of the family became manager in Sydney, and by the 1880s the firm owned branch factories in Melbourne and Adelaide. In 1888 a United States consular report commented on the Cameron Brothers' activities in Australia: "One secret of the success of this firm is the advantage it possesses in having all their American leaf selected and cured by their own firms in Richmond and Petersburg, Virginia."[3] Control of the raw materials must have also been a strong consideration influencing the Camerons to set up a factory in Australia. Other American and British overseas firms were also making pipe tobacco and cigarettes in Australia, and by 1900 they possibly controlled at least half the output of manufactured tobacco. In 1903 and 1904 the main firms combined in various ways to form a powerful trust to control the importing, manufacturing, and sales of tobacco products in Australia.

H. L. Wilkinson's little known book titled *The Trust Movement in Australia*, published in 1914, devoted a sketchy chapter to "The Tobacco Trust." Being a civil engineer by profession, Wilkinson was not a sensationalist or a muck-raker. He concluded that at least seven-eighths of the tobacco trade in Australia was controlled through subsidiary companies by a British-American trust and that in Australia the trust was fixing the price of tobacco and "making huge but unascertainable profits."[4]

Such trusts and monopolies were not easily dismantled in Australia because in 1909 the High Court ruled—a ruling henceforth largely accepted—that the constitution of the Commonwealth of Australia did not really empower the Commonwealth government to control corporate monopolies.[5] I have not found a history of the tobacco industry in Australia—one of many fields of Australian economic history in which research has barely begun.

II. The Role of New Technology and New Products

The canning of meat also attracted British as well as Australian capital. Australia traditionally had a large surplus of meat and mutton. The country produced far more meat than its people could eat but had no safe and palatable way of supplying that meat to Europe. The Franco-Prussian War of 1870–71 increased the demand for canned meat and, perhaps because the United States had not fully recovered from its civil war, Australia was in a favorable position to supply Europe. D. Hogarth & Co., a meat canner in Aberdeen, Scotland, formed the Hogarth Australian Meat Preserving Co., Limited in 1870 with Scottish capital as well as capital subscribed by Australian colonists who had retired to live in Britain. The new firm began to slaughter sheep and cattle near Toowoomba in southern Queensland in April 1871 and employed Polynesian labor recruited from the nearby Pacific Islands to introduce an unusual pressure-cooking method of preserving the meat.[6]

In April 1870 the Central Queensland Meat Preserving Company Limited was formed in London and it built the biggest meat-preserving plant in Australia at Rockhampton. Of the capital subscribed before January 1873—by then the company was heading for collapse—just over three-quarters came from English investors, mostly those living in London, and the remainder from Australians. By 1874, with the European boom in canned meat only a memory, the big preserving plant at Rockhampton in central Queensland was closed and the smaller Toowoomba plant was idle. The decline of the overseas market, and the public's distaste for canned meat in preference to fresh meat, hampered these two overseas ventures. Remote control, the problem of running a factory on the other side of the world, also weakened the Central Queensland firm. "Some inexplicable decisions were made in England concerning supplies of tin plate and ingot tin and lead for solder," writes one historian.[7] Similarly, decisions involving the remittance of funds across the world and the establishing of credit were also unwise. If there were adequate records of overseas ventures in Australia, we would probably find that the problem of management from afar was often crucial.

One of the few British firms to set up a factory in Australia in the 1880s and to leave behind some of its records was the Bristol firm of John Lysaght Limited. About 1884 it decided to set up a factory near Sydney in order to make wire netting. At that time a plague of rabbits numbering hundreds of millions, infested the grasslands of much of southeastern Australia and competed with the sheep for grass; their competition was costly because sheep wool was Australia's main export. To curtail the spread of rabbits and to prevent them from reentering areas from which they had been successfully eliminated, sheep owners were spending heavily on fences made of wire netting. There was thus an increasing demand for wire netting in Australia, but this bulky and easily damaged product occupied much space in the British ships coming to Australia and accordingly required high shipping costs. An obvious solution was to import the coils of unprocessed wire from England and weave the wire into netting in an Australian factory on one of the machines that the British firm of Lysaght had developed.

Another incentive to build a factory near Sydney was provided by the New South Wales government which imposed a duty on imported wire netting. These three main reasons—the natural protection afforded a bulky product, the real protection of an import duty, and the soaring market in Australia for wire netting—have been outlined by economic historian Professor Schedvin, who wrote a brief history of this firm.[8]

The early history of this wire netting factory is incomplete. The factory began operations near Sydney about 1884 and was unprofitable. Management was probably poor. The new machines probably had mechanical troubles. The head of the Bristol firm, John Lysaght, actually made the long voyage to Australia in 1886 to examine his investment. He added capital, reorganized the business, set it up as a separate company called Lysaght Brothers & Company, and owned most of the shares. When he returned to England, management of the Australian company fell largely into the hands of his nephew; by the mid-1890s it seems to have had few links with the English parent and from 1897 it decided that most of the wire which was the raw material for its weaving machines should be bought in Germany rather than in England. The Australian factory was now very profitable and in a typical year of the

1890s paid a dividend of 30 percent, which was too high in view of the firm's subsequent management and financial difficulties. In 1902 and 1903 a severe drought in New South Wales temporarily reduced the plague of rabbits and also limited the ability of sheep owners to afford wire netting for new fences. The Lysaght company lost so much money that it had trouble in paying its 200 employees. Soon it fell into the arms of its creditors—The Bank of Australasia, a London bank operating throughout Australia, and a Sydney firm of merchants and financiers called Gibbs, Bright & Co., part of the large London-centered firm of Antony Gibbs & Sons. Gibbs, Bright & Co. took control of Lysaghts in 1905 and turned it into a sounder venture, gained control of most of the Australian market for wire netting, and began to manufacture barbed wire (which competed with imports from the United States), nails, and zinc white. Perhaps half of the shares in Lysaghts were still held directly and indirectly in England; and some of the firm's policies were probably decided by Antony Gibbs & Sons in London rather than at the directors meetings in Sydney. When Lysaght Brothers & Company was about to sell out to the Australian-owned steelmaker Broken Hill Pro-prietary Co. in 1929, the company could still be called, by some definitions, part of a multinational empire.

New products and new technology were probably crucial to most of the multinational manufacturing ventures set up in Australia before 1914. This was true of canned meat and galvanized wire netting. It was also true of several other overseas manufacturing ventures established in the period 1880 to 1900 in Melbourne, which was then Australia's largest city.

Melbourne was one of the first cities in the world to build sky-scrapers of eight, ten, or twelve stories in height. The tall building boom ran from about 1886 to 1892, and Melbourne was probably third to New York and Chicago in the erection of tall offices and hotels. These buildings depended on safe and efficient elevators which were driven not by gas, steam, or electricity but by high-pressure water pumped through undergound pipes beneath the city streets. John Coates, a partner in the London engineering firm of John Coates & Company, visited Melbourne in 1887 with his neph-ew George Swinburne and obtained from the local parliament the right to build a large pumping station and construct high-pressure water mains beneath the city streets.[9] To finance their venture they floated the Melbourne Hydraulic Power Company with its head office in Melbourne and with a substantial English shareholding. John Coates & Company were the consulting engineers as well as large shareholders. George Swinburne, the nephew, remained in Australia to run the project.

The venture was highly successful and manufactured and supplied hydraulic power for most of the passenger and goods elevators in Melbourne until the era of the electric elevator arrived. How long it could be defined as a multinational venture I do not know. More research is required on these isolated episodes of direct British involvement in Australian manufacturing.

The demand for elevators, especially the lavish elevators installed in Melbourne's new office buildings, attracted overseas manufactures. The New York firm of Otis apparently supplied the technology—presumably in return for shares—to a new company floated in Melbourne in 1887 to manufacture Otis elevators. Otis, however, did not control or manage the Melbourne company. This probably increased that company's prospect of success.

London's largest maker of lifts, Richard Waygood & Company, exported high-grade passenger lifts to Melbourne. In 1888 it acquired half of the shares in a new company, the Australian Waygood Elevator Company, which began to make and assemble elevators in a new workshop in South Melbourne. The Melbourne subsidiary quickly dominated the elevator business in Australia and within a year had received orders for about one hundred lifts. But when the building boom began to end in Melbourne in 1891 and the economy sagged in most Australian cities, the new firm was in trouble. Henry Walker, the chairman of the parent firm in London, made the slow voyage to Melbourne to see whether he could rescue the business. He decided instead to sell the Australian Waygood Elevator Company, in return for shares, to a Melbourne engineering company established in the 1850s by Peter Johns, a new immigrant from England. Peter Johns decided that the name of Waygood was perhaps more valuable than its other assets; in 1892 his company changed its name to Johns & Waygood Limited. The London firm of Waygood was only a minor shareholder in the Melbourne company and had virtually no influence in its management. It would be easy to attribute Waygood's failure solely to the depression that hit Melbourne's building industry, but the causes of its failure were probably more complex.[10]

The role of new products and new technology in multinational manufacturing was visible also in the power supply industry. In Australia the production and distribution of gas was essentially financed by Australian capital, but the introduction of electricity and its more sophisticated technology gave an opening for British capital. At the start of this century two of the largest Australian cities, Melbourne and Adelaide, were supplied with electricity by London-owned companies. These two companies appear to have occupied the same office in the city of London and they had the same chairman and directors. Kalgoorlie, the largest gold-mining city in Western Australia, was also served by a company floated in London in 1899 and known as the Kalgoorlie Electric Power and Lighting Corporation Limited. Kalgoorlie's prosperity slowly waned, and in the years before 1914 the Kalgoorlie Electric's ordinary shareholders, as distinct from preference shareholders, received no dividends. To provide electricity to big cities like Melbourne and Sydney was a safe investment, but power companies were liable to be nationalized. In Australia the federal, state, or municipal governments have tended to own the main public utilities and eventually they acquired the British-directed electricity companies operating in Australia.[11]

By 1908 there were special incentives for British manufacturing companies to build factories in Australia. The Commonwealth of Australia was increasing its tariff on imported goods in order to foster local factories. Moreover, the Commonwealth had virtually created a common market so that the whole territory of Australia was now available on favorable terms to the Australian manufacturer. With increasing signs of tension in Europe, the Commonwealth Government was also eager to strengthen British rather than American or German manufacturers. Australian politicians knew that the security of Australia depended on a strong British navy and that a strong British navy in turn depended on strong British industry in steel or ship building, explosives or engines and did nearly everything in their power to keep Britain industrially powerful. Accordingly, British imports into Australia were given preferential

treatment by the tariff.[12] Whether that preference discouraged them
from setting up factories in Australia is an important but elusive
question.

The Manufacturers' Association of Great Britain, an industrial
lobby and information bureau with offices near the Houses of Parliament in London, decided to investigate the Australian market in
1908 and sent Ben H. Morgan to report. He carefully looked at
factories and markets, spoke to leading politicians and even lobbied
successfully for a reduction in the import duties on certain British
products entering Australia. On his return home, he quickly filled
a book of 250 pages with his hopes and fears. Britain, he said, supplied 61 percent of Australia's imports. But how long, he warned,
could Britain retain her large share in the face of growing competition from German and American firms.[13] "Undoubtedly," he
wrote, "there are exceptional openings for starting factories in Australia and New Zealand at the present time."[14] He listed many of
the opportunities, ranging from steelworks to woolen mills. Steel
was the biggest opportunity that was ignored by English firms. Australian capital financed this key industry.

III. Obstacles Facing Overseas Investors before 1920

Manufacturing was now a fast-growing sector of the Australian
economy but it was still dominated as late as 1920 by Australian-
owned firms. There were exceptions, however, and the exceptions
were increasing. But manufacturing so far had been far less attractive than mining and banking to overseas firms.

What were the main deterrents to overseas firms thinking of opening a factory in Australia? Why, for instance, did manufacturing
companies in England hesitate to come to Australia whereas hundreds of mining companies came? Both manufacturing and mining
industries in Australia posed a problem of management for firms in
faraway London. It was not easy for a London company to assess
the advice of its Australian management, to supervise that management, or to decide when the management was inefficient.

Manufacturing, I believe, had special problems. Whereas a typical
London-owned mining company in Australia exported its produce
to a world market, the typical London-owned factory in Australia

sold its products only in Australia. Local knowledge, not London's knowledge of the world commodity markets, was therefore vital for Australian factories. In addition, most Australian factories were labor intensive and offered less scope for investors. Mining, however, was becoming deeper, metallurgically more complex, and larger in scale; therefore, it was becoming capital-intensive. The typical factory in Australia was far too small to justify an investment from overseas, whereas by the 1880s and 1890s the typical mine on the rich Australian fields such as Broken Hill and Kalgoorlie was a larger production unit and greedy for capital. It is also reasonable to believe that for English investors and firms, their own nation still offered opportunities in manufacturing but few opportunities in mining. Australia, in contrast, was an exciting field for mining investment, and many of the mineral opportunities in Australia arose at times when the English stock exchanges were slack.[15] Much of the British buying of Australian mines, especially gold mines, occurred in cheap money years when the short-term business cycle in England was near the trough or in the early phase of an upswing. Those were the years when profits in English manufacturing, banking, and shipping firms were lower. They were also the times when gold mines were relatively attractive, because during the era of the gold standard the price of gold was fixed, so the real price of gold was unchanged at the time when the prices of all other commodities were falling.

The manufacturing industry in Australia, at least until 1920, placed other obstacles in front of English companies. The market was restricted by the small population of only five million in 1920 and the geographical dispersal of people. The creation of a national market and the forming of the Commonwealth of Australia in 1901 were partly offset by the rapid increase in freight rates on the long Australian coast in the next twenty years, because the new Commonwealth had increased shipping costs by giving a virtual monopoly of coastal, as distinct from the overseas, shipping to Australian-manned ships. In addition, British factory owners were reluctant to set up new factories in Australia because the new factories in Australia would usually eat into their own export market. Many British manufacturers delayed too long, thus allowing American or Australian owners to build factories which were sheltered behind a new and permanent tariff wall and prohibited British goods from entering their traditional market.

A protective tariff was essential if most Australian factories were to prosper. To obtain a favorable tariff from the Australian colonial parliaments before 1901 and from the Commonwealth parliament after 1901 required knowledge of Australian politics and sometimes, lobbying or influence. Political influence was more likely to be wielded by Australian citizens than by a company operating from London. Political influence or alertness was more essential in manufacturing than in mining, though today it is essential in both fields of investment in Australia. Absence of political knowledge is one of the reasons that help to explain why few overseas firms created factories in Australia in the period to 1920.

It may well be that an undue proportion of this paper is devoted to discovering and assessing the obstacles limiting overseas-owned factories in Australia in the period when overseas participation was weak. But in trying to understand the complex forces that affect the multinational ventures in manufacturing, we probably learn as much looking at a period where the retarding forces were strong as we learn studying the postwar period when the accelerating forces were strong.

IV. The Middle Years, 1920–45

After the First World War manufacturing boomed in Australia. In the mid-1920s manufacturing passed the primary industries as a contributor to gross domestic product and was already far ahead as an employer of labor. Manufacturing was now approaching the peak in its share of employment and was employing about one quarter of the work force. It was still labor intensive and its contribution to the standard of living was not as conspicuous as the jobs it created. By 1939 manufacturing was at its peak in the percentage of employment it provided. Indeed the years 1932–33 to 1938–39 formed the last period in which manufacturing employment was to increase at a faster rate than employment in the rest of the economy.[16]

The years 1920 to 1945 were not highly profitable for Australian manufacturers. The world depression hit Australia, and the factories suffered more than the farms and mines. The Second World War was far more stimulating to manufacturing than the First World War (Australia was too isolated to be a vital supply base), but the wartime economy was closely regulated and did not permit high profits. Nonetheless, the war extended—some critics would say "overextended"—the range of Australian manufacturing. At the end of the war Australia had many advanced industries, including a large military aircraft industry with 44,000 employees.[17]

Overseas manufacturers, especially those from the United States, had quickened their interest in Australia in the 1920s and 1930s. Whereas before 1920 a big overseas-owned factory in Australia was rare, many of the large factories of the following two decades were overseas owned. The Ford Motor Company of Canada and General Motors from the United States moved into the automobile industry and began making car bodies and components and assembling vehicles with imported engines. Many English firms set up Australian factories, especially near the B.H.P. steelworks at Newcastle, and made steel wire, rods and tubes, axles and wheels, pipes and galvanized iron from Australian iron and steel, or chemicals from the byproducts of steelworks and coke ovens.[18] A small steelworks was built south of Sydney at Port Kembla in the late 1920s by an alliance of Australian capital and the two British steel firms of Dorman & Long and Baldwin. Imperial Chemical Industries, the huge English merger of 1926, became the most versatile of the multinationals in Australian manufacturing, and by 1940 its subsidiary companies in Australia were making explosives, sporting ammunition, artificial fertilizers, alkali products, plastics, leather cloth, paints, and a variety of other products. A history of this enterprise's activities in Australia would tell us much about the role of multinationals and their successes and failures. I tried back in 1958 to write such a history using the company's records, but the company holds the copyright on the manuscript.

At the end of the Second World War, Australian factories were still overwhelmingly the property of Australians. But in many expanding sectors of manufacturing, overseas firms were now strong. No statistics are available, but it may well be that in 1945 one-eighth to one-tenth of the factory output, and rather less of the factory employment, was controlled by overseas firms, and most

of those firms had come to Australia since 1920. Overseas ownership, however, was not yet a divisive political issue. The left-wing
groups directed more ammunition against the Broken Hill Proprietary Company, the biggest of all manufacturing companies
which were Australian, than against any foreign-owned company.
In several Australian states, especially in Western Australia, overseas-owned factories were virtually unknown and their absence was
more a cause for regret than applause among Western Australian
politicians. Factories were job creators and were widely welcomed.

Obviously the high obstacles to overseas ventures in Australian
manufacturing must have become less forbidding in the 1920s and
1930s. The Australian tariff against imported manufactured goods
had become larger and induced American and British exporters to
set up plants in Australia. The United States too had become a
vigorous exporter of capital, and capital provided competition for
Britain in exporting manufactured products or in protecting export
territories by erecting branch factories in Australia. Many of the
new fields of manufacture had a sophisticated technology and required heavy investment. That gave an overseas firm some advantage over small Australian firms which might otherwise have entered
or expanded into these new fields. Another important change was
quietly occurring, a change particularly visible in Australia but
relevant to the growth of multinationals in every part of the world.
That change was simple: world markets were shrinking.

V. Factory Doors Open Wide, 1945–80

Australian factories were transformed in the 1950s and 1960s.
Factory productivity had always been disappointing, and output for
each employee had probably increased by less than one percent a
year in the period 1850 to 1900 and by about one percent a year
between 1900 and 1930.[19] Traditionally, productivity in Australia's
rural and mining industries was much more impressive. Between
1949–50 and 1967–68, however, manufacturing acquired new efficiency and vitality, and the productivity of each employee is estimated to have risen annually by four percent a year. Capital poured
into factories where formerly the power of wrists and arms and legs
had been decisive. Moreover, the new industries were capital inten-

sive. Professor H. F. Lydall has estimated that in the 1950s about 40 percent of the increase in productivity came from technical progress including some gain from economies of scale, and about 60 percent came from the injection of capital. Of course, the inflow of new techniques often came with the capital.[20] Much of the increased output of factories came from more recent industries—iron and steel, automobiles, chemicals, electrical and electronic equipment. In less than two decades their share of manufacturing output had leaped from one-fifth to one-third. They were also major contributors to the Australian factory exports, which were of small volume in 1950, but by the early 1970s provided about 20 percent of Australia's export income. Another merit of the factory boom was its capacity to employ many immigrants from Europe; in the early 1970s four out of every ten of the workers in factories were immigrants. Manufacturing in the period 1947 to 1966 employed a steady 27 or 28 percent of the work force (compared with the United States' 24 percent) and then began to slowly decline. Simply by retaining for so long its share of a fast-growing work force, manufacturing provided work directly and indirectly for a new army of workers.

The increasing efficiency of manufacturing was accompanied by and partly a result of the widening activities of multinational companies. In the period 1945–53 perhaps 45 percent of the investment in Australian factories came from overseas, though in the next period this percentage was not so high.[21] By 1962–63, the first year for which adequate statistics on foreign capital are available, 22 percent of the value of output in manufacturing came from companies that were controlled from overseas. Four years later the percentage had increased to 26 percent, and it is higher today.

Overseas control centered on the big companies rather than on the mass of small factories. The Australian Bureau of Statistics examined manufacturing for the year 1972–73; it looked closely at the 200 largest enterprise groups and calculated that 87 of the 200 were foreign controlled.[22] The Bureau's working definition of foreign control was pragmatic rather than legal, and it regarded a firm as under foreign control if at least 25 percent of its shares were "held by one company, or by a group of associated companies, incorporated in one overseas country." In short, the dividends from many of these firms probably were distributed to Australian as well as overseas shareholders, and in a few firms most of the dividends went to Australians, but effective control of the firms lay overseas. These foreign-controlled companies produced nearly one quarter of the value added by all Australian factories. If we take a more rigid definition of foreign control and apply it only to companies in which at least 50 percent of shares were held overseas, then sixty-eight of the top 200 manufacturing companies were foreign controlled. Among the smaller firms, foreign control was much less common.

Most overseas-owned Australian manufacturing enterprises in 1945 were still British but by 1970 such firms were almost as likely to be U.S. firms as British firms. A survey in 1971 of the 113 largest foreign-owned manufacturing firms in Australia counted fifty that were mainly owned in Britain and forty-five owned in the United States.[23] Moreover, those firms based in Switzerland, Germany, Holland, France, Sweden and countries of continental Europe were far more prominent than they would have been in 1945. The strong Japanese interest in Australian manufacturing was to come in the late 1970s. In the financial years of 1979–81, Australia was ranked second and third as the main outlet for Japanese overseas invest-ment, and much of that capital flowed into Australian manufac-turing. Of Japan's total investment in Australia, 37 percent has been in mining and 29 percent in manufacturing—especially trans-port equipment, iron and steel, and other metals.[24] Mining, it should be added, even more than manufacturing, was the goal for multi-national companies coming to Australia in the 1960s and 1970s.

The most thorough report on Australian manufacturing in recent years was the Jackson Report in 1976. Commissioned by the Com-monwealth Government, backed by effective research, and pro-duced by a committee of leading citizens led by Gordon Jackson, an industrialist, the report examined manufacturing in elaborate detail. The report also surveyed foreign-owned firms and concluded the following main advantages:[25]

They provided effective access to overseas technology, including management skills and techniques.

They were a vital source of funds for large projects and indus-tries new to Australia.

Many of the overseas-owned firms had specialist staff in indus-trial relations and were "advancing the skills of the Australian manufacturing sector in the field of company/employee relations."

While many Australians argued that foreign-owned firms were unlikely to export strenuously for fear of entering the overseas markets of the parent company, the American companies in Australia in 1972 were probably exporting more successfully than the Australian-owned firms (if I have read correctly the confusing figures in the report).

The Jackson Report also listed neutral and negative conclusions:

The aims and interests of foreign firms seem to be "as much in tune with Australian aspirations" as are those of comparable Australian firms. Australians dominate the boards and the chief management posts in most foreign-owned firms, but those firms in which a foreign citizen holds the chief post do not seem less independent than those where Australians are in the majority.

If foreign-owned firms persist in practices "disadvantageous to Australia," the government should curb those practices.

Foreign firms should be persuaded to increase their Australian equity, but should do so voluntarily rather than by government decree. The latter policy would strain Australian financial resources and impair industrial development by frightening away firms "closely tied to parent technology or products."

Such conclusions were tentative rather than definitive. The issue is complex, the evidence is incomplete, and cause and effect cannot always be disentangled with ease. Some critics would argue that the Jackson Report, though illuminating, was perhaps too sympathetic to overseas-owned firms on several issues.

I think that public hostility in Australia is weaker toward overseas ventures in manufacturing than overseas ventures in mining. The public mistakenly saw mining as an industry of luck. Why, people thought, should Australians not enjoy most of the benefits of that luck? Mining was also a larger target for criticism because its profits, especially with the slump in manufacturing in the late 1970s, seemed more spectacular. Moreover, mining disturbed the rocks and the soil and to fervent nationalists that was akin to rape. Uranium mining, in particular, was a controversial industry. Many mines were on lands which Aboriginals laid claim, so mining was contested. In Australia the mines, even more than factories, were also hosts to foreign companies. For all these strong reasons, the multinationals in manufacturing usually arouse less unease and less emotion than those in the mining sector, even today.

A young nation that seeks rapid economic development while maintaining a high standard of living must borrow from other nations. Australia has usually been a heavy borrower. From 1861 to 1900, private borrowing accounted for just under 50 percent of the capital inflow. From 1901 to 1939, private borrowing was less than 20 percent of the capital inflow. And during the years 1945 to 1969, private borrowing leaped to about 90 percent of the capital inflow.[26] These fluctuations are astonishing and also involve ideological fluctuations. In periods of heavy public borrowing, the right-wing politicians say, "beware, beware of the great interest burden." And in some years their warning has been timely, because the interest payments going overseas have almost strangled the economy. In three separate periods the property income paid to overseas lenders exceeded 33 percent of Australia's merchandise exports, in other words, one-third of the export income from wool, gold, and all other products simply went into defraying interest on overseas borrowings. Those high-debt years were in 1886–90, 1891–95, and in the world depression years of 1929–30 to 1933–34 when the interest-exports ratio reached a record 39 percent.[27] In contrast, the strong periods of private overseas borrowing, such as the years after 1945, have provoked from the left-wing politicians the warning, "beware, beware of the great dividend drain." There is no simple answer to these warnings. If Australia borrows at fixed-interest rates, the obligation to repay is heaviest in the depressed years. If Australia borrows through the multinational companies and other private investors, however, the total price paid will be higher, but the higher price will be paid mainly during the prosperous years when Australia can more easily afford to pay. The great constitutional crisis in Australian politics in November 1975 was partly triggered by the dilemma of whether Australia should allot its mineral resources largely to the multinational companies or whether the Commonwealth of Australia should borrow massive sums overseas at fixed-interest rates, develop these mineral deposits, and bear the losses and reap the rewards.

VI. Hidden Preconditions of the Multinational Era

When we see some of the specific difficulties of overseas companies that opened factories in Australia in the nineteenth century, or even as late as 1940, we can glimpse at the effects of Australia's isolation. Many British and American companies must have been deterred from opening a factory in Australia by the sheer difficulty of communicating with a land so far away. If they did open a factory, their inability to supervise it adequately was often a reason for the failure of their investment. In 1880, for instance, a Birmingham factory owner who thought of opening a factory in Australia and decided to make his own investigations spent thirteen weeks travelling in the fastest mail steamship from England to Melbourne and back again.[28] He would require four weeks, at the minimum, in Australia to assess the local market, the quality of the casual labor, the prospect of obtaining a protective tariff against imports, the likelihood of obtaining skilled foremen, and the suitability of sites for a factory. Even the four weeks in Australia would hardly have been long enough, because he would have to visit both Sydney and Melbourne to meet ministers and opposition politicians and ascertain the views of local bankers and merchants to whom he carried testimonials. In all he would be away from his own business in England for at least four months. He would be on the ocean for many weeks and out of touch with the world. Thus it was difficult to set up a business in Australia, and if the business drifted into debt, the journey to Australia to investigate was equally slow and dislocating. I mentioned earlier two British-owned factories in Australia that ran adrift in the period 1880–1900. In both crises, the chairman had to come from England to assess and decide what action to take.

The international telegraph had reached Australia in 1872, so a visiting businessman was not completely out of touch with England. Yet there was always a possibility that the single telegraph line, which ran through the interior of Australia and on to a tropical sea bed, would accidentally break and remain out of service for days or weeks. There was no alternative telegraph line to Australia until 1901 when a cable was successfully laid from South Africa via Mauritius and Cocos Island to Western Australia.[29]

Nonetheless, the international telegraph, for all its cost and uncertainty, did shorten the distance between Australia and the main source of capital, the British Isles. It is significant that the first vigorous British investment in Australian mines occurred in 1886–87 soon after the telegraph had become cheaper and more reliable.[30]

Even in the 1930s, isolation placed a burden on those few residents of England who controlled important Australian companies. Almost every year W. S. Robinson, managing director of Zinc Corporation (a direct ancestor of the powerful Rio Tinto Zinc Corporation), made the long voyage to inspect Australian mines, smelters, and industrial plants. His willingness to travel was considered exceptional, and he made amends by travelling in style with his personal servant. At every port he cabled extensively and at sea —the Marconi system now being in vogue—he sent radiograms as if they were Christmas cards.[31] When Australian prime ministers had to visit England they still travelled by sea. James Scullin, prime minister of Australia during the depression in 1930, was away from his country at a time of political and economic crisis for four and a half months and over half of that tour was spent in ocean liners. Essington Lewis, managing director of Broken Hill Proprietary, which was Australia's biggest manufacturing company, was considered an astonishingly well-travelled Australian businessman. A man who managed to the last inch, he periodically made the long voyage to inspect overseas steelworks and shipyards and to meet industrial leaders in many lands. His overseas trip of 1934 occupied seven months, during which time he observed the rearming of Japan.[32] Lewis was one of the first foreigners to appreciate the industrial might and military potential of Japan.

In the late 1930s it was possible to travel by flying boat between Australia and England, but few made the flight. It was still slow and considered by many to be hazardous. The postwar era made flying between Australia and Europe practical for businessmen and politicians. Eventually, quick and cheap international telephone and telex, television, and satellite have reduced the distance even more. The political leaders of the Australian state governments in the 1950s and 1960s increasingly made quick air journeys to Europe and North America to woo multinationals to their own states.

Some persons may sensibly point out that Australia had been abnormally isolated in the era before fast aircraft and that its isolation tells little about the general problems of multinational companies in that era. Yet the isolation of Australia merely showed in extreme form an isolation that had once existed on both sides of the Atlantic and at the far ends of Europe.

Significantly, United States firms moved into Canada with vigor long before they moved into Europe and its more populous markets. The original investment decision was more easily made, and the management difficulties more soluble, if the branch factory was in Canada rather than in France or Italy. Moreover, since successful investment in a factory overseas depended on an ability to predict and influence the level of tariff protection and to gauge the local market, physical closeness to the investment was an aid to understanding as well as to access. It was also easier to persuade an able "resident manager" to live in a foreign country if it was not too far away.[33]

I believe that geographical proximity greatly aids the operations of multinational companies. But proximity and distance are not merely physical measurements in miles or travelling days but represent cultural distance as well as geographical distance. A land is culturally distant if its language, commercial laws and social customs, markets and incentives, and motivations and energies are different. If we could devise a Beaufort Scale for distance—a scale combining both geographical and cultural distance—we would probably find that those lands where the amalgam of geographical and cultural distance was narrow were most likely to attract multinational ventures in manufacturing. Australia, culturally close though geographically remote, attracted British capital well ahead of American and French capital. Indeed, Australia would have attracted much British capital even if Britain had not been the world's greatest lender a century ago. Likewise, before 1914, Canada vigorously attracted United States manufacturing capital even when the United States was not a large lender. Czarist Russia, another example, enticed French capital into a variety of business ventures because in many aspects the cultural distance between the two nations was not wide.

In the last sixty years the geographical and economic distance between nations has dramatically shrunk, thus aiding the overseas flow of investment. The cultural distance also has shrunk perhaps even more quickly. Japanese investment in Australia and Indonesia in the early 1980s probably bridges a cultural gap which would have been prohibitively wide sixty years ago. Investors setting up a project in a foreign land want a degree of economic security. Knowledge of the land and society where they invest and a fast flow of news from the site of their investment are vital ingredients of that sense of security. An ability to travel quickly in crises to and from the land of their investment is also an aid to investment.

Decentralization of management and decision making was a vital way of bridging geographical and cultural distances in the years when the world was wider. England's East India Company gave great power to its officials geographically far away in India during the centuries when sailing ships had go around South Africa. The East India Company also eased the difficulties of operating in a difficult environment by becoming, in effect, the governor of parts of India, not only a trading company but a company of occupation as well. Similarly, when the English banking companies of the Bank of Australasia and the Union Bank were floated in London in the 1830s to open banks in Australia, they solved the problem of physical distance and the minor problem of cultural distance by a large decentralization of power. These banking companies succeeded in establishing one of the most dispersed networks of branches in the world and by 1890 each company had a head office in London and a chain of branches in Australia and New Zealand which covered a far wider area than western Europe. Much of their success came from delegating power; the head office in London delegated much power to boards of advice in the main Australian cities and to an Australian chief executive who did not visit London nor receive any visits from London directors in the late nineteenth century. In the various scattered branches of the bank, the local manager had a considerable margin of discretion.[34]

It seems reasonable to suggest that a joint-stock company with its bureaucracy and its special mode of government was specially suited for bridging distances. The increasing role of joint-stock companies has aided the spread of international manufacturing ventures. In contrast, in the nineteenth century a dynamic businessman who created a successful factory by his own efforts was less likely to open factories in other lands, since he was unlikely to open a factory in a land that he could rarely visit. The modern joint-stock company, where the salaried managers rather than the rich owners have the dominant say and occupy most of the seats on the board is especially suitable for international ventures. These managerially controlled companies tend to be more interested in the prestige of the company, its longevity, and its role as a career vehicle than simply as a vehicle of profits.[35] Projects in other lands are likely to satisfy all these goals.

Finally, political and economic security help to bridge global distances. The period 1945 to 1980 was relatively peaceful for advanced western nations and was an aid to the growth of multinational companies. At the same time, the rise of many independent nations, especially in the tropical zone, and the political instability and economic nationalism of some of these nations has restrained the activities of multinationals there. The heavy overseas investment in Australian mining in the 1960s was partly a result of the diversion of capital from insecure lands with excellent mineral prospects but with a risky economic and political climate. Global companies prefer to operate in lands where the mineral prospects are less attractive but the company's prospect is high of retaining what mineral wealth it found.

VII.　The Sardines and the Whales

The activity of multinational companies has aroused intense interest and concern. Observing the worldwide companies, we are possibly inclined to think that something unprecedented and even freakish is happening. In fact, a version of the same process has been going on for at least one hundred years in small business enterprises. The sardines were busy crossing the world long before the corporate whales caught our attention.

In every decade between the 1830s and the 1880s, scores of Eng-

lish manufacturers gave up one-man or two-man businesses or
wages work in the British Isles, migrated to Australia, and sooner
or later became manufacturers again. This international flow of
thousands of individuals carrying their skills and tools of trade and
a little capital was more significant than we readily appreciate. We
concentrate nowadays on the big firm, but one hundred years ago
the small firm was the heart of manufacturing.

There was little incentive for a prosperous British manufacturer
to risk everything by migrating across the seas to Australia in the
nineteenth century. Most of those who did migrate were young or
had failed at home. They were blacksmiths, wood carvers, coach
builders, wheelwrights, weavers, or tanners—members of ancient
and modern trades.

By migrating they hoped to lift themselves to a higher social
standing. Most worked in Australia for wages before starting their
own business. There were few direct transfers of a manufacturing
business from Britain to Australia, but if we could piece together
the evidence, indirect transfer would be on a large sacle. A few examples of the migration of manufacturing follow. John Letham, a
native of Park Head in Scotland, was a blacksmith who acquired
enough money to buy iron goods and migrate in 1854, during the
gold rush, to Melbourne. He sold his goods at a profit, became a
blacksmith and maker of stonemason's tools, and by the 1880s was
a prosperous citizen.[36] The firm of Eilenberg and Zeltner, makers
of waterproof clothing in Melbourne, was founded by Eilenberg
who had had long experience in the trade in England and South
Africa as well as in Paris, Vienna, and Berlin. He reached Melbourne in 1882, set to work with himself and a hired boy, and
quickly took on twenty more employees.[37]

Sometimes the migration was two-way or three-way. Arthur
Ferne worked in the tailoring trade. Ferne was apprenticed to the
woollen trade in London and later migrated to New Zealand and
then to Australia where he became manager of a large tailoring
business in Melbourne. He set up his own tailoring business with
half a dozen branches in Melbourne's suburbs, sold that business
and set up a similar business in the inland gold city of Ballarat,
sold that and, in poor health, returned to London where he set up
in the same line of business. By 1888 he was back in Melbourne as

owner of the London and American Tailoring Company, a mix of the manufacturing and the retail.[38] The flow of manufacturing skills to Australia was only one avenue of this movement. These manufacturers, tradesmen and artisans went to the United States, Canada, Argentina, Chile, South Africa, New Zealand, Algeria, and many lands of European settlement—long chain of people and skills spanning the world. This exodus was not simply to the new world; it was also a movement within Europe, especially the westward exodus of Jews from Russia and the movement from country to city in central Europe.

The flow of individuals, skills, and fragments of large firms and whole little firms was surprisingly like the migration of multinationals in recent decades and brought overseas technology, especially new technology, and imported skilled labor and capital. The flow also provided competition for the staid, sheltered industries in the new lands of immigration. Some may argue that the multinationals were not like last century's migrants with their boxes of tools and leather aprons and several gold coins sewed in the inside of their vest pockets. But the similarities can be carried further. Just as the multinationals send away dividends, so individuals of a century ago sent home their remittances to aged parents, or the fare money to relatives who were hoping to emigrate. Many owners of little factories in Australia went home to the British Isles, having sold their business in Australia. The exodus of individual artisans had other resemblances to the forays of the multinationals. Complaints that the multinational company makes decisions with the homeland, not Australia, in mind neglect to consider that a century ago in Europe, the decision of the individual baker, brickmaker, and blacksmith to emigrate was made in a foreign land and with the individual's interests rather than the interests of the land of adoption in mind. Most of the immigrants arrived in the new world were loyal to a foreign land. In contrast, the multinationals at least appoint Australians to the high offices—partly as camouflage but more often as an exercise in decentralization.

Was the migrant, like the multinational, an alien in a new land? Most immigrants had a transition period when their loyalty to their homeland remained strong and then passed through a transition phase during which they imagined that someday they might return to their homeland. The typical migrant with factory skills was even more transitory than a multinational company. The big multinational company opening a factory, smelter, or refinery in Australia in 1982 has a larger and a less revocable commitment to the new land than did the one-man business of 1882 which was so portable and so embodied in one family that it could leave whenever it wished. It is easy to sell a bakehouse or blacksmith's forge but not always easy to sell a huge factory with an international marketing and technological network. Certainly, if the local government becomes hostile, a multinational cannot put its factory under its arm and leave the country.

There are also dissimilarities between the individual migrants and the multinational. The multinational is huge and is often a monopoly. The technology it brings is often complex and it is often financially secretive. It is thus a conspicuous and sometimes a deserving target. Nevertheless, the multinational factory is a large-scale version of an old process. Nationalists instinctively realize this fact and often direct against the multinationals the very arguments which they direct against new immigrants coming from distant lands.

Notes

I would like to express my gratitude to Dr. John Fogarty of the economic history department of the University of Melbourne for his discussion of this topic with me.

1. G.J.R. Linge, *Industrial Awakening: A Geography of Australian Manufacturing 1788 to 1890* (Canberra, 1979), p. 18.
2. For early manufacturing ventures, see Linge, *op. cit.*, pp. 101, 116, 145 and 578. For dividends of English and Australian Copper Company, see R. L. Nash, *The Australasian Joint Stock Companies' Year Book* (Sydney, 1913–14), p. 236.
3. G. W. Griffin, *New South Wales: Her Commerce and Resources* (Sydney, 1888), p. 196.
4. H. L. Wilkinson, *The Trust Movement in Australia* (Melbourne, 1914), p. 49.
5. G. Sawer, *Australian Federal Politics and Law 1901–1929* (Melbourne, 1972), pp. 83–84.

6. Linge, *op. cit.*, pp. 686–87; K.T.H. Farrer, *A Settlement Amply Supplied: Food Technology in Nineteenth Century Australia* (Melbourne, 1980), p. 122.

7. Farrer, *op. cit.*, pp. 122–23.

8. C. B. Schedvin, "Rabbits and Industrial Development: Lysaght Brothers and Co. Pty Ltd., 1884 to 1929," *Australian Economic History Review*, vol. 10 (March 1970), pp. 27–55. The date of opening is given as 1883 in *The Cyclopedia of Victoria*, vol. 1 (Melbourne, 1903), p. 534.

9. G. Blainey, *One Hundred Years: Johns & Waygood Limited 1856–1956* (Melbourne, 1956), pp. 22–23.

10. G. Blainey, *op. cit.*, pp. 33–35.

11. Nash, *op. cit.*, pp. 137–55, discusses the financial details of all Australian gas and electricity companies.

12. W. M. Corden, "The Tariff," in A. Hunter, ed., *The Economics of Australian Industry* (Melbourne, 1963), p. 187.

13. B. H. Morgan, *The Trade and Industry of Australasia* (London, 1908), pp. 64–69.

14. Morgan, *op. cit.*, p. 64.

15. G. Blainey, "A Theory of Mineral Discovery: Australia in the Nineteenth Century," *The Economic History Review*, vol. 23 (1970), pp. 306–10.

16. E. A. Boehm, *Twentieth Century Economic Development in Australia* (Camberwell, Australia, 1971), pp. 123–24, 129.

17. G. Blainey, *The Steel Master: A Life of Essington Lewis* (Melbourne, 1971), p. 167.

18. H. Hughes, *The Australian Iron and Steel Industry 1848–1962* (Melbourne, 1964), pp. 82, 85, 106; G. Blainey, *The Steel Master, op. cit.*, p. 115.

19. W. A. Sinclair, *The Process of Economic Development in Australia* (Melbourne, 1976), pp. 214–15.

20. Boehm, *op. cit.*, pp. 132, 155; Sinclair, *op. cit.*, 221–25.

21. E. L. Wheelwright, "Overseas Investment in Australia," in A. Hunter, *op. cit.*, p. 144.

22. *Policies for Development of Manufacturing Industry* (Jackson Report), vol. 1 (Canberra, 1976), p. 96.

23. Jackson Report, vol. 3, pp. 121–22.

24. Study by Australia-Japan Economic Institute, reported in *The Australian* (Sydney), 24 Sept. 1981, p. 22.

25. Jackson Report, vol. 1, p. 100; vol. 3, pp. 159–63.

26. Boehm, *op. cit.*, pp. 118–10.

27.   Boehm, *op. cit.*, p. 116.
28.   G. Blainey, *The Tyranny of Distance: How Distance Shaped Australia's History* (Melbourne, 1966), p. 222.
29.   G. Johnson, ed., *The All Red Line: The Annals and Aims of the Pacific Cable Project* (Ottawa, 1903), pp. 45–49.
30.   G. Blainey, *The Rush That Never Ended: A History of Australian Mining* (Melbourne, 1979), p. 102.
31.   W. S. Robinson, *If I Remember Rightly: The Memoirs of W. S. Robinson 1876–1963* (Melbourne, 1967), especially pp. 166–67.
32.   G. Blainey, *The Steel Master, op. cit.*, chapter 9, entitled "A Fortnight in Japan."
33.   A 1919 memorandum written by W. S. Robinson about the creation of a white lead factory in Sydney noted, "the difficulty of finding suitable technical men and managers to send out from here was great in pre-war times," see Fraser Papers, University of Melbourne Archives, box no. 1/28/20/3.
34.   S. J. Butlin, *Australia and New Zealand Bank: The Bank of Australasia and the Union Bank of Australia Limited 1828–1951* (London, 1961), passim.
35.   G. Blainey, "The Politics of Big Business: A History," pamphlet (Academy of Social Sciences in Australia, Canberra, 1976).
36.   Anon., *Victoria and its Metropolis: Past and Present*, vol. 2 (Melbourne, 1888), p. 609.
37.   *Ibid.*, p. 601.
38.   *Ibid.*, p. 710.

COMMENTS

Takeshi Yuzawa
Gakushuin University

Professor Blainey's excellent paper describes the conditions that made Australia a capital-recipient country from the second half of the nineteenth century. He not only comprehensively treats the main characteristics of Australian economic development but also presents valuable case studies on foreign firms branching into Australia. Special emphasis is placed on the difficulties foreign firms experienced investing directly in manufacturing fields, in contrast to the booming investments in mining. These difficulties seem to stem primarily from conditions peculiar to Australia such as its historical relationship with Britain, remoteness from Europe and the United States, relatively large distances between major cities, and scarcity of labor.

Comparative business history provides several examples of possible ways to solve these problems. These problems were tackled at least with some success in other countries through protective tariff policies for infant industries, channeling governmental money to major firms, and encouraging immigrants. The position of Japan, which is also remote from industrially advanced European countries and the United States, has resembled that of Australia. The United States has solved the problem of large distances between major cities composing the domestic market by its frontier movement and the ardent promotion of railroad construction.

But to understand the basic causes of Australian industrialization, it is first necessary to examine the following questions from the viewpoint of business history. What were the principal motives of investors for overseas firms to make direct investments in Australia? Was this done to acquire natural resources, to control the host country's market, to avoid tariff barriers, to employ cheap labor, or for other reasons? A firm's eventual purpose in moving to foreign countries is, generally speaking, to gain more profits. Professor

Blainey states: ". . . British factory owners were reluctant to set up
new factories in Australia because the new factories in Australia
would usually eat into their own export market." Theoretically,
however, British manufacturers certainly could have built new
factories in Australia if they had assurances of higher profits from
such investments than from merely exporting to Australia and
other countries from their home base in Britain. Professor Blainey
refers somewhat tentatively to the Jackson Report, which concluded that American-owned companies in Australia exported more
successfully than Australian-owned firms. What is the reason for
this seeming contradiction?

Regarding the host country, to what degree was the Australian
government eager to develop the economy by Australian-owned
firms even after 1901? I can not understand why the government
reduced import duties in 1908, even though import duties were
lobbied for by Ben H. Morgan, representing the Manufacturers'
Association of Great Britain. Was it difficult for the Australian government to insist on its own interests when promoting local firms at
this time? Moreover, I would like to know the attitude of Australian businessmen toward foreign firms. Were Australian businessmen ready to take over the management of foreign companies?
Their attitude should be compared to the mentality of the businessmen in Australian-owned firms such as the Broken Hill Proprietary
Company.

Australia, in a sense, is a relatively young and untraditional country, much like the United States. It might be useful to compare the
process of industrialization in these two nations. As shown in Chandler's study, American big business first came into being in the field
of processing agricultural products and related industries, then urbanization contributed to the transport revolution and the rise of
heavy industries. We can see the same process of economic development in Australia as in the United States. As described by Professor
Blainey, Australian urbanization began in the last quarter of the
nineteenth century and was after development of the tobacco,
canned meat, and wire netting industries. Urbanization promoted
new industries such as skyscraper construction, hydraulic elevators,
and gas and electricity services. But why did urbanization in Australia not accompany the rise of heavy industry? Did the Australian

people with their rich mineral resources already enjoy a high standard of living even before industrialization?

Foreign Business Activities and the Chinese Response, 1842–1937

Tien-yi Yang
Asia University

China's fate was changed by her modern encounter with the West. The Western impact on China was politically and spiritually so immense and deep as to shape the course of her modern history. Yet materially foreign investment in China played only a marginal role because it was small in aggregate amount and was confined in the treaty ports. Foreign investment was mainly responsible for calling forth a small modern sector on the fringes of the Celestial Empire and touched merely a fraction of the Chinese economy without transforming it in keeping with the Western model. This limited effect was not only because modernization was exclusively of foreign origin but also because the special position and imperialist behavior of the foreigners made them resented rather than admired, and the innovations that they brought and attempted to push onto China were accordingly resisted. Most Chinese, unlike the Japanese, did not see a need for Western technology, which they regarded as not belonging to the domain of culture, and were able to satisfactorily continue their viable and self-sufficient traditional system. Thus, two systems, one Western and the other Chinese, were separate and only incidentally tangential; the structure and character of Chinese economy as a whole were left unaltered. Moreover, a weak, unstable and bankrupt Chinese government that could not control internal and foreign intrigue or harness foreign trade and investment to serve national development was thought to be a crucial factor in China's failure in initiating industrialization.[1]

I.   An Outline of Foreign Investment in China

According to Remer's estimates,[2] foreign investment in China reached $788 million in 1902, $1,610 million in 1914, and $3,243 million in 1931; according to a Japanese source,[3] it was $3,483 million in 1936. At current prices, foreign investment doubled from 1900 to 1914 and redoubled from 1914 to 1931. Deflated by the available wholesale price index, it increased by about 90 percent from 1902 to 1914, and only 20 percent from 1914 to 1931.[4] Remer's study provides an analysis of total foreign investment by purpose or nature of the business and makes the customary distinction between loans and direct investment.

The Chinese government raised large loans abroad to pay the indemnities of the Sino-Japanese War in 1895 ($200 million) and the Boxer Uprising in 1900 ($334 million). From 1898 to 1911, China also raised large sums abroad chiefly for railroad construction. Loans for general administrative and political purposes dominated the period 1912–26. Between 1861 and 1938, 44 percent of the foreign loans to the government, as expressed in constant prices, were for military and indemnity purposes; 20 percent were for general administrative purposes, largely for interest payments; 31 percent were for railroads; and only 5 percent were for industrial development.[5] These foreign borrowings tended to be economically sterile, inflationary, and burdensome.

Direct investment, being always predominant, grew from 63.9 percent of total foreign investment in 1902 to 78.1 percent in 1931. Table 1 shows the fields in which these investments were employed. Investments were primarily used in fields related with foreign trade (import and export trade, banking and finance) and transportation (mainly railroads). Not many investments went into manufacturing (primarily cotton textiles), very little into mining (chiefly coal and iron), and none into agriculture. C. M. Hou's recalculation of Remer's data indicates that in 1931 the direct investment portion of total foreign investments was distributed as follows: import and export trade 19.4 percent; railroads 16 percent; shipping 7.7 percent; manufacturing 14.9 percent; real estate 13.6 percent; banking and finance 8.6 percent; mining 4.4 percent; communications and public utilities 4 percent; and miscellaneous 11.3 percent.[6] The

TABLE 1   Foreign Capital in China by Use (US$ millions; percent in parentheses).

Use	1914		1931	
Government administration	330.3	(20.5)	427.7	(13.2)
Transportation	531.1	(33.0)	846.3	(26.1)
Communications and public utilities	26.6	(1.7)	128.7	(4.0)
Import-export trade	142.6	(8.8)	483.7	(14.9)
Banking and finance	6.3	(0.4)	214.7	(6.6)
Mining	59.1	(3.7)	128.9	(4.0)
Manufacturing	110.6	(6.9)	376.3	(11.6)
Real estate	105.5	(6.5)	339.2	(10.5)
Miscellaneous	298.2	(18.6)	282.8	(8.7)
Obligations of foreign municipalities	0.0		14.2	(0.4)
Total	1,610.3	(100.0)	3,242.5	(100.0)
Direct foreign investments included in above	1,067.0	(67.3)	2,493.2	(78.1)

Source: C. F. Remer, *Foreign Investment in China* (New York, 1933), pp. 70, 83.

TABLE 2   Foreign investments in China by Country, 1902–1936 (US$ millions; percent in parentheses).

Country	1902		1914		1931		1936	
Great Britain	260.3	(33.0)	607.5	(37.7)	1,189.2	(36.7)	1,220.8	(35.0)
Japan	1.0	(0.1)	219.6	(13.6)	1,136.9	(35.1)	1,394.0	(40.0)
Russia	246.5	(31.3)	269.3	(16.7)	273.2	(8.4)	0.0	
United States	19.7	(2.5)	49.3	(3.1)	196.8	(6.1)	298.8	(8.6)
France	91.1	(11.6)	171.4	(10.7)	192.4	(5.9)	234.1	(6.7)
Germany	164.3	(20.9)	263.6	(16.4)	87.0	(2.7)	148.5	(4.3)
Belgium	4.4	(0.6)	22.9	(1.4)	89.0	(2.7)	58.4	(1.7)
Netherlands	0.0		0.0		28.7	(0.9)	0.0	
Italy	0.0		0.0		46.4	(1.4)	72.3	(2.1)
Scandinavia	0.0		0.0		2.9	(0.1)	0.0	
Others	0.6	(0.0)	6.7	(0.4)	0.0		56.3	(1.6)
Total	787.9	(100.0)	1,610.3	(100.0)	3,242.5	(100.0)	3,483.2	(100.0)

Source: For 1902–1931, see Remer, *Foreign Investments*, p. 76. For 1936 (excluding Manchuria but including Hong Kong), see Tōa Kenkyūjo, *Rekkoku tai-shi tōshi to Shina kokusai shūshi* (Tokyo, 1944), pp. 2, 72–73, 131, 200.

distribution of foreign investment in China by country is shown in Table 2.

The chief investing countries in China were Great Britain, Germany, and France in the last century and Britain and Japan in the

1930s. British investment, which was most important both in ab-
solute amounts and in relative share, consisted mostly of direct investment, although loans to the Chinese government were very important in the nineteenth century. Direct investment was 58 percent,
66 percent, and 81 percent of total British investment in the years
1902, 1914, and 1931; and 50 percent of direct investment was in
fields directly associated with trade in 1931. Geographically, 77
percent of direct investment was in Shanghai in 1929.

Japanese investment increased rapidly after 1905 when Japan
defeated Russia and acquired Russian territorial and economic privileges in South Manchuria. Of Japan's total direct investment, 69
percent and 63 percent were in Manchuria in 1914 and 1930 (31
percent in 1914 and 25 percent in 1930 were in Shanghai). The
South Manchuria Railway Co. was formed in 1906 and 50 percent
of its capital stock was owned by the Japanese government, which
also controlled the company by appointing the principal officers.
This railroad company owned 79 percent of Japan's direct investment in Manchuria in 1914 and 60 percent in 1930. Japanese investment in China was mainly direct investment, which accounted
for 100 percent of the total in 1900, 98 percent in 1914, and 77
percent in 1931. After becoming firmly entrenched in Manchuria,
Japan grew to become the largest investor in China in 1936.

Russia's investment in China was accounted for almost entirely
by the Chinese Eastern Railway owned by the Russian government. Russia's direct investment in China was concentrated in
Manchuria and Outer Mongolia. French investment was characterized by loans to the Chinese government that remained more
than half of the total investment. French direct investment was represented partly by the Yunnan Railway, which was largely under
the control of the French government. German investment was the
third largest investment in China before 1914, when Germany
owned an increasing interest in the development of Shantung
province. American investment, which had begun earlier in the
1870s, did not grow large. Although it increased after 1914, it never
constituted more than 7 percent of total foreign investment in
China before 1937. Forty-nine percent of American investment was
direct investment, chiefly in fields related with trade.

II.   Various Fields of Foreign Investment in China

1.   Trade and Banking

Foreign investment in China originated in China's foreign trade. Some of the largest British trading firms such as Jardine, Matheson and Co., David Sasson and Co., and Dent and Co. first appeared in China in the 1830s and 1840s. Mackenzie and Co., Mustard and Co., and Butterfield and Swire came in the 1860s. American trading firms such as Russell and Co. and Olyphant and Co. also participated in China's external trade as early as the beginning of the nineteenth century. The hope of economic gain first brought these foreign companies to the Middle Kingdom. They displayed a pioneering spirit and introduced a number of Chinese products into the international market while also opening the Chinese market to foreign products.

The growing volume of external trade created a demand for the establishment of financial institutions in China to finance imports and exports. From 1848 to 1872 several foreign banks opened branches in Shanghai. The Hongkong and Shanghai Banking Corporation was founded in Hongkong in 1864 by merchants of many nationalities (British, German, American, Persian, and Chinese) and began to operate in Shanghai in 1865. Later it became an entirely British-owned company and grew to become the largest bank in China. This corporation, together with British banks, had a virtual monopoly on the finances of China's foreign trade until the end of last century. The other important banks that were established in the 1890s were Yokohama Specie Bank, a Japanese concern which opened branches in Shanghai and later in Manchuria; the Russo-Chinese Bank (later reorganized as the Russo-Asiatic Bank), whose immediate purpose was financing the Chinese Eastern Railway in Manchuria; the Deutsch-Asiatishe Bank; and the Banque de l'Indochine. During and immediately after the First World War, Japanese banks started an extensive drive to establish a branch bank in China and American banks also made progress in this direction.

2.   Shipping

Not long after the opening of the five ports in 1842, the number of treaty ports increased and coastal and inland areas were opened to foreign navigation. The first foreign shipping company in China was the Shanghai Steam Navigation Co., which was founded in Shanghai in 1862 by an American trading firm named Russell and Co. with the help of capital supplied by Chinese and foreign merchants in China. This concern was very successful and virtually monopolized steam traffic on the Yangtze River from 1867 to 1872. In 1877 it withdrew from Chinese waters by selling its entire fleet and properties to the newly established Chinese firm of China Merchant's Steam Navigation Company.

Butterfield and Swire founded the China Navigation Co. in Shanghai in 1872, and Jardine, Matheson and Co., using the capital of Chinese comprador merchants and British merchants in China, founded the Indo-China Steam Navigation Co. in 1875. These two British firms, together with the one Chinese firm, became known as the Big Three and dominated Chinese steam shipping until 1907. In that year the Nisshin Kisen Kaisha was founded. This Japanese firm grew to be another giant in Chinese shipping and was heavily subsidized by the Japanese government in its initial years.

3. Railroads

The Chinese government persistently opposed railroad construction in the early years because it feared that railroads would penetrate the interior and cause unnecessary troubles. However, this negative point of view gradually changed after 1895 when China, defeated by Japan, began eagerly to imitate Western technology. The practical value of railroads was understood, and a chapter that has been called the scramble for the railroad concession in China was opened from 1895 to 1903. The right of railroad construction came to be regarded as a prize of international profits, and foreign governments began large-scale construction in China.

The earliest railroad concession was obtained by France in 1895 for the Yunnan Railway. Russia obtained a concession in Manchuria in 1896 for the Chinese Eastern Railway; in 1898 the line became a part of the South Manchuria Railway. The South Manchuria Railway was transferred to Japan, and the Chinese Eastern Railway was also sold to Japan in 1935. In 1897 Germany obtained the right to build a line known as the Kiaochow-Tsinan Railway.

Britain obtained the concession for the Canton-Kowloon Railway in 1906.

The aim of the imperialists to construct railroads in China was for gaining spheres of influence in China and for transporting troops into China, if needed, to protect their respective interests and also maintain a balance of power. The Chinese government also constructed several railroads with foreign loans in the ensuing years. However, apart from the high service costs of these foreign obligations (interest, discounts, and commissions), it is questionable whether these railroads were of any advantage to the Chinese economy. Commercial profit was of little if any concern. For instance, before the construction of the Yunnan Railway, there was little trade between Southern China and Indochina. Not only were the foreign lines unrelated to China's economic needs at that time, but their usefulness was limited by frequent civil wars and disturbances. Moreover, the provisions in the loan agreements prevented efficient central management by establishing boundaries within which the several lines were treated as separate enterprises. Nevertheless, foreign lines did influence the later development of China's railroads, because the network of the nation's railroad system, as shaped during this period, lacked planning and coordination.

4. Mining

With the opening of the treaty ports, foreign steamers frequented the coastal and river ports. When they found that the native coal was too expensive or poor in quality, foreign merchants wanted to develop modern coal mines. They frequently requested the right to mine coal but were turned down by the Chinese government. At that time, the native people believed that the opening of a mine (as well as the construction of a railroad) would disturb the spirits, destroy *feng shui* ("wind and water," a good sign in geomancy), and bring misfortune. Because of this superstition, the Confucian and patrimonial bureaucrats were in constant fear of people's opposition to such foreign undertakings. Thus, mining was prohibited.

Foreigners made fruitless efforts to mine coal, iron, and silver before 1895 but finally succeeded in obtaining mining rights and founded many mines either entirely on their own or through joint ownership with Chinese from 1896 to 1913. But mining meant that foreigners had to leave the treaty ports and go into the Chinese interior. Because they were permitted by treaty to trade and manufacture only in the ports, they had to undertake special negotiations and make special agreements with the Chinese government to observe Chinese mining regulations.

The British interests were in two large mines, the Kaiping coal mine and the Peking Syndicate. Japan obtained her mining interest through direct investment and through loans. The three largest iron mines and ironworks in China—the Hanyehping, the Anshan, and the Miao-Er-Kou—were all connected with Japanese capital.

The first modern iron and steel plant, the Hanyang, was completed in 1893 under the leadership of Chang Chih-tung, the governor-general of Hupei and Hunan. From 1890 to 1896, more than 5 million taels of government funds were spent, but little iron or steel was produced or sold. The government was reluctant to provide more funds, and the enterprise fell into great difficulties. Meanwhile, through a complicated reorganization, the Hanyang ironworks became the Hanyehping Coal and Iron Company in 1908. Still more money was required and left no alternative except to borrow abroad. The principal source of loans was Japan. From 1902 to 1930, sixteen loans were secured from Japanese sources, and the terms for repayment of the loans was to be executed by the sale of iron ore and pig iron to the Japanese government ironworks at Yawata. The problem was that Hanyehping was unable to repay these loans in the manner provided.

In the 1904 agreement, for example, the first year's interest on a ¥3 million loan at 6 percent was ¥180,000. At the agreed price of ¥3.00 for first-grade ore, Hanyehping had to export 60,000 tons of first-grade ore to Yawata in order to pay the interest alone. In 1913 Hanyehping borrowed ¥15 million through the Yokohama Specie Bank and was to repay the loans by the sale of ore and pig iron at a fixed price per ton; this fixed price sometimes fell below the market price and sometimes even fell below the Chinese cost of production. Hanyehping thus obtained much less than the market price, especially during World War I when the price increased sharply. In addition to the fixed price for their repayment, Hanyehping was to sell to Yawata 17 million tons of first-grade ore and 8 million tons of iron during the 40-year term of the loans. This tonnage represented about 70 percent of the total ore reserves of the mine. Increased supervision of Hanyehping by Japanese advisers was provided in later loans, and Hanyehping gave the Yokohama Specie Bank a prior option for further loans during the life of the 1913 agreements. As Hanyehping fell deeper and deeper into debt to its Japanese creditors, it became obvious that the company could never export enough ore to repay both the interest and principal on the loans. In 1934 the outstanding principal and interest on the loans was estimated at more than ¥40 million—one and one-half times the original principal. Hence Japan secured control over Hanyehping and transformed it into primarily a supplier of raw materials for Japanese heavy industry. The history of Hanyehping[7] is indeed a tragedy, and the lesson learned is that the bite of the imperialist wolf is as bad as his bark. But who hopelessly mismanaged the business and let the Japanese in the first place? The Chinese.

In the development of foreign interests in mining in China, Britain and Japan were the most active and obtained the most substantial results. Their investments were almost exclusively in coal and iron. Foreign investments in other minerals such as lead, antimony, or gold were small.

5. Manufacturing

One hundred and three foreign-owned industrial enterprises were inaugurated in China prior to 1895. These enterprises were illegal under the treaties, but they existed nevertheless; most of the enterprises were in the Shanghai foreign concessions but a smaller number were at other treaty ports. Ship repairing, shipbuilding, and processing for export constituted the major manufacturing activities of foreign enterprises in these early years. Two of the four largest foreign shipyards were built in the 1860s; the other two were built at the turn of the century. Processing for export, chiefly of tea and silk, was undertaken by foreign merchants in China as early as the 1850s and grew very rapidly before 1895. Other products were not important in those years, but they covered a wide range, such as drugs, sodas, flours, lumber, soap, and ice.

Encouraged by legalization of the foreign establishment of manu-

facturing firms in the Treaty of Shimonoseki in 1895, foreign investment increased and reached $111 million by 1914, as estimated by
Remer. Investment in shipyards and processing for export continued
to grow, although the emphasis apparently shifted to the production
of consumer goods principally for the Chinese market. Textiles,
food, drink, and tobacco were the main fields for foreign enterprises to exploit. While the establishment of British, French, German, and Russian firms was evenly distributed over two decades,
most of the Japanese enterprises were begun in 1904 and later, a
result of Japan's increasing economic penetration in Manchuria
after the Russo-Japanese War. Britain and Japan accounted for all
of the engineering firms and shipyards and for a very high proportion of the firms in other fields.

A host of goods were manufactured for domestic consumption.
Some products were largely for the residents, both foreign and
Chinese, of the treaty ports and were manufactured by foreign firms
in China. The products for Chinese mass consumption did not appear until after the market had been reasonably well established
through imports. Cotton goods were among the leading Chinese
imports. After several unsuccessful attempts by foreign merchants to

TABLE 3. Foreign Investments in Manufacturing in China by Country, 1936 (US$
millions; percent in parentheses).

Manufacture	Britain	United States	Germany	France	Japan	Total	
Textile	64.6	1.2	3.9	0.0	112.4	182.1	(54.7)
Metal, machinery, equipment	20.8	3.6	0.1	0.5	4.1	29.1	(8.8)
Chemicals	63.0	1.7	2.0	1.0	6.8	74.5	(22.4)
Lumber, woodworking	4.0	0.5	0.0	0.0	0.9	5.4	(1.6)
Printing, bookbinding	0.3	0.3	0.1	0.0	0.8	1.5	(0.5)
Food, drink, tobacco	23.3	1.1	0.9	0.5	5.8	31.6	(9.5)
Others	3.7	1.1	0.1	0.0	3.3	8.2	(2.5)
Total	179.7	9.5	7.1	2.0	134.1	332.4	
	(54.1)	(2.9)	(2.1)	(0.6)	(40.3)		(100.0)

Source: Tōa kenkyūjo, *Rekkoku tai-Shi tōshi to Shina kokusai shūshi*, pp. 7–8, 99, 102–
4; Tōa kenkyūjo, *Nihon no tai-shi tōshi* (Tokyo, 1943), pp. 278, 282, 284,
289, 305.

Note: Hong Kong is included; Manchuria is not.

open textile factories in Shanghai, the first foreign factory, Ewo Cotton Spinning and Weaving Co., was founded in 1897 by Jardine, Matheson and Co. in Shanghai. In the same year a British, an American, and a German firm were founded in Shanghai. These four foreign firms had a total of 160,548 spindles. The Japanese also sought to open textile factories in Shanghai in 1895 but soon found textile factories unprofitable to operate in China and withdrew. The foreign cotton mills in China at that time did not make much profit and declared no dividends, especially after 1899. This probably accounted for the scarcity of new factories by British or American firms in later years. By 1913 eight foreign firms in China were owned mainly by the British and Japanese. Foreign investments in manufacturing are shown in Table 3.

III. The Salient Features of Foreign Investment in China

The amount of foreign investment in China, as shown before, was $3,483 million in 1936. Taking the Chinese population in 1936 at 500 million, the per capita amount was still less than $7. This figure is notably less than that in other underdeveloped countries; in 1938, for example, the figure for India was $20; Latin America was $86; and Africa (Union of South Africa excluded) was $23. It is evident too that in contrast to the typical pattern of foreign investment in many underdeveloped countries, very little foreign capital in China was used for mining or plantation agriculture. Virtually no foreign capital went into tea, sericulture, soybeans, or the other agricultural products which made up most of China's exports. Though a target of Western exploitation, China never became a colony and did not possess the characteristics of a monoculture. Apart from silk, bean and its products (grown largely in Manchuria), no single item formed more than 10 percent of China's total exports by 1931.

Although the foreign trade of China Proper increased (the real increase from 1870 to 1931 may be four times at most), it never exceeded 1.5 percent of the total value of world trade. In per capita terms, it remained negligible, and probably smaller than that of any country in the world.[8] Moreover, China was in a low level of development, as it still is today, and had abundant and varied resources and a large domestic market, factors that reduce a country's involvement in foreign trade, China's foreign trade could not grow large by its nature. As a consequence, foreign investment in China could not have grown large because of the small volume of trade, a concomitance of the low level of national income.[9]

In order to increase national income, investments have to be made primarily in fields that enlarge the capacity to produce for either home consumption or export. But foreign investment in both fields is small in China. As pointed out above, the foreign direct investment was largely related with China's external trade and most was made by the trading firms and foreign banks. However, trade alone was not a sufficient agent of transformation. It did not produce innovation or the equivalent of modernization in a premodern economy. The foreigners in China treaty ports did not significantly alter the nature of existing trade, let alone affect the conditions or commodities of production. They left the Chinese economy little changed from the state, manipulated by the Chinese, it was in when they found it. The foreigners and their Chinese imitators also had a dominantly speculative attitude; they were neither free nor interested in trying through investment and management to improve production or to develop the Chinese economy. Like traditional Chinese merchants, foreigners were more often content to compete for slices of the cake rather than try to make the cake bigger. Thus the growth of China's foreign trade was merely a symptom of increasing commercialization and exchange beyond traditional levels; in many cases it bypassed or superseded the traditional centers.

Furthermore, foreign investments in China (except in Manchuria) were mainly made by private individuals. These individuals were not often persons who came to China with large capital. In fact, most of the private individual investors made their fortunes in China and enlarged their businesses by reinvestment. This was particularly true of the British merchant. The growth of Jardine, Matheson and Co. over the course of a century, from a small agency house in the 1830s to the largest trading company with many industrial and financial interests in China, illustrates this process quite well. As Remer observed, some of them "started on a shoe string" or were "built up from nothing." Such examples were abundant at that time. At first, foreign merchants had high hopes of exploiting what they believed to be an almost unlimited market in China. Immediately after the Opium War, British business circles believed that the Chinese market for textiles would exceed the entire European market. Therefore, they were active in investment in almost all fields related with trade and also active in other fields. J. M. and Co. had investments in such divergent industries as silk reeling, packing, cold storage, engineering, shipping, shipyards, insurance, breweries, and cotton textiles. But the rate of return on investment was not as high as expected.

C. M. Hou's study of 115 financial statements for foreign firms in China from 1872 to 1932 shows that the profit net worth ratios were mostly 5 to 20 percent; about 41 percent of the firms had profit rates of less than 10 percent, about 64 percent of the firms had ratios less than 15 percent, and 13 percent of the firms had ratios 25 percent or higher. In a study of fifty foreign business firms in China in 1930, Remer found a rate of profit on investment of between 10 and 20 percent in "years of prosperity." A Japanese study of eighty-nine Japanese manufacturing concerns in China in 1927 reports an average rate of 5.5 percent; another study of seventy-seven Japanese manufactureres in Manchuria from 1907 to 1916 and from 1921 to 1926 puts the average annual rate at 9.4 percent. All this is evidence of manufacturing firms earning the lowest profit rates; around 10 percent can be accepted as a crude approximation of the normal profit rate in this sector.[10] This explains why no substantial amount of foreign investment was employed in manufacturing (only 15 percent of total investments). Even more important, manufacturing was not as profitable as appeared because of the nature of the market in China. For the products that the Chinese masses could afford to buy, the traditional handicrafts proved to be an effective alternative to products of modern technology. For the products that were beyond the reach of traditional handicrafts, the market was limited because of the poverty and low purchasing power of the masses. The lack of purchasing power of the masses was one of the main causes for the few inducements to investment in manufacturing. In brief, foreign trade and investment in China were much smaller than in other underdeveloped economies and also contributed little to China's national income.

IV. Geographical Confinement of Foreign Investment in China

Not only were both the amount and inflow of foreign capital small for China, but they were geographically restricted to the treaty ports. When a foreigner sought out trade and investment opportunities outside the pale of Western civilization, he often encountered various obstacles and strong opposition to his activities. To realize opportunities for trade and investment, he had to rely on the economic and military superiority of his native country (gunboat diplomacy) and employ limited aggression against countries. However, this aggression served only to introduce a reaction against the West in the undeveloped countries and called forth an even greater antiforeign resistance. Increased resistance of the peoples in turn often led to the outright colonization by a Western power. China, because of the international power struggle, never became the colony of a single power but had a semicolonial position and was the scene of open rivalry between the Western powers and Japan.

Foreign powers sought to open the China market and, once this was accomplished by military victory, they demanded economic privileges to establish a legal and institutional framework that would facilitate and protect the business interests of their nationals. Recurring patterns in the unequal treaties were China's lack of tariff autonomy, extraterritorial rights, concessions, leased areas, spheres of influence, foreign troops, and special rights that China was forced to grant to the various powers. Therefore, the special position and imperialist behavior of the foreigners lead the Chinese to resist and regard their presence on Chinese soil as a symbol of invasion. The Chinese government often believed that whatever profit foreign marchants made was at the expense of the Chinese. They also feared that foreign economic penetration would cause many Chinese to lose their livelihoods and would upset the Chinese economy.

In China a vigorously self-conscious cultural nationalism, national identity, and tradition of an integrated national state and culture had existed for some two thousand years before Westerners arrived. The Western challenge merely reinforced existing sinocentric pride. The Chinese, at that time, regarded all foreigners as barbarians to whom China had been willing to condescend. (This attitude was fully betrayed in the tribute system before 1840.) After the Opium War foreigners revealed themselves also as bandits—clever and effective in certain ways but alien and frequently evil.[11] Very naturally, the Chinese felt themselves greatly humiliated by the foreign powers and were always suspicious of and hostile to foreign investment in China. This sharp opposition to foreigners' development of China became a decisive obstacle and has remained a negative force to this day. The Chinese government first tried to confine the foreigner's activities in the treaty ports and stop foreign economic penetration of the interior. For economic activities that had to take place outside the treaty ports—such as railroad construction, mining, and plantations—foreigners had to negotiate with the Chinese government. Foreign nationals, with the exception of missionaries, were not permitted to own or lease land outside the treaty ports. The treaty port system was to a large extent an enclave economy and created a dualism. There was no blending of China and the West but only a sharpening of confrontation.[12] This system in China merely refocused and sharpened the traditional Chinese insistence on a self-sufficient and self-satisfied identity and exacerbated the traditional resistance to foreign models.

Though the number of designated ports grew steadily, increasing from the original five named in the Treaty of Nanking to seventy-three by 1930, many were merely "ports of call," and a foreigner's movements were restricted. Shanghai was by far the most important, since it accounted for more than one-third of the foreign investment in China in 1931. This geographical confinement of foreign economic activity, along with legal restrictions on foreigners' movements, severely limited the points of contact between the foreign sector and the large domestic economy. With few notable exceptions, a foreigner conducted his business at the treaty port with a Chinese merchant who was also located there.[13] Isolated from the Chinese producer and consumer, foreigners were effectively prevented from such activities as directly inducing desirable innovations and technical changes in production, organizing the collection, discrimination, transportation, and merchandising of trade goods, and carrying out significant market research for new trade goods and investment opportunities.

In other words, the traditional indigenous system in China managed to continue functioning right through the nineteenth century and into the twentieth century. The traditional Chinese merchants were fully able to protect themselves against foreign encroachments; they controlled the treaty ports and maintained control over the internal marketing even of foreign goods, including those that were genuinely new to China such as kerosene, factory-made matches or cigarettes, and machine-spun yarns. There was no product vacuum the foreigners could fill. The foreign goods were sold in the standard markets along with traditional Chinese goods, and there was no need and no room for foreigners to establish a modern marketing system along Western lines or with the participation of modern merchants.[14]

V. The Impact of the Treaty Port Foreigners on China's Modern Sectors

The foreigners' activities, though feared as evil, probably strengthened China's economy far more than they weakened it. Much of the capital generated in the treaty ports was drained off as profits or reinvested abroad, but there was significant new net investment in China. More importantly, foreign efforts to wider external markets were certainly accompanied by increased Chinese production of foreign trade goods, even if this increase was not a large proportional increase over traditional levels of production. Undoubtedly, foreign trade increased the stimulus of commercial production for export, even in long-established export industries such as tea and silk. The foreigners tapped these industries and created an expanded overseas market for them as well as for commodities like tung oil, eggs, bristles, wool, hides, peanuts, and straw braid in later years. But the increased exports did not stimulate the production of other goods in China, because these exports did not rely to any appreciable extent on the products of other sectors and were used extensively as inputs in other sectors. In summary, none of the export increases represented a new departure or new sector whose growth significantly changed the nature or operation of the economy. The goods diverted into external channels only slightly increased supplies of goods that had previously been circulated more domestically. They involved only a small fraction of the Chinese economy as a whole.

Concerning imports, the possible beneficial effects of foreign trade suffered from similar limitations. A major share of China's imports were final manufactured or processed products destined for consumption. Besides opium, which is clearly a drain or a dead weight on the Chinese economy, imports such as cotton goods, cereals, and sugar could supplement domestic supplies of consumer goods. The availability of machine-spun yarn benefited indigenous production and improved its ability to compete. Due in large part to this reason, the Chinese were reluctant to buy foreign goods or adapt foreign business methods or technology, because traditional goods and methods were equal or superior, especially in cost. The only significant exceptions, which will be examined later, were kerosene, cigarettes, and cotton yarn. However, cigarettes and cotton yarn, like matches and a number of other lesser goods of originally foreign manufacture, came increasingly from Chinese producers using Chinese raw materials by 1915.

The import of producer goods does of course involve a significant linkage effect, but these imported goods represented only a small part of China's total imports. Machinery, iron and steel and other metals, chemicals and dyes and pigments, and transportation equipment accounted for only 5 percent of imports in 1900 and 17 percent in 1928. In addition, some of these goods were imported for use in the foreign sector itself, and a large share of the machinery and equipment were for the textile industry, which was one of the few important light industries producing consumer goods. Obviously, foreign capital was dominant in the modern sector of the Chinese economy and was responsible for the initial appearance of most modern industries. Nevertheless, the forward and backward linkage of all these industries was very limited; their inputs were acquired directly from the agricultural producer, and their output (except for cotton yarn) went directly to the consumer. Strictly speaking, there were no heavy industries in China before 1937.

Although foreigners' activities were confined to the treaty ports, they enjoyed the fullest degree of freedom there and had no reason to fear Chinese laws or other Chinese control. As an investor, the foreign firm possessed certain advantages: access to foreign capital abroad, technological sophistication, entrepreneurial talent, managerial efficiency, and political and diplomatic privileges accorded by the unequal treaties. It is often said that foreign firms with their superiority could easily compete and oppress their Chinese counterparts. But, on the other hand, foreign firms, as the precursors of many Chinese industries, also set an example for Chinese entrepreneurs and demonstrated the usefulness of business practices. Moreover, foreign firms performed an important function of technology transfer to China and provided a training ground for managers as well as an emerging industrial labor force. Their most important function was the entrepreneurial function performed by the compradors who served as representatives of foreign firms in conducting business with the Chinese. These compradors not only acquired knowledge about Western enterprises but also earned a very handsome income from the foreign firms in China; they figured prominently in the establishment of modern enterprises. Some bureaucrats, traditional merchants, and gentry also invested in varying degrees in modern enterprises.

These treaty port Chinese, who benefited from the foreign presence, were in part a new kind of Chinese who promised to be the indigenous agent for the remaking of China along Western lines in trade, finance, transport, industry, politics, and ideology. They enjoyed the new entrepreneurial freedom offered in the treaty ports: security of property and accumulation, the protection of nonparticularistic law, a stable civil order, the ready availability of capital at low rates of interest, and expanding opportunities for constructive as opposed to parasitic use of capital.[15] They were not slow in making use of capital, because there existed an individual rationality that was economically sound in the conditions prevailing in China, especially after 1860. Where innovation offered reliable and immediate rewards, Chinese never hesitated to adapt it. The best illustration is the almost instant response to the introduction of steamship enterprises, which attracted the earliest major Chinese investment outside of trade. Chinese merchants subscribed about one-third of the original capital for the first three foreign steamship companies founded in Shanghai between 1862 and 1868; in 1873–74, nearly 80 percent of the initial capital of the China Merchant Steam Navigation Co., the first such enterprise—and the largest single shipping fleet in East Asia at that time—was owned and operated by Chinese. There was a well-known Sino-Anglo-American Steamship rivalry in China among these three companies in subsequent years.[16]

This was an outstanding example that Chinese merchants were quick to recognize the value of the insurance that could be obtained on the cargoes steamships carried. Chinese merchants began traveling on and then shipping their goods by these safer and faster ships. The development of steamship companies reduced the cost of transportation, increased the extent of the market of goods, and made it possible for many industries to grow owing to access to a larger market.

By 1894, Chinese investors and managers were represented in about three-fifths of the foreign firms in China.[17] Chinese investors began to fully perceive and act on changed circumstances that made foreign-managed innovative enterprises an attractive outlet, and they were followed in time by Chinese-managed enterprises. After 1911, industrial investment became more popular among Chinese merchants. Data suggest that the Chinese merchant-capitalist-investor was becoming more willing to risk his money in modern enterprises because many of the earlier objections to such investment were losing their force: profitability and security were proportionately less for the traditional use of capital (land, usury, and speculation) and proportionately more for industrial investment.[18] Accordingly, large amounts of Chinese capital were invested in new mining and manufacturing enterprises, principally cotton textiles and tobacco. Before comparing these two most successful Chinese industries with their foreign counterparts and examining the fiercest sino-foreign rivalry that ever existed in China, I would like to look into how aggressively American firms penetrated the China market.

VI. Foreign Business Activities and Chinese Response: a mixture of acceptance and resistance

1. Standard Oil Co. in China[19]

In the early years of the twentieth century, Standard Oil was one of the most successful American enterprises in penetrating the China market and promoting petroleum sales there. Unlike most American firms that relied on European commercial houses in the treaty ports, Standard built up its own modern efficient distribution complex. By dispatching its specially trained men into the heart of China and introducing an improved and cheaper kerosene lamp, it increased its sales and enhanced its reputation. In the process, it formed close ties with native merchants and became a household word to many Chinese. Meanwhile, its products, mostly kerosene, formed a large and vital part of America's annual exports to China.

Standard began to export kerosene to China in the late 1870s and enjoyed a virtual monopoly in the market. By 1889 its exports reached 15 million gallons, about 2 percent of total American kerosene exports. During this period it was content to sell its products on consignment to local Chinese merchants, who took the speculative risks in dealing with unreliable and irregular demand, and thus its sales net was loosely and primitively organized. In 1890, Standard took the first tentative step toward a more effective marketing strategy, because the company was challenged by Russian oil and the development of oil fields and refineries in the Netherlands East Indies. In trying to protect its position in China against the competitor, Standard upgraded the quality of its products, marketed cheaper brands to match the popular Russian products, transported and stored its goods in bulk, advertised widely the virtues of kerosene, and introduced small and cheap lamps suitable to the Chinese market. The most important of these innovations was an elaborate marketing network. In the mid-1890s the company sent its own agents to Shanghai and Hong Kong, expanded its China network of competent and experienced agents, and gave agents considerable room for local initiative. In 1899 Standard established a profitable station at Chungking, deep in the interior, and by 1905 had thirteen offices staffed by American agents.

Standard was also challenged by the Asiatic Petroleum Co., a Royal Dutch-Shell enterprise, which commanded a marketing system in China and enjoyed closer sources of crude oil in Sumatra and Borneo. Standard fought fiercely to maintain its supremacy in the China market by price cutting. But, after a brief period of competition, it reached at emporary agreement to divide the Far Eastern market with the Royal Dutch. However, this price war with its rivals convinced Standard that it had to establish an integrated

oil industry in China based on local crude. Despite its efforts, however, the company ultimately failed due to the various barriers in
China.

Standard's initiatives in marketing, together with its early cuts in
the cost of kerosene, enabled it to improve its position against its
rivals. Its exports increased from about 34 million gallons (nearly
half the market) in the 1890s, to 80 million gallons in 1905; 96
million gallons (60 percent of the market), or nearly 15 percent of
its sales, was outside North America by 1910. Kerosene accounted
for half of American total exports to China in 1914 and was the
only major item that did not meet Japanese competition in China.
Standard and Texaco, which entered the China market around
1910, together recorded sales as high as 231 million gallons, equal
to 88 percent of the market in 1928. By the late 1920s Standard
had invested $43 million in its marketing system in China, then
consisting of six major regional offices, eighteen subagencies, and a
widespread distributing network composed of Standard's own Chinese agents and local Chinese merchants. While the agents handled
sales from company warehouses in the interior, the merchants selected by Standard and guaranteed by other wealthy merchants
sold to the ultimate consumer on a commission basis.

But Standard was not unopposed in the China market. In the early
years, the resistance that Standard encountered came initially from
officials sympathetic to complaints that imported kerosene was dis-
placing native vegetable oils. For instance, in 1887 Chang Chih-
Tung, the governor general of Kwangtung and Kwangsi, requested
a ban on kerosene imports on the grounds that kerosene was unfair
competition to the peasants who grew peanuts, the processors who
extracted oil from peanuts, and the merchants who sold peanut oil.
"The livelihood of our people is at stake and we are obliged to pro-
hibit imports," he argued. At the turn of the last century, Chinese
erected an imposing combination of obstacles; municipal regulations
against the use of kerosene, the refusal of merchant guilds to handle
it, opposition to the establishment of storage tanks, and illegal taxation. However, kerosene gave a stronger, steadier lighting and length-
ened the work day for many peasants engaged in handicrafts during
the long winter season of confinement indoors. At the same time,
it had a price advantage over native vegetable oils, especially as the

overseas demand for it, both as a foodstuff and as an industrial component, increased. Exports of vegetable oil climbed steadily from the early 1890s and spectacularly from the late 1900s and into the 1920s. Kerosene was demonstrated to be superior to domestic alternatives without being substantially more expensive.[20] And because of these reasons, the force of opposition diminished and the consumer accepted kerosene as an attractive new alternative fuel.

Standard adapted itself to Chinese conditions and succeeded in reaching the extensive interior market. In attempting to conquor the China market, they had to surrender, to a degree, to it. This meant that their agents had to learn the language and customs of the people, their products and advertisements had to appeal to Chinese tastes, and their goods had to travel along established Chinese marketing patterns and through the hands of Chinese merchants. It also meant that they had to be solicitous of public opinion, which meant cultivating good will by contributing flood and famine relief, sponsoring agricultural schools, and so on. The firm was always under the pressure of Chinese economic nationalism, which manifested itself in efforts to impose taxes on foreign firms. Standard often accepted economic nationalism, because prolonged negotiations hindered company business and imperiled good will. There was often some condemnation against "capitalistic imperialism," or various controversies on treaty rights between the Chinese and the firm, but to continue operations, Standard thought temporary restrictions were easier to accept than the possibility of being shut out of the China market.

The China market was not as vast as Westerners fancied and neither was it impenetrable. The potential for trade did exist for those firms with an attractive product superior to its competitors, but to realize a profit they had to possess adequate capital, persistence, and flexibility in reaching out to Chinese customers. For example, Western firms were often accused of constructing bulk storage tanks which posed substantial fire hazards as well as being prominent symbols of foreign intrusion. Faced with protests against their storage tanks, Standard agents generally bided their time until local passions cooled and they could work out some mutually satisfactory agreements with local authorities. The agents had to accommodate themselves to established Chinese business practices, the preferences of their customers, and the force of Chinese nationalism. The experience of Standard reveals that aggressive and innovative marketing and a strong financial base were the essential factors for success in the China market.

2. A Sino-Foreign Rivalry: The BAT and Nanyang Cigarette Co.[21]

A second striking example of foreign penetration was the cigarette industry, which grew after the market had been opened up by imports and very quickly replaced manufactured imports. In 1890 the American Tobacco Company's agent, Mustard and Co., began to import cigarettes into China from Great Britain and found cigarettes were widely accepted by the Chinese. After the giant British-American Tobacco Co. (BAT) came into being in 1902, one of its subsidiaries, the British Cigarette Co., established several cigarette manufacturing plants in China—first in Shanghai, Hankow, Mukden, and Harbin and later in Tientsin and Tsingtao. At first the company had to import tobacco for its plants because Chinese tobacco was unsuitable for cigarettes. Within ten years, however, it was able to cure Chinese-grown leaf to be used in a mixture with American tobacco. The company continued its efforts to substitute Chinese leaf for imported leaf. It distributed American seed to the Chinese farmers and taught them improved methods of culture and preparation. After investigations, it found that Shantung possessed the most favorable conditions for tobacco growing and this province became the main center of the culture. The introduction of a new crop called not only for much patient experimental work but also tactful propaganda in overcoming the initial suspicions of the peasantry. When the company's agents first brought American seed to the farmers, they found little enthusiasm, and their offer of contracts was coolly received. But as soon as the farmers saw that the results far exceeded their expectations, they inundated the company with applications for contracts; after a few years nearly all the wheat fields in the vicinity of Fangtze (Shantung) were converted to American tobacco plantations.

BAT had numerous curing factories in the tobacco-growing districts. The staff of these establishments included foreigners, many of whom were leaf experts with experience in tobacco production in the United States. Each establishment had a comprador who supervised the Chinese staff and acted as a link between BAT and the growers. Usually the land on which the curing factories and collecting stations were built was held in the comprador's name, as foreign firms were still not permitted to own land outside the treaty ports. Moreover, it was necessary to provide the farmers with working capital, especially as the growing and treatment of American tobacco required the application of more labor and capital per acre than did Chinese-style tobacco. The compradors provided seed, bean-cake as fertilizer, and coal for curing on credit. These loans were usually made through the intermediary of the local gentry in the tobacco growing business. By the 1930s home-produced leaf was able to satisfy most of the domestic demand and replaced the imports. By 1934 there were about 300,000 families engaged in growing American tobacco, and tobacco became the chief cash crop in the three main centers—namely, Wei-hsien in East Shantung, Fengyang in North Anhwei, and Hsuchang in Central Honan.

By 1915 BAT had investments in China totaling $20 million, and its production climbed from 1.25 billion cigarettes in 1902 to 12 billion in 1916. By 1916 BAT had a net annual profit of $3.75 million. In 1919 it had capital of $250 million in silver. In the mid-1930s, it had seven cigarette factories that employed about 25,000 Chinese workers and warehouses in some 547 countries and municipalities in China. Inasmuch as its products were for Chinese domestic consumption, BAT had a very comprehensive marketing system. Its selling agents were primarily Chinese and could be found all over the country. As early as 1916, its network already extended well into Sinkiang (Chinese Turkestan), Mongolia, and other bordering provinces. In many areas, especially the interior, cigarette smoking was introduced by these agents. (Smoking was at least a cheap pleasure for poor peasants.)

As the cigarette business prospered, several Chinese firms were established in imitation. Cigarette consumption in China was vastly expanded; it is estimated to have been 300 million in 1900, 22,500 million in 1920, and 88,500 million in 1933. The expansion was primarily by domestic production, because imports declined sharply during World War I and thereafter. As already observed, Chinese regarded foreign penetration as intolerably humiliating. After the turn of the century, the antiforeign atmosphere encouraged the purchase of articles and consumption of commodities produced by Chinese firms. This "buy Chinese" sentiment intensified as the technique of boycott came into more frequent use. The first large-scale Chinese boycott of 1905 was directed against American goods and followed the exclusion of Chinese labor from the United States in 1904. As the century advanced, a series of international events kept Chinese nationalistic feelings alive. There were the Twenty-One Demands in 1915, the Shantung question at the Paris Peace Conference in 1919, and the May 30 Incident in 1925. All these were construed by the Chinese as national humiliations and prompted them to buy Chinese goods.

The supremacy of BAT was challenged by the Nanyang Brothers Tobacco Company, which had been established by overseas Chinese. This firm came into existence during the anti-American boycott of 1905 and enjoyed tremendous public good will by being a Chinese concern, especially when the 1911 Revolution broke out. Nanyang Brothers aroused so much enthusiasm among the overseas Chinese that they patronized Chinese cigarettes despite their poor quality. Taking advantage of the national crises and number of boycotts, Nanyang Brothers greatly increased its sales and doubled and tripled its assets. In 1918 it moved its head office from Hong Kong to Shanghai and by 1921 it had nine plants. It really emerged as a serious competitor during the First World War; later it used the anti-British boycotts of the 1920s to advance sales at the expense of its foreign rival.

BAT responded to the threat by using aggressive business tactics. After the boycott of 1905, BAT blocked the development of any significant competitor within China's industrial sector until 1915. Using its monopoly control over the market, the company set prices that yielded a high profit—18.75 percent on net sales in 1916, for example—a profit rate higher than that of most foreign manufacturing firms in China. After 1915, when Nanyang Brothers penetrated South China, the lower and middle Yangtze, and North China, BAT tried to bar its entrance into these regional markets. Once it had overcome barriers to entry, BAT tried to reduce Nanyang Brothers to submission by using a variety of competitive tactics its Western owners had previously used in the West. First, it used price wars and smear propaganda alleging that Nanyang was associating with Japanese interests, just when Nanyang Brothers was experiencing a boom in the aftermath of the Twenty-One Demands of 1915. This coercive campaign seemed to be more vigorously conducted in 1919 after the May 4 Movement. Pressure from BAT was immense. At one time Nanyang Brothers was unable to find, even on consignment basis, any retail outlet in Shanghai, because all shops were committed to its rivals. BAT offered an attractive merger to buy the company out. Nanyang Brothers, convinced that BAT could ruin them at any time through a price war, thought the only saving grace was to accept the proposed merger offer. But the negotiations constantly bogged down over the matter of price and finally ended in 1922. In the early 1920s, when Nanyang Brothers was well established in China, BAT appealed for cooperation only in failure, and the competition between the two reached its peak. But after the mid-1920s, the rivalry declined as Nanyang Brothers weakened and suffered large losses after 1928. By 1930 the era of serious commercial rivalry ended.

Nanyang Brothers was never able to overcome BAT's economic advantages and shake its commanding position. Although Nanyang had arrangements similar to those of BAT for distributing seed and establishing collection stations and curing factories in tobacco-producing areas, it had less control over production than did its rival. The quality of Nanyang Brothers cigarettes seldom measured up to BAT's standard, whereas the quality and flavor of BAT cigarettes were admired and envied by all Chinese competitors. Thus BAT had a head start on its Chinese rivals and kept it. BAT produced 45.9 percent of all cigarettes made in mainland China in 1932 and 59.4 percent in 1935. Nevertheless the embarrassment caused by the boycotts was sufficient for BAT to establish a sales subsidiary under a Chinese name in 1921, divide the firm into several companies in 1934, and cease to use the name BAT in China thereafter. Some of the companies that took over the former sales departments were placed under Chinese management.

BAT opened the China market for cigarettes and created new sources of tobacco. In fact, BAT relied primarily on its Chinese compradors and agents to carry out these two tasks. Working through its Chinese employees and merchant associates, BAT employed innovative advertising techniques, pushed its sales along traditional Chinese channels of trade, and induced Chinese peasants to produce quality tobacco to meet the company's production needs. Well-paid and well-trained Westerners in BAT introduced a new method of production of cigarettes by installing in China the latest models of cigarette-making machinery and organized the industry along new lines. They also introduced two major innovations. The first was integrated mass production and mass marketing. The other was an organizational innovation: a decentralized system with regional offices at the core of each of China's major marketing areas, each equipped to perform its own manufacturing, marketing, and administrative functions independently of the others. Whereas the Chinese at BAT gained far more experience as commercial managers than as industrial managers.

Both BAT and Nanyang Brothers adapted to the circumstances that faced business in China by recruiting the appropriate Chinese to guide its product through the existing market structure and adjust its advertising to suit the political atmosphere and cultural milieu. The best evidence of their adaptability and the significance of the cigarette market may be found in their advertising. Nanyang Brothers, for example, fully recognized the commercial significance of Chinese patriotism. They saw in the "Chinese-made" label the only key to their success. The rival firm BAT also recognized this significance: it established sales organs under Chinese name and ceased to use the name BAT in China. Nanyang Brothers also effectively employed advertising that had been unknown in China. During the 1915 flood in Kwangtung, it distributed relief by a steamboat with a huge company flag on its mast. Again, during the 1920 North China drought, it donated to relief five dollars for every case of cigarettes sold during a period of five months. Their mission was accomplished efficiently and in grand style. The public was impressed and the demand for Nanyang Brothers cigarettes soared. Donations were also made to education by establishing a school and selecting and sending forty-five students to study in the United States. Nanyang Brothers also subsidized newspapers to influence the public through news and editorials. It distributed gifts and lottery tickets to consumers and even lobbied to have its cigarettes used at official functions. All these activities undoubtedly made the market grow rapidly.

This advertising seems to have been the key to Nanyang Brothers' and BAT's commercial success and was pressed on consumers in intensive campaigns. It attracted enough smokers to make a market for cigarettes in China. In short, using advertising designed and distributed by Chinese in both companies, Nanyang Brothers and BAT showed not only their abilities to use existing commercial structures but also their awareness of popular traditions, regional differences, political development, and other features of Chinese life. They performed all tasks that made for a business acceptable to Chinese society at all levels, regional and local as well as national.

BAT and Standard Oil both adapted themselves to Chinese conditions and proved that both Chinese transport and Chinese merchants were satisfactory means of reaching the extensive interior market. The profits were there for any businessman who seized the opportunity, if he possessed adequate capital and persistence and flexibility in reaching out to Chinese customers. The experiences of BAT and Standard indicate some resistance stemming from a mixture of nationalism and economic self-interest but also considerable acceptance from Chinese consumers and merchants. While Chinese economic nationalism only slightly hampered the activities of the BAT and Standard, it placed much more heavy emphasis on creating a domestic cotton industry for turning back the tide of foreign manufactured imports. Consequently, there was a firm resistance by Chinese-owned cotton mills and Chinese handicraft industries to the activities of Japanese-owned mills in China (*zaikabō*, as they are usually referred to).

3. The Activities of the Japanese-owned Cotton Mills in China[22]

The Sino-Japanese War revealed the weakness of China to the world and, at the same time, aroused a nationalistic sentiment and indignation inspired by the establishment of foreign-owned mills in Shanghai after the Shimonoseki Treaty. These circumstances served to stimulate the construction of mills by the Chinese. Seven cotton mills were founded before 1895 and eight were begun by 1899. All these mills experienced initial difficulties in technological and organizational aspects, though their products appeared to be welcomed by customers in various inland provinces. Just the same, the obstacles in introducing modern cotton mills to China were no less formidable even to Westerners. The four foreign mills erected in Shanghai in 1897 (as already observed) managed to pay 3 or 4 percent dividends for a year or two and then were compelled to discontinue the dividend payments for several years. Accordingly, no Western-owned mills were established until one British mill was opened up in 1914.

No Japanese mills were built in China immediately after the signing of the Shimonoseki Treaty. In 1895 there were two Japanese firms actively preparing for construction of mills in Shanghai, but they quickly changed their minds in view of the difficulties encountered. The Japanese capitalists proceeded very cautiously in the matter of operating cotton mills in China. In 1902 Mitsui and Co. first bought a bankrupt mill in Shanghai as a trial and two years later it bought another Chinese mill. The operations of these two mills were quite successful, owing to the introduction of management methods that proved to be successful in homeland. It was not until 1911 that Japanese textile manufacturers built their first mill in China in accordance with their own design. Up to 1913, it was just a trial period for the three groups of Chinese-owned, Western-owned, and Japanese-owned mills.

Although the First World War provided impetus for both Chinese and foreigners to invest in China, because imports declined and profits rose, little foreign investment took place. Britain was busy with the war and Japan was enjoying prosperity at home. There were sharp changes, however, in the situation of the cotton industry, both in China and Japan, which forced the major textile companies in Japan to shift their attention to China as a new frontier.[23] First, the Chinese tariff revision in 1918 imposed higher duties upon the coarse yarns which Japan had been exporting to China. More importantly, the recent developments in China seemed to indicate that the country would sooner or later recover its tariff autonomy and eventually exclude Japanese cotton goods. Probably no other country in the world was so dependent upon export markets as was Japan. At that time Japan was entirely dependent on the China market for its prosperity. In 1914 the China market consumed 92 percent of all Japanese yarn exports, or about one-quarter of the total national production, and about 70 percent of all cotton piece good exports, or about 8 percent of total domestic production, though less in the weaving industry. The China market changed significantly after reaching a peak in 1915; cotton yarn exports to China declined steadily and at a rate faster than the overall decline in cotton yarn exports. Second, the midnight shift in cotton mills was banned in Japan, but this practice remained legal in China. This led the Japanese to reconsider comparative production costs and moved them to take advantage of cheap labor in China. Third, the cotton industry in Japan was depressed after 1920, while in China the boom was still continuing. All these reasons served as inducements to open mills in China. The cotton manufacturers in Japan seemed to feel that the prosperity of the nation was identified with the prosperity of the cotton industry. As one eminent manufacturer observed, "it is to the advantage of the empire to throttle the development of the Chinese cotton industry." The China market was large and growing, Japanese manufacturers were confident that the competent Japanese managers could easily compete with the poorly organized Chinese-owned mills as well as the mills of the British.

Thus, in 1914–18, the existing Japanese firms in China added several new mills, and another wave came in 1921–22 when six new mills were formed in Shanghai and three in Tsingtao. At the end of 1922, the spindleage of these mills exceeded one million and reached more than 1.3 million with 7,200 looms by 1925. There were a total of fifteen mills and forty-two factories. Including all the cotton mills in China, the period 1914–22 witnessed an increase from 1,031,297 to 3,610,720 in total spindleage and from 5,488 to 19,228 looms. The rates of increase, more than 300 percent, were the highest in the world for that period. In 1925–31 there were no new entries, and after 1931 another rush of establishing cotton mills was seen, especially in Tientsin, North China, which became another center for cotton mills.

As the relative share of British-owned mills in China was reduced to a negligible point (about 4 percent in spindleage and 6.9 percent in looms in 1936), the focal point of the contest was between the Japanese manufacturers and the Chinese manufacturers, whose rela-

TABLE 4   Number of Cotton Spindles and Power Looms in China.

	Chinese	Japanese	Western	Chinese	Japanese	Western
1897	276,929	0	160,548	3,016	0	896
	(63.3%)		(36.7%)	(77%)		(23%)
1913	520,993	111,936	232,848	2,707	886	1,210
	(60.2%)	(12.9%)	(26.9%)	(56.4%)	(18.4%)	(25.2%)
1922	2,272,098	1,080,756	257,866	12,459	3,969	2,800
	(62.9%)	(30%)	(7.1%)	(66%)	(20%)	(14%)
1936	2,919,708	2,485,352	230,006	25,503	28,915	4,021
	(51.8%)	(44.1%)	(4.1%)	(43.6%)	(49.5%)	(6.9%)

tive growth is shown in Table 4. Although both groups of manufacturers were expanding, the Japanese group grew at a faster rate and improved its share year after year. The ordinary Chinese manufacturers were unable to fully utilize their capacity and had a high failure rate, as evidenced by the fact that in 1923-31 there were nineteen mills reorganized, five taken over by creditors, eleven bankrupt, and seventeen sold to others. The situation reached the worst point in 1935 when twenty-four of the ninty-two Chinese-owned mills collapsed and another fourteen units reduced their production schedules. During the depression in those years, a larger number of bankrupt Chinese-owned mills, especially in Tientsin, North China, passed under Japanese ownership. It is clear that the failure of Chinese-owned mills was mainly because of the Japanese presence.

The Japanese opted for a complex international division of labor in the China market. The Japanese-owned as well as Chinese-owned mills satisfied the demand for coarse yarn in China against foreign imports (including Japanese yarn), and the homeland mills competed in the import market for medium and high-count yarn and finer cotton piece goods against the Western supplies. The operational cost of Japanese mills was significantly lower than those at home, but their productivity was generally higher than either Chinese-owned or Western-owned mills.

The Japanese were systematic and aggressive businessmen. Since Japan did not possess an advantage in cotton supply and textile technology, the success of Japanese textile producers depended entirely upon their systematic and coordinated activities. It is true that all of them were affiliated in one way or another with *zaibatsu* (business cliques)—the giant corporations from which they received financial as well as technological support. More importantly, they had also developed excellent management systems, a marketing organization, and raw material procurement organizations. It did not take them long to apply these organizational principles to their plants in China. The Boseki Rengokai [Japan Spinners Association] entrusted three major cotton importers to buy raw cotton from India and China. Their large-scale and advance purchases provided considerable cost savings. These three big cotton importers dispatched their procurement agents to the interior areas of India and China to deal directly with cotton farmers or local cotton merchants. In north China they often extended credit to Chinese cotton farmers in the spring so that the farmers became bound by the contract to deliver cotton at the harvest time. On behalf of its member firms, the Association reached an agreement with the Japan Steamship Co. whereby the member mills were entitled to a freight rebate of 30 percent on all cotton shipped from India. Thus the Japanese spinning mills could obtain their raw materials at a cost even lower than the prevailing spot market prices in cotton-producing countries.

In addition, Japanese mills were renowned for their skill in blending cotton, a technique of mixing different varieties of raw cotton in making yarn. This ability enabled them to buy cheap varieties of cotton, an important cost-saving advantage, and yet maintain a constant yarn.

As is well-known, currency, weights, measures, and the language in China represented major obstacles to business. The China market was huge and regionally varied; the prices, standards of quality, consumer patterns, buyers or sellers and their credit ratings, and regulations or exactions could not be sorted out by foreigners acting on their own. Local officials and guilds had their own systems of control, taxation, squeeze, production and management to which all commercial dealings had to adjust. Trade was competently managed by sophisticated merchant guilds within a network in which long-standing personal connections were paramount and where direct and indirect official ties were also often important; hence, there was no place for outsiders. To most foreigners the China market was an unknown world in which they could not attempt to function, except for a very few who learned Chinese and acquired some knowledge of the market and its varied characteristics. Most treaty port Westerners declared, virtually as a point of pride, that it was impossible and somehow not even fitting for a civilized person to learn Chinese.[24] The language barrier was so formidable that the services of the comprador were essential.

Apparently, the difficulties encountered by the Western-owned mills in the early stages of development were formidable. It is by no means an easy task for a foreign concern, even with superior technology, to run a modern manufacturing enterprise in a strange and backward land where other complementary modern economic institutions are absent. In the case of Westerns in China, these difficulties were aggravated by the language barrier and drastic cultural differences. The learning process was extremely slow and painful for them, which in part helps to explain why Western-owned mills earned rather thin profit margins in the first fifteen years or so.

Thus Westerners had to rely extensively upon the expensive comprador system for a long period. The British did not know how to handle Chinese workers properly and had to do everything through Chinese foremen and brokers. The mill signed contracts with foremen for recruitment and gave them the freedom to set wages (usually piece rates) for the workers they recruited. Due to the lack of an effective and direct supervision system, the quality of the products sometimes was not quite up to standard. In comparison, Japanese quickly learned to adapt to Chinese conditions, probably because of the high degree of cultural and linguistic similarities between the two countries. The Japanese managers had received some professional as well as language training and directly supervised Chinese workers. They recruited and trained their own workers, hence the discipline among workers was much better. In many ways, Japanese mills in China operated like their counterparts in Japan; for instance, they built similar dormitories, mess halls, hospitals, nurseries, recreation rooms, baths, and schools for the welfare of workers.

Furthermore, the Japan Spinners Association obtained an agreement in 1892 from the Japan Steamship Co. to reduce the freight rate by 40 percent for textile shipments to China. In 1906 Mitsui

Bussan formally organized the Japan Cotton Export Guild for conducting unified selling activities abroad. The Japanese government also provided financial assistance to textile exporters through the Yokohama Specie Bank. Indeed, the businesses, government, and banks formed a trinity to pursue national interests aggressively and systematically. Moreover, the Cotton Export Guild maintained branch offices or retained representatives in a large number of Chinese inland cities, whereby Japanese goods could reach every corner of the country. The Japanese carefully cultivated their market, regulated supply to meet demand, and eliminated costly middlemen by delivering goods directly to retail dealers. The Japanese not only could get in closer contact with markets, but also could exchange information on markets, blacklist dishonest Chinese dealers, and extend credit to their customers.

Extending credit to buyers was an important promotion technique used by the Japanese distribution system in China. The sales representatives of Mitsui Bussan were authorized to accept Chinese native products like soybeans or beancakes as payment. The sales credit appealed strongly to Chinese dealers who were financially poor. Once American exporters of cotton goods attempted to form a direct-selling mechanism in Manchuria by sending their own representatives to local markets. This endeavor failed in part because the firm insisted on cash transactions. Because Westerners had no means of judging the buying capacity or financial standing of native dealers, virtually all transactions had to be carried out on a cash basis. It was only natural that they relied heavily on the comprador who took the responsibility of guaranteeing and enforcing payments from Chinese dealers. In dealing with Chinese dealers, Westerners not only used compradors as intermediaries but also shipped goods first to Shanghai and then distributed the goods in a roundabout way through the hands of several dealers at greater cost.

Thus, Western firms remained in effect commission agents, as they had been since their first trading contacts with China. This was by no means a cheap selling method. For instance, Japanese trading firms were content with a 1 percent profit markup on greys and delivered the goods directly to retail dealers in the consuming areas, whereas Western traders asked for a 3 percent markup on the same kind of greys. Moreover, Western traders had to pay a 1.5 percent commission to their compradors and further markups had to be made by the distributing dealers. The total cost incurred in the whole distribution process was estimated to range from 8.5 to 17 percent. In 1930 the distribution cost for British textile exporters was estimated to be about 3.5 times that of Japanese goods. This large difference stemmed partly from the long-distance transportation charges. A Japanese weaving firm could fill a special order within weeks, whereas it usually took months for a shipment to come from England.

In summary, the strong competitive power of Japanese textiles stemmed, to a large extent, from its superior organization of production and distribution mechanism in China, which made it possible to sell goods at relatively low prices, and also from a vertical integration of the operations of procuring raw cotton, producing cotton goods, and distributing goods, especially in the overseas market. The main advantages of Japanese mills in China over Western mills lay in these capabilities. When Japanese textile producers rushed to China to build mills or subsidiaries in the 1910s and 1920s, Western-owned mills, except for the British firm of Ewo Cotton Spinning and Weaving Co. were quickly reduced to marginal firms in the industry. They had no power to endure the acute competition after World War I and collapsed one by one.

In confrontation with the sharp competition of Japanese mills, which had always been able to count upon effective military-diplomatic support from the Japanese government to back their claims, Chinese mills were only able to resist the Japanese by taking advantage of the spontaneous boycotts that had often occurred as a means of expressing people's indignation against foreign powers. Between 1908 and 1932, boycotts were carried out nine times against Japan. Naturally, cotton goods produced by Japanese mills in China were apt to become one of the chief targets of boycotts. From 1918 to 1933, there were forty-five labor disputes or strikes in Japanese mills in Shanghai. These anti-Japanese protests delivered a severe blow to both Japanese imports and mills in China. But these movements did not last long, and Chinese mills did not necessarily come out as winners. At the outset of the movement, many Chinese distributors who were anticipating an acute shortage from Japanese mills of the Japanese-made products favored by certain Chinese consumers rushed to the market and piled up inventories of goods, which they sometimes sold disguised as Chinese-made. Ironically, the prices soared and unsold inventories quickly found buyers in anticipation of and immediately after the movements. However, more importantly, the Chinese mills during the boycotts were unable to satisfy demand in the market which was hitherto supplied with Japanese products.

Despite the fear that foreign firms would beat their Chinese counterparts, there were factors that made them coexist in the modern sector during the years before 1937. Chinese and Japanese cotton mills in China had a fair degree of division of labor; the Chinese mills largely engaged in the production of coarse yarn or cloth and the Japanese manufactured finer products. The reason that Chinese firms were primarily engaged in the production of articles of lower quality is simply due to the division of the market. The finer products were sold mainly in the treaty ports to the wealthier and more Westernized minority, while the coarse products were sold to rural residents, who accounted for over 90 percent of the population. Accordingly, the two products were not close substitutes and had separate markets. Chinese firms were unable to compete effectively with their foreign counterparts in the field of fine products but they had advantages in exploiting the market for the rural population and the urban poor. The low cross elasticity of demand for the coarse and fine products certainly diminished the vigor of keen competition between them. This was also true of other industries.

VII.   Concluding Remarks—Foreign Impacts on Chinese Economic Modernization

The successful firms like Standard Oil Co. and the BAT were a few significant exceptions in China market, as well as the Japanese-owned cotton mills whose success was far more striking, but none of these foreign firms transformed nor seriously deranged the Chinese economy. In other words, the Chinese economy as a whole underwent no significant transformation and, at best, there occurred only a partial development.

Foreign investment is expected to play a catalystic role to over-come initial difficulties of development and serve as a necessary agent to start the Chinese economy on the road to modernization. Foreign capital was dominant in the modern sector of the Chinese economy, and there were practically no modern industries in which foreign capital was not to be found. But the size of capital, even if the Chinese domestic investment is included, was not of a magnitude to initiate industrialization or to provide a threshold level for sus-tained economic development. Moreover, the slight modernization and innovation occurred in the treaty ports were mainly con-fined there, leaving the indigenous system, largely inviolate, to con-tinue its vigorous survival and even invade the treaty ports with some success. Eventually the impact of extremely limited foreign investment was unable to cause the cumulative forces of develop-ment, and the vast predominantly rural bulk of the country was only marginally affected. Foreigners' contributions were too mar-ginal to be seen as aspects of transformation.

The total contribution by the modern sector to national income is estimated to have amounted to about 10 percent in the 1930s, a period when the traditional sector (handicrafts, small mines, junks, and so forth) remained overwhelmingly dominant.[25] The reason the indigenous sector could survive modern competition was because the traditional technology employed more labor relative to capital. Since the price of labor was very low, especially for household labor (nearly zero-cost labor for female piecework) with limited capital to produce goods for use or for the market to supplement the fami-ly's income, the unit cost of production was much lower. Con-sequently, modern technology could only concentrate on products that were beyond the reach of traditional technology. Since these products were more expensive, they were also beyond the purchas-ing powers of the Chinese masses.

When machine-spun yarn was first imported into China, the de-mand for indigenous hand-spun yarn dropped drastically. The poor peasants were forced to abandon hand spinning and hold fast to hand weaving by taking advantage of the machine-spun yarn (origi-nally imported from India and Japan but later obtained in greater quantity from domestic factory production). Thus the poor peasants resisted the imported machine-made cloth by engaging in hand-

weaving with labor and toil. However, to be sure, the Chinese
farmers were not opposed to the foreign cloth because of patriotism.
Quite the opposite was the case; they had to find ways to survive
the danger of being hit with the wave of imports. In any case, cheap
labor and the poverty of the masses were the basis for the survival
of the traditional sector. Chinese resistance to new commodities or
any innovations was in many respects rationally selective but not
blind; it rested on calculated self-interest rather than on unthinking
reaction or xenophobia. Since kerosene, for instance, was the first
truly Western product to capture the China market, it was easily
acceptable. But imports such as cotton goods, cigarettes, and sugar
could be supplemented with domestic supplies.

The machine-spun yarn revitalized handicraft weaving and enabled it to retain a large share of the rural market into the 1930s
against competing machine-made cloth, whether of foreign or domestic origin. The most illustrative case is the hand-weaving industry in
the Kaoyang and Ting-hsien area in Hopei. The cloth of these two
regions was sold in places where imported cloth or factory-made
cloth in China was also available, yet the industry in both regions
witnessed a rapid growth. In Hopei, as late as the 1930s, the hand-
loom weavers still accounted for four-fifths of the total cloth production.[26] In the country as a whole during the mid-1930s, 60 to
70 percent of total cloth production was still hand-woven.[27] As for
domestic factory-products, Chinese-owned factories accounted for
over half of total cloth production in the mid-1930s. The cloth was
sold everywhere, either by local shops directly or through mer-
chants-travelers sent out from the provincial centers to lay in stock.
The system was clearly economically rational and commercially
successful.[28]

The resistance of indigenous production so late, and its ability
to adjust to changing conditions by taking advantage of technological innovations, tell us something about the reasons for foreign
failure either to corner a significant share of the market (except for
kerosene and cigarettes) in the face of the superior competitive position of traditional production or to see their technologies triumph
even in Chinese hands. Hand-woven Chinese cloth preserved a
strong opposition to manufactured cloth into the 1930s and continued to enjoy an enormously greater sale because it was more

durable and cheaper by weight than foreign machine-made cloth.

Finally, it is worth mentioning that in semicolonial China, there were two systems, foreign and Chinese, which, though competing in the same market at least within the treaty ports and their immediate environs, remained for the most part separate. As China had developed a different value system and different ways of doing business during its long period of isolation from the West, most Chinese at that time did not see much need for Western commercial, technological, and institutional innovations that were foreign and alien to them. This alienation was aggravated by an urban-rural split. The treaty ports represented a new and exclusively urban phenomenon following a Western model, while the rest of China remained little altered, except that it was better able to resist foreign efforts to invade it. The two systems touched one another very little, and the Western system did not spill over into the traditional Chinese system. The backwash or multiplier effects of economic growth, let alone innovation, in the treaty ports were also limited by the degree of separateness of the two systems. The foreign impact was concentrated in external trade and in the sale to Chinese merchants of a few originally foreign goods—kerosene, yarn, and later small amounts of machinery. None of these products ever involved more than a small fraction of the Chinese economy, whose nature was not significantly altered by their presence.[29]

NOTES

1. Albert Feuerwerker, *The Chinese Economy, 1912–1949* (Ann Arbor, 1968), p. 73.
2. Carl F. Remer, *Foreign Investments in China* (New York, 1933), pp. 69, 76, 82, 124.
3. Tōa Kenkyūjo, *Rekkoku tai-shi tōshi to Shina kokusai shūshi* (Foreign Investments in China and China's Balance of Payments) (Tokyo, 1944), pp. 2, 72–73, 131, 200.
4. Chi-ming Hou, *Foreign Investment and Economic Development in China, 1840–1937* (Cambridge, Mass., 1965), p. 14.
5. Chi-ming Hou, *op. cit.*, pp. 24–38.
6. Chi-ming Hou, *op. cit.*, chap. 3.
7. Albert Feuerwerker, "China's Nineteenth Century Industrializa-

tion: The Case of the Hanyehping Coal and Iron Co. Limited," in C. D. Cowan, ed., *The Economic Development of China and Japan* (London, 1964), pp. 79–110.

8. Rhoads Murphey, "The Treaty Ports and China's Modernization," in Mark Elvin and William Skinner, eds., *The Chinese City between Two Worlds* (Stanford, 1974), p. 49; idem., *The Outsiders: The Western Experience in India and China* (Ann Arbor, 1977), pp. 204, 272.

9. Chi-ming Hou, *op. cit.*, pp. 97–101.

10. Chi-ming Hou, *op. cit.*, pp. 112–17.

11. Rhoads Murphey, *The Chinese City between Two Worlds*, pp. 31–32.

12. Rhoads Murphey, *The Outsiders*, pp. 179, 225; Chi-ming Hou, *op. cit.*, chap. 7.

13. Tōa Kenkyūjo, *Nihon no tai-shi tōshi* (Japanese Investments in China) (Tokyo, 1943), pp. 72–73.

14. Rhoads Murphey, *The Chinese City between Two Worlds*, pp. 27, 36; idem., *The Outsiders*, pp. 117, 227.

15. Rhoads Murphey, *The Chinese City between Two Worlds*, pp. 20–21, 38; idem., *The Outsiders*, pp. 106, 122, 125.

16. Kwang-ching Liu, *Anglo-American Steamship Rivalry 1862–1874* (Cambridge, Mass., 1962); idem., "British-Chinese Steamship Rivalry in China," in C. D. Cowan, *op. cit.*

17. Ching-yü Wang, "Shih-chiu-shih-chi wai-kuo ch'in-hua chiy-yeh chung ti hua-shang fu-ku hou-tung" (The Rise of Chinese Merchants as Investors in Foreign-controlled Enterprises in the Nineteenth Century), *Li ship yen chiu* 4 (1965), pp. 39–74.

18. Rhoads Murphey, *The Outsiders*, p. 191.

19. Thomas J. McCormick, *China Market: America's Quest for Informal Empire, 1893–1901* (Chicago, 1967); Mira Wilkins, *The Emergence of Multinational Enterprises: American Business Abroad from the Colonial Era to 1914* (Cambridge, Mass., 1970); idem., *The Maturing of Multinational Enterprise: American Business Abroad from 1914 to 1970* (Cambridge, Mass., 1974); Ralph W. Hidy and Muriel E. Hidy, *Pioneering in Big Business, 1882–1911* (New York, 1955); George S. Gibb and Evelyn H. Knowlton, *The Resurgent Years, 1911–1927* (New York, 1956); Noel H. Pugach, "Standard Oil and Petroleum Development in Early Republican China," *Business History Review* (Winter 1971); Michael H. Hunt, "Americans in the China Market: Economic Opportunities and Economic Nationalism, 1890s–1931," *Business History Review* (Autumn 1977).

20. Rhoads Murphey, *The Chinese City between Two Worlds*, p. 30.
21. Chinese Science Academy and Social Science Academy of Shanghai, ed., *Nanyang hsiung-ti yen-ts'ao kung-ssu shih-liao* (Historical Materials on the Nanyang Brothers Tobacco Company) (Shanghai, 1958); Sherman Cochran, *Big Business in China: Sino-Foreign Rivalry in the Cigarette Industry, 1890–1930* (Cambridge, Mass., 1980); Hanseng Chen, *Industrial Capital and Chinese Peasants: A Study of the Livelihood of Chinese Tobacco Cultivators* (Shanghai, 1939); Senzo Ōi, *Shina ni okeru Ei-Bei tabako torasuto no keiei keitai* (The Form of Management of the BAT in China), *Tōa kenkyūshoho* 26 (February 1944); Ch'eng-chin Huang, "Ts'ung Nan-yang hsiung-ti Yen-ts'ao kung-ssu lai k'an min-tsu tzu-ch'an chieh-chi ti hsing-k'o" (Insights into the Character of the National Capitalist Class Based on the Nanyang Brothers Tobacco Co.), *Hsueh-shu yueh-k'an* (October 1958); Y. C. Wang, "Free Enterprise in China: The Case of a Cigarette Concern, 1905–1953," *Pacific Historical Review* (November 1960); Hsi Wang, "Ts'ung Ying-Mei yen kung-ssu k'an ti-kuo chu-i ti ching-chi ch'in-lueh" (BAT as a Case Study in Imperialist Economy Exploitation), *Li-shih yen-chiu* (August 1976).
22. H. D. Fong, *Chung-kuo chih mien-fang-chih-yeh* (China's Cotton Textile Industry) (Shanghai, 1934); idem., *The Cotton Industry and Trade in China*, 2. vols. (Tientsin, 1932); Chih Wu, *Hsiang-tsun chih-pu-yeh ti i-ke yen-chiu* (A Study of the Rural Weaving Industry) (Shanghai, 1936); Chung-p'ing Yen, *Chung-kuo mien-fang-chih shih-kao* (A Draft History of China's Cotton Textile Industry) (Peking, 1963); Kang Chao, *The Development of Cotton Textile Production in China* (Cambridge, Mass., 1977); Wellington K. Chan, *Merchants, Mandarins, and Modern Enterprise in Late Ch'ing China* (Cambridge, Mass., 1977); Naosuke Takamura, *Nihon bōsekigyoshi josetsu* (A History of the Japanese Cotton Textile Industry), 2 vols. (Tokyo, 1971).
23. H. Higuchi, *Nihon no tai-shi tōshi kenkyū* (A Study on Japanese Investments in China), (Tokyo, 1939), pp. 259–82.
24. Rhoads Murphey, *The Outsiders*, p. 103.
25. Ta-chung Liu and Kung-chia Yeh, *The Economy of the Chinese Mainland: National Income and Economic Development, 1933–1959* (Princeton, 1965).
26. H. D. Fong, The Cotton Industry and Trade in China, *op. cit.*, vol. 2, p. 230.
27. Chung-p'ing Yen, *Chung-kuo mien-fang-chih shih-kau, op. cit.*, p. 311.
28. Yoshihiro Hatano, "The Organization of Production in the Cotton

Cloth Industry in China after the Opium War," in *Chūgoku kindai kōgyō-shi no kenkyū* (Studies on the Early Industrialization in China) (Kyoto, 1961), pp. 529–48.

29. Rhoads Murphey, *The Outsiders*, pp. 123, 185–88.

REFERENCES

The Major References in Section I.–V.

a. Carl F. Remer, *Foreign Investments in China*, New York, 1933.

b. Tōa Kenkyūjo (East Asian Research Institute), *Shogaikoku no tai-Shi tōshi* (Foreign Investments in China), Tokyo, 3 vols., 1942–43.

——, *Nihon no tai-shi tōshi* (Japanese Investments in China), Tokyo, 1943.

——, *Rekkoku tai-shi tōshi gaiyō* (An Outline of Foreign Investments in China), Tokyo, 1943.

——, *Rekkoku tai-shi tōshi to Shina kokusai shūshi* (Foreign Investments in China and China's Balance of Payments), Tokyo, 1944.

c. Hiroshi Higuchi, *Nihon no tai-shi tōshi kenkyu* (A Study on Japanese Investments in China), Tokyo, 1939.

d. Chi-ming Hou, *Foreign Investment and Economic Development in China, 1840–1937*, Cambridge, Mass., 1965.

e. Yū-t'ang Sun, ed., *Chung-kuo chin-tai kung-yeh-shih tzu-liao, 1840–1894* (Source Materials on the Modern Industrial History of China, 1840–1894), 2 vols., Peking, 1957.

f. Ching-yū Wang, ed., *Chung-kuo chin-tai kung-yeh-shih tzu-liao, 1895–1914* (Source Materials on the Modern Industrial History of China, 1895–1914), 2 vols., Peking, 1957.

g. Chen Ch'en et al. Comps., *Chung-kuo chin-tai kung-yeh-shih tzu-liao* (Source Materials of Chinese Modern Industrial History), Peking, 6 vols., 1957–61.

h. Tse-yi P'eng, ed., *Chung-kuo chin-tai shou-kung-yeh-shih tzu-liao, 1840–1949* (Historical Materials on Chinese Modern Handicraft Industries, 1840–1949), 4 vols., Peking, 1957.

i. Ch'eng-ming Wu, *Tikuo chu-i tsai chiu Chung-kuo ti t'ou-tzu* (Investments of Imperialistic Powers in Old China), Peking, 1958.

j. Chung-ping Yen, ed., *Chung-kuo chin-tai ching-chi-shih t'ung-chi tzu-liao hsüan-chi* (Selected Statistical Materials on the Economic History of Modern China), Peking, 1955.

k. Ping-ti Ho and Tsou Tang, eds., *China in Crisis*, 3 vols., Chicago, 1968.

l.   Albert Feuerwerker, *China's Early Industrialization: Sheng Hsuan-huai (1844–1916) and Mandarin Enterprise*, Cambridge, Mass., 1958.
     ——, *The Chinese Economy ca. 1870–1911*, Ann Arbor, Michigan, 1969.
     ——, *The Chinese Economy, 1912–1949*, Ann Arbor, Michigan, 1968.
     ——, *The Foreign Establishment in China in the Early Twentieth Century*, Ann Arbor, Michigan, 1976.

m.   John K. Fairbank, *Trade and Diplomacy on the China Coast: The opening of the treaty ports 1842–1854, 1953*, Cambridge, Mass., 1964.

n.   Michael Greenberg, *British Trade and the Opening of China 1800–1842*, Cambridge, 1951.

o.   G. C. Allen and A. G. Donnithorne, *Western Enterprise in Far Eastern Economic Development: China and Japan*, London, 1954.

p.   Yu-kuci Cheng, *Foreign Trade and Industrial Development of China*, Washington, D.C., 1956.

q.   E. C. Carlson, *The Kaiping Mines 1877–1912*, Cambridge, Mass., 1957.

r.   Edward LeFevour, *Western Enterprise in Late Ch'ing China: A Selective Survey of Jardine, Matheson & Company's Operation, 1842–1895*, Cambridge, Mass., 1968.

s.   Yen-p'ing Hao, *The Comprador in Nineteenth Century China: Bridge between East and West*, Cambridge, Mass., 1970.

t.   Robert F. Dernberger, "The Role of the Foreigner in China's Economic Development, 1840–1949," in Dwight H. Perkins, ed., *China's Modern Economy in Historical Perspective*, Palo Alto, Calif., 1975.

COMMENTS

Keijiro Ishikawa
Doshisha University

Professor Yang's paper emphasized five points that are surprising and challenging to our knowledge of China. I would like to raise five questions on these points:

1. Foreign direct investment in China left the structure and character of the Chinese economy as a whole unaltered, although there were successes such as Standard Oil, BAT, and Japanese cotton mills.
2. The two systems, Western and Chinese, touched one another very little.
3. Foreigners' activities (direct investment in China) were confined to the treaty ports and were marginal.
4. Some of the foreign firms performed an important function of technology transfer to China and acted as a training ground for managers.
5. Direct investment in China by Standard Oil and BAT was successful because of pushing their sales along traditional Chinese channels of trade; on the other hand, Japanese cotton mills also succeeded without using traditional channels of trade and marketing.

Questions:

1) Why could the direct investment of Japanese cotton mills succeed without the use of Chinese traditional channels of trade, which were the most important reasons for the success of Standard Oil and BAT?

2) It is probably true that foreign direct investments in China were confined to the treaty ports and were marginal, but I think that these treaty ports were also important points of growth for the Chinese economy or business. If so, we must consider that foreign direct investments were significant for the

invasions of foreign powers. At least, we must not underestimate the influence of foreign direct investments in China.

3) What happened to Western technology and trained managers in China after 1937?

4) Why did China accept foreign direct investments? Was it only because they were persuaded by the military strength of foreign powers?

5) Regardless of the size of their influence, did many foreign direct investments in China succeed?

Foreign Investments and Technology Transfers: The Case of the French Chemical Industry in the 1950s and 1960s as Viewed by the Direction des Industries Chimiques

François Caron
University of Paris-Sorbonne

In the 1950s and 1960s, the French chemical industry showed a rate of growth well above other French industries. Such growth went along with a major effort to diversify and to adapt the industry to the new technologies that had emerged in the 1940s, since France had lagged behind in technology to a considerable extent in the war years. This episode highlights a few influences, and first and foremost being the role of great multinational firms in the chemical industry. Regarding these foreign investments, an appraisal of the attitude of the Direction des Industries Chimiques (Department for Chemical Industries or DIC) of the French Ministry for Industry is highly relevant to the issue. Access was kindly granted by the staff of the Archives Nationales responsible to the Ministry for Industry to examine the minutes of meetings of the Comité des Investissements Etrangers (Commission on Foreign Investments), which, from 1956 to 1969, included Ministry officials, various reports, and some of the relevant correspondence files. I shall start by investigating the DIC's standpoint, then examine its action within the Comité des Investissements Etrangers, and conclude with an endeavor to assess its influence.

I. The General Stance of the DIC

The DIC's standpoint reflected two main questions: (1) Is foreign investment in any way beneficial to the French economy? and

(2) Does it constitute a threat to the nation's independence in any particular branch of the economy? The relative emphasis on and significance of these two queries varied, mainly because of the opening up of trade barriers and the setting up of the Common Market. In February 1966 the Ingénieur-général des affaires extérieures (Engineer-general for Foreign Affairs or IGAE) held that "foreign investments may contribute to the development of the country's industrial potential and to an increase of the national income wherever French home investments are inadequate, either due to the sluggishness of certain sectors, or as a result of a narrow national capital market." A paper issued by the DIC in February 1965 stressed, in a similar vein: "Wherever the products involved are not being manufactured by French firms [techniques that are the exclusive propriety of a foreign group and are not open to the outsiders or involve technical or commercial risk into which French industrialists are reluctant to venture], foreign investment is, as a rule, beneficial. The manufacture of chemicals is such an involved process that any novel operation fuels the expansion of the whole."[1] One may thus speak of an "imperative of growth," requiring that foreign investments be accommodated, which resolves into three distinct arguments: the balance of payments argument, the technology transfer argument, and the full-employment argument. The IGAE went on to mention "the benefit of improving the industrial fabric of the nation by shaking up, with the help of the foreign investing firms' vitality, some of the sluggish sectors of activity." This was a rather theoretical point, and individual departments within the Ministry for Industry, such as the DIC, are usually not overanxious to put in jeopardy the promotion of modernization and reform and reconstruction by agreeing to unwelcome and inopportune investments.

Indeed, foreign investments can be fraught with "dangers." They may "kill off profit-making enterprises" should the relevant sector be saturated; they may "jeopardize the independence of rival companies on the home market" or even "bring about a position of preponderance in one sector of [manufacturing] activity," according to the IGAE. To quote further, such circumstances are particularly prejudicial "in the key sectors of the economy and especially in sectors using advanced technology" or situated "upstream, feeding a line of industry, due to the subsequent growth of the initial investments." The insistence on preserving the independence of the upstream sectors is a long-standing feature of foreign investments and constituted a major strand in the industrial policy implemented in the 1950s and early 1960s. From 1963 to 1964, however, it became apparent that insufficient regard had been given to the downstream sectors: "The position in certain branches manufacturing the more elaborate chemicals [*chimie fine*]," the DIC warned in 1965, "is becoming disquieting, as foreign interests hold too large a stake; indeed, control of these secondary activities inevitably affects the growth of that general chemical industry of which they form an extension." The outlook of the earlier position is thereby altogether reversed. The big French chemical producers, alongside the higher echelons of government, were forced to concede that the activities of paint shops, household chemical preparations retailers, and pharmacists had a bearing on their brief, and conceivably somewhat belated, admission.

As a matter of fact, the opening of the Common Market had seriously restricted the scope for action by French government agencies; after outlining the basic tenets of an investment policy, the IGAE was led to mention that "such a policy may only be effective if it is allowed to develop within the Common Market . . . for if an investment is to be denied in France only to be effected in the neighboring country . . . we find ourselves with all the drawbacks and none of the advantages." In March 1970 an EEC committee, while taking a stance against United States investments, was to lament the "subsidy warfare" prevailing between the various member states.

The attitudes in French government have changed over time. In 1968 the vice-chairman of the DIC wrote to the Directeur général de la production industrielle (Director-General for Industrial Production) that "phases of liberalism have given way to restrictive phases, and there are no more than word-of-mouth directives from cabinet to government agencies on the matter."[2] As a matter of fact, policy did take a definitely restrictive turn from 1963 to 1964 onward. One memo, dating from 1970, considers that the switchover occurred in 1965: "The decision was made to exercise closer control over foreign investments to allow the firming up of only

those investments which involved a technological or economic contribution unquestionably beneficial to the French economy."[3] The
emergence of this stance coincided with the first United States program of voluntary cutbacks on capital exports. By the end of 1967,
however, a more liberal stance was once again in evidence. The
only caveat was that no such investment was to "jeopardize independent growth in sectors of activity underpinning future developments." Subsequent policy turned out to be much more dynamic.
The assent to foreign investments went hand in hand with a policy
favoring French investments abroad. Notwithstanding some manifest misgivings on the part of the Bank of France, these investments
went through a particularly vigorous phase of expansion during the
late 1960s. That same policy strove to bring about an internal
restructuring of vulnerable sectors. The "Propositions for a Policy"
("Elements d'une politique") put forward by the DIC in November
1970 as a contribution to the drawing up of the Sixth Plan show a
new spirit at work: "New foreign investments should not be opposed, as they are needed to sustain the growth rate of industry,
[particularly] should the investment contribute to the economic
equilibrium of some new base in the chemical industry."[4] However, "one should preserve, in every sector wherever still feasible,
the independence of one or more leading enterprises that are capable of providing centers of reconstruction for small firms." The safeguard against the threat of subordination had become a counter-
thrust.

II.   The Action of DIC within the Comité des
        Investissements Etrangers[5]

However far-reaching these changes in policy may have been,
they are not so sweeping as to preclude a general investigation of
the DIC's practice. Its action was prompted, whatever the shifts in
government policy, by the desire to ensure the takeoff of the French
chemical industry as a reasonably balanced, self-sufficient whole,
having as many lines of technology as possible at its command. The
Comité des Investissements Etrangers (Foreign Investment Commission or CIE) was set up to give rulings on applications for permits concerning foreign investments in France. These powers came

under the Office des Changes until 1966 and under the Act of January 27, 1967, thereafter. The cases submitted to the Commission are those involving operations over a given amount of money. (This amount was set at 500,000 francs from March 1962 to October 1969.) The Commission plays a consultative role. For the purpose of my limited investigation, I do not intend to separate the various categories of cases submitted; indeed, most of these cases presented a combination of features involving a package of equity investments, a loan, and a transfer of technology. The Commission scrutinizes all forms of investment, such as the setting up of a new venture, the buying of shares in an existing one, or an increase in capital. As noted earlier, its stance is determined by one of two imperatives: growth or independence.

III. The Imperative of Growth

1. The Balance of Payments Imperative

In the 1950s and 1960s, foreign investment was at first used to implement a policy of import substitution. The Ministry for Industry wished to ensure that France be endowed with the factories for producing as many of the main staple products for domestic consumption as possible to avoid being forced to import them. The favored means of penetration for such basic products, as far as the DIC was concerned, was the joint subsidiary, in which the foreign corporation contributed its expertise and the French company brought it into operation. For example, the Société Industrielle des Silicones was set up in 1949 as a 50–50 subsidiary of Saint-Gobain and Dow Corning of the United States. DIC itself had instigated this development as early as 1947, when it faced repeated demands for imports of this product. In 1956 another joint subsidiary with equal shares of equity, this time set up by Saint-Gobain and CIBA —the Société des Produits Chimiques de l'Allier (Prochal)—was approved on the grounds that it was to manufacture melamine resins for varnishes and laminates and "the home production of such resins should in principle eliminate some imports." In 1957 completion of the Shell-Saint Gobain plant at the Berre was to "bring about savings in currency which are appreciated by the Commission."

The late 1950s and early 1960s witnessed the establishment on French soil of a number of new factories which expanded the range of domestic products. These factories were set up by wholly owned foreign subsidiaries or joint ventures whose aim was to develop the synthesis of organic compounds with special emphasis placed on synthetic rubber, carbon black, and plastics. Instances of directly owned foreign subsidiaries are Cabot, United Carbon, General Tire, Firestone, Goodyear, and Philips Petroleum; instances of joint subsidiaries would include the establishment, for the purposes of G.R.S. manufacture, of General Tire and Kuhlmann in 1959; Progil, Bayer and Ugine in the same year to set up a plant whose products included polyether isocyanide; and Pechiney and Dow Chemical to produce Styron and Saran. The list could be extended to cover many other examples.

The DIC was anxious that the proposed investments would be capable of generating a flow of exports and frequently demanded, as a precondition to acceptance, that an undertaking export a proportion of output. This attitude became systematic with the opening up of the Common Market. For instance, the Canadian firm Polymer Corpo experienced little difficulty in obtaining a permit in 1960 to establish a synthetic rubber plant, since it had agreed to export 75 percent of output. In 1961 the United States corporation Interchemical bought a share of equity in a French firm producing inks, since its intention was "to take a foothold in Europe through a previously established firm to serve as its base for further ventures." The aim was to avoid importing American manufactures while ensuring that the joint venture was on a scale commensurate with operation in the European market. In 1962 the complete takeover of Monsanto-Boussois, effected by Monsanto, was deemed to be "part and parcel of the overall strategy of Monsanto within the Common Market." A plant set up by Sandoz at Huningue in the Vosges in 1963 was "to supply the entire Common Market;" this was also the case for the Kodak plant set up in 1964 at Chalon-sur-Saône: it was "intended to produce the new film base for the Common Market and the U.K." A certain community of interests may emerge between the states where multinational corporations have established operating bases and the local branches of these corporations. As a typical instance of just such a process, in 1967 the management of the French subsidiary of a major Swiss chemicals firm successfully invoked the risk of an Italian operation becoming established for the production of azoic dyes to vindicate their application, in the face of opposition from French dye producers, for a loan and an increase in capital.

2. "Useful Technologies"

In most cases, foreign investment is accompanied by a transfer of technology; for that reason, the determination of an investment policy may not be attempted without reference to the determination of a research policy. After World War II, the decision of French policy-makers was to favor in principle a policy for basic research that would cover most ground, so that truly French technologies might be evolved. In its report for the First Plan in 1947, the Commission de Modernisation des Industries Chimiques (Committee for the Modernization of the Chemical Industries) considered that "the creation of a new line in the field of chemicals is always the result of three successive operations [the discovery of a product or process, the pilot study and construction of production operations, and full-scale production]; of these operations, only full-scale production is directly profitable, and there is a temptation to disregard the first two [and] to purchase licenses."[6] Such an attitude was deemed counterproductive, and it was felt that France had to strike a "reasonable balance" between these operation so that home manufacturers "might always have at their disposal products equal to the best on the world market."[7] This somewhat sanguine outlook tended to result in preference being given to an all-embracing research policy, over and above the systematic purchase of licenses. In many areas, however, the purchase of foreign technologies was inevitable. A chemicals development working group (groupe de travail chimie-développement) set up in 1963 within the DGRST (Délégation Générale à la Recherche Scientifique et Technique) reported: "After [the Second World] War, an overriding priority was given to securing manufacturing capacity for the new products (which had appeared during the war) in France, so as to avoid resorting to imports"; in this respect "it became apparent that it is costly and pointless to invent all over again what has been done already." At the time of the Third Plan (1957–1960), however, the notion still prevailed that French industry should develop French patents in every domain.

In the early 1960s the discussions which had been conducted within the DGRST committees resulted in two general conclusions: (1) what was needed was to "direct research to untried areas" rather than to expend efforts on "problems where others have already got a lead on us" and (2) what was called for to achieve true mastery in a technical domain was to "promote development operations," for "in the chemical industry, expertise, that sum of technical knowledge acquired through the development of a process at the pilot stage and which is a prerequisite for the smooth operation of an industrial unit, is as a rule of far greater value than the patent to which it relates."[8] This research policy, at once more discriminating and more development orientated, was largely arrived at through an analysis of the exchanges between France and other countries in the field of patent rights.

Two sources, the Ministry for Industry and the Bank of France,[9] are helpful to retrace from 1961 to 1969 the technological exchanges in chemicals between France and other countries. Up to 1967 no

TABLE 1   Receipts of Expenditures in Technological Exchanges (millions of francs).

	DIC Data						Bank of France Data	
	General Chemicals		Total Chemicals incl. Glass				Total Chemicals	
	Rec.	Exp.	Rec.	Exp.	Rec.	Exp.	Rec.	Exp.
1961	......	......	......	......	......	......	62.0	66.3
1962	......	......	......	......	......	......	57.4	89.0
1963	......	......	......	177.7	......	......	94.7	133.3
1964	107.5	172.5	146.9	217.2	11.0	6.3	92.3	150.7
1965	113.9	188.5	157.3	234.6	12.6	6.1	117.4	163.8
1966	92.8	223.5	138.7	272.8	14.4	7.3	114.8	190.4
1967	105.0	212.9	136.0	273.8	30.3	11.7	111.8	154.9
1968	125.0	227.3	153.7	296.6	25.4	12.0	55.7	151.9
1969	156.3	208.7	192.6	336.8	31.9	13.4	63.4	194.2

Note: In DIC data "Total Chemicals" include : General Chemicals (heavy industry), Parachemicals (secondary industry but without perfumes and transformation of plastics) and glass (given here to permit comparisons ; these figures are included in "Total Chemicals").

serious discrepancy showed up between the two sources. The discrepancy becomes quite marked, however, in 1968 and 1969. The DIC statistics were drawn "from information available to it" and cover patents, technical assistance, and development costs. The Bank of France statistics cover patents and royalties.

These somewhat crude figures do not allow for any intertemporal comparisons. They do support, however, the conclusion that the chemical industries usually show a fairly important deficit, being on the order of 50 to 67 percent, but that this deficit is the outcome of a conjunction of "a fairly high remittance in royalties" and of "a not insignificant receipt of revenues," according to H. Couturier.[10] Such revenues "are collected by a very few companies," which have managed to develop a particular technology, in which they keep a leading position (this is the case, for instance, for Air Liquide, Rhône Poulenc, and Saint-Gobain). Patents, as such, made up a minuscule proportion of the aggregate exchanges, when comparing their contribution to the figures for royalty payments, and thus vindicates the development-orientated policy that had emerged. According to the 1963 report of the Chemicals Development Working Group, firms purchasing their technology abroad come under three headings: (1) foreign subsidiaries, (2) "ventures set up as joint subsidiaries by the big chemical firms, in partnership with oil companies," and serving mainly as the medium for the introduction of new technologies (organosynthetic chemicals, plastics, synthetic rubber and textiles), and (3) medium-sized companies. In point of fact, the cost of technology transfers is lower when technology purchases are effected through the medium of subsidiaries, whether jointly owned or otherwise; as J. Dunning has noted, "one further possible advantage of knowledge transmittance via direct investment is that the parent company may charge its subsidiary less than the market price for the knowledge it transmits."[11]

In such cases as the above, however, the lower cost of the transfer of technology was not due to any goodwill on the part of the parent company—whose propensity was indeed to call for higher royalties to achieve lighter taxation on profit—but rather to the DIC's insistence that in all events the rate of royalty payment should never exceed 3 to 4 percent, at most, of turnover. In the 1950s a great many joint subsidiaries were set up on the basis of the foreign parent company contributing patents and expertise whose value was accounted for as part of its equity stake. Subsequently, the DIC was to become outspokenly critical of this formula. It was in such a manner that the previously mentioned Société Industrielle des Silicones was set up; in 1966 it broke its ties with the U.S. parent company and, after fifteen years of technological subordination, set up its own research department. Technology had indeed been "naturalized."

As a matter of fact, quite a number of technologies were transplanted into France along similar lines, either as joint subsidiaries or directly owned subsidiaries as starting points. That is the way France developed, from the late 1950s onward, its petrochemical industry, synthetic rubber industry, and production of the basic materials going into plastics. All these companies constituted at the same time to a massive transfer of technology and were the instrument of a policy of import substitution. No government agency, any more than the French Cabinet, could ignore France's need for huge transfers of technologies. From such a position, rather than pay heavy royalties to acquire production licenses, it was more rational to agree to the establishment of foreign operations which, on the one hand, gave scope for a reduction in the burden of royalty payments and, on the other hand, provided the basis for the development of these technologies in a French situation and with French expertise. This latter scheme agrees well with the product cycle described by Vernon.[12] A 1967 memo issued by the Finance Ministry[13] mentions that foreign investments peaked off between 1964 and 1967, whereas remittances on royalties increased. This trend, which is deemed to be damaging, is explained as resulting from the evolving of "a new strategy in certain U.S. firms who, rather than invest into sectors where competition is too harsh, prefer to draw royalties." To sum up, foreign investment was entertained primarily to reduce the cost of the transfer of technology, which it did as long as the procedure could be kept under control.

In many instances, although the Ministry for Industry is in principle set against foreign investment in the form of the buying of equity shares into an established French firm, such operations are allowed when it can be argued that the French firm has let itself be technologically outpaced by its foreign competitors. In 1962

CIBA took over a long-standing firm specialized in movie and photographic equipment and accessories in the Lyons area. The move was approved on the grounds that the company "has been on the decline for some years, because of insufficient technological research and industrial and commercial initiative." That same year, Diamond Alkali took over a French firm manufacturing water softeners; sanction was given because this company had "no proprietary technology," whereas Diamond Alkali "owns patents in the international league," which allowed it to stand up to the German competition. When, in 1964, Grace Corporation took over the firm of DAREX, manufacturers of "special organic materials," it was pointed out that "production processes are based on technologies owned by the Grace Corporation. The intended operation is therefore quite in order." In 1965 a French firm specializing in the manufacture of amylated products was taken over by a Dutch firm whose share of equity went up from 25 to 50 percent; this takeover was agreed to since "the French firm was lacking in technology . . . whereas the Dutch firm has built up quite extensive research facilities." These various cases show that when it depends on foreign technology, the medium-sized firm is in danger of being taken over, in the short run, by the firm that supplies it with its patents. Such cases lead us to consider a new angle: foreign investment for safeguarding ailing enterprises.

3. Bailing Out an Enterprise

In the course of the 1960s, the Ministry for Industry found cause to be disturbed in the proliferation of the practice of buying equity shares in an existing firm at the expense of setting up new ventures and came out strongly in favor of the latter solution. My research has turned up many instances of small or medium-sized French firms being bought up by foreign firms, because they were experiencing serious financial difficulties or because strained finances did not allow them to meet a buoyant market demand, or if an estate presented problems of succession. In such cases, the DIC as a rule calls for a moratorium so that it may find a French partner to substitute for the aspiring foreign firm—a fruitless search more often than not.

When considering an application for final acceptance, the argument that jobs were to be safeguarded was just as decisive as the regional development argument for the establishment or expansion of a plant. In this respect, it would seem that foreign enterprises were granted no immunity from the guidelines laid down by French policy-makers; on the contrary, the permits procedure afforded ample leverage to these officials to influence decisions about locating the plants. As a last point on this matter, whereas I found few cases where foreign operations were established to create competition for French producers, the DIC sought to avoid any one foreign producer getting sole control of the market for a particular product. The exemplar in this respect was detergents. One might also mention the case of boron, a product for which a joint subsidiary was set up in 1961. At that time only one producer, the subsidiary of a British firm, was operating and the opinion was that "the presence of a second producer can not but be fruitful."

4. The Striving for Independence

In the course of the 1960s, the DIC was quite explicit in its dismay that the parachemical sectors (pharmaceuticals, paints and varnishes, and perfumes) were in danger of passing completely under the sway of foreign interests as had happened with detergents. To counter this threat, a strategy was drawn up as part of the Fifth and Sixth Plans. This strategy was a dynamic policy of reform and reconstruction that would not stand in the way of penetration in these sectors but would allow the setting up of a balancing concentration. In the 1950s and early 1960s, investments in the pharmaceutical sector, stimulated by the obligation for medicinal preparations to have been produced in France, did not apparently cause any particular anxiety until 1963 onward. To give a revealing instance, in January 1965 the "powerful American corporation of Smith Kline and French Laboratories" wished to buy out a small French laboratory. The DIC voiced its fear that this corporation was "taking advantage of the rescuing of this paltry little business to flood the French market with its products," and "wondered whether it might not be better to let it die." In 1966 the proposed expansions of Eli Lilly France and Sandoz were welcomed with open arms, as they were to create regional establishments which the DATAR (Délégation à l'Aménagement du Territoire et à l'Action

Régionale) had deemed highly desirable. That same year, however, the DIC was to sound the alarm when faced with the takeover by Universal Oil Product of a large firm producing essential oils in Grasse, and the financial standing of this firm was very sound. The DIC warned that the Grasse industry was in a weak position since few synthetic products were manufactured in France, and because the industry "is made up of family enterprises which hinder reorganization and facilitate forcign penetration." The DIC put forward a policy advocating a linkup between the Grasse companies and the setting up of groupings drawing on the big pharmaceutical corporations and also secured a three-year moratorium. However, to the best of my knowledge, the deal was never resubmitted to the Comite. Nonetheless, in 1967 Merck France took over the Clevenot laboratories, as it thought that these laboratories "lacked adequate research teams, hardly being of much use to a French firm in the pharmaceutical sector." In 1968, in particular, the Ministry for Industry had to give way on the buying of equity shares by Hoechst in Roussel Uclaf, the second French pharmaceutical firm "whose profit margins are inadequate" and "which has been kept away from some important areas in therapy." Laboratory takeovers by foreign firms in 1969 were even more numerous. The DIC could not help emphasizing "the disquieting position of pharmaceutical laboratories" and "regret the ever-increasing foreign penetration." The DATAR answered with some animus, "foreign investments in the sector of pharmaceutical products have, in the course of the past few years, helped to solve many problems posed to regional developers."

This final clash sums up the dilemma I have sought to highlight. In my opinion, the Ministry for Industry did succeed by its persistence in determining and implementing a policy which was no longer defensive but rather took the initiative in supporting French investments abroad, reforming and reconstructing various sectors, and building up a research capability ready to seek out opportunities. In summary, a deliberate policy of foreign technology transplant was implemented, particularly in the field of synthetics and plastics, but the process was much less under control in the sectors producing the more elaborate products (*chimie fine*, for example) for want of an early resolve to keep it under any control.

IV. Foreign Investments in the 1960s: A Balance Sheet

As far as inflows and outflows are concerned, the data drawn up by the Ministry from 1963 to 1969, on the basis of "information available to it" only, cover the sector of chemicals as a whole (including pharmaceuticals, paints, and rubber). From 196 million francs in 1963, chemicals rose between 1964 and 1968 to an average of some 300 million francs, showed a sharp upswing in 1969 (757 million francs), and soared further upward by 1973. This rise was, to a considerable extent, offset by French investments abroad, which rose from an average of 86 million francs in 1965–1967 to 269 million francs in 1968, and to 577 million francs in 1969. These figures illustrate the switchover from a defensive strategy to dynamic offensive strategy.

Be that as it may, it would be of some interest to make an overall balance sheet of such investments. Such a balance sheet covering 1963 was drawn up by the DIC in 1965. This study only covers 342 companies, with a turnover above 10 million francs, accounting for 85 percent of the trade in chemicals. Of these, 126 companies have a turnover above 30 million francs, realizing 67 percent of aggregate turnover. Of the 342 firms considered, 77 (22 percent) operate with foreign capital, and 59 have more than 50 percent foreign equity. Corresponding turnover figures account for 23 percent of aggregate. Foreign equity also increases with size; of the 126 firms with a turnover above 30 million francs, 38 (30 percent) operate with foreign capital and 31 have a foreign majority share of equity. These 38 firms account for 25 percent of the aggregate turnover of firms in this class. United States investments represent the largest element, whether one considers the number of firms involved (60 percent) or the corresponding share of turnover (54 percent). The only major Common Market investment is from Belgium, owing to the size of Solvay's French operation, which was set up well before World War II. Actually, the DIC was not over-enthusiastic as far as Common Market establishments were concerned, and it appears instead to have favored operations originating in the United States. The justification by the DIC for such a stance is given in one of its reports for the drawing up of the Sixth Plan in 1970: "Contrary to what one finds to be the case with

TABLE 2 Percentage Share of Turnover within the Chemical Industry in 1963.

Sector	Turnover total (million francs)	Firms with a turnover of 30 million francs or more					Firms with a turnover between 10 and 30 million francs				
		Number	Turnover total	Foreign firms			Number	Turnover total	Foreign firms		
				Number	Turnover	Percent			Number	Turnover	Percent
		I	II	III	IV	IV/III	I	II	III	IV	IV/II
Pharmaceutical products	3,700	27	1,990	9(1)	409	20.5	65	1,150	12	219	19
Paints	1,680	8	468	1	57	12	29	458	2	31	7
Phytosanitary products	475	5	334	3	136	40	4	80	2(2)	27	34
Detergents cleaning materials	1,475	6	1,022	3	818	80	5	99	2	44	44
Sensitized materials	550	3	472	2	472	100	2	45	1(3)	12	30
Abrasives	210	3	134	1	101	75	4	61	—	—	—
Dyes	247	2	193	1	42	22	2	18	1	6	33
Synthetic rubber	258	4	250	4	250	100	—	—	—	—	—
Blacks	82		73	2	71	99		—		—	
Plastics	1,813		1,556	4(4)	253	16.3		150	3(5)	21	14
Petrochemicals	10,010	68	7,338	3(6)	339	11.4	105	1,629	2(7)	20	16
Organic synthesis				2(8)	435				6(9)	136	
Other chemical industries				1					8(10)	107	
Total	20,500	126	13,830	38(11)	3,443	25	216	3,690	39(12)	623	17

(1) Two are 50:50.
(2) One is 50:50.
(3) A 50:50 society.
(4) Two are 50:50.
(5) All are 50:50.
(6) One is 50:50.
(7) All are 50:50.
(8) All are 50:50.
(9) One is 50:50.
(10) Three are 50:50.
(11) Seven are 50:50.
(12) Two are 50:50.

certain American investments, Common Market investments are often of little benefit to the French economy; in most cases, the subsidiary is turned into simply an appendage of the group and the center of decision remains within the parent company, which implements the policy most favorable to itself regarding supplies and exports and without much regard for its subsidiaries." This passage shows the contrast in strategies between that favored by United States firms, which quite readily allow their subsidiaries to "walk on their own legs," and that of European firms at the time. And, whatever the merits of the case, the report is quite frank and outspoken.

Taking the various sectors into account, one finds the most clearcut feature of foreign investments in the French chemical industry (see Table 2) to be their tendency, already apparent at the time, to go for the more elaborate chemicals (*chimie fine*)—"those which flow into the consumer market." Foreign firms have shown a marked preference for downstream operations such as pharmaceuticals, parachemicals, phytosanitary products, and plastics. Such a strategy agreed well with the avowed purpose of the Ministry for Industry, where it was deemed far more important in the 1950s, to secure control of the main staple products of industry rather than the more sophisticated products. This attitude only mirrored the prevailing attitude within the French chemical industry—an attitude shared by French industrialists as a whole; for too long, French industrial policy has rested on the myth of "basic sectors." As a matter of fact, a form of division of labor was effected at the European level and, as the DIC's vice-chairman noted in 1970, the big international corporations in general chemicals have favored Benelux sites: "Their operations in France did not go beyond joint subsidiaries set up with French groups, almost always with a view to controlling a share of the market for certain products."

This analysis called for a more detailed investigation inquiring into the motivations of foreign investors. The DIC singled out four considerations (setting up production plants close to their markets, adapting products to local tastes, taking advantage of lower labor costs, and evading tariff barriers) which in themselves explain both the preponderance of investments from countries outside the Common Market—relative to investments from member states—and the preference shown for "branches of secondary chemistry, i.e., those which include a large part of labor and for which marketing problems are of great importance." To refine this analysis of modes and to attempt a form of typology, one may consider the three distinctive cases below.

1. For general chemicals, the petroleum-refining companies previously established in France and expanding into heavy petrochemicals (Esso, Shell, and British Petroleum) should be treated separately. French policy-makers and officials have never allowed these companies to gain total control of any one product; in 1970, for example, Esso and Shell together only held 27 percent of the market for ethylene and 34 percent of the market for propylene. In the organosynthesis industries, such as the plastics industry, the most common procedure was to set up a joint subsidiary with equal shares of equity being held by a French partner. This method was used to gain entry in the French market by the big German, Swiss, or American groups or by oil companies that did not have refineries in France, such as Standard Oil of California. As for heavy petrochemicals, one is liable to find markets shared between wholly owned foreign subsidiaries and French firms. To give one example of such a juxtaposition, production of polystyrene in 1970 was distributed among wholly French firms (Aquitaine Organico and Courrières Kuhlmann) accounting for 49 percent of aggregate output, one wholly owned foreign subsidiary, Monsanto (29 percent of output), and a subsidiary of Dow Chemicals (the parent company holding 51 percent of equity) named Plastichimie (22 percent). For any one product, distribution is the outcome of complex arbitrations and, above all, of an evolution over time where failures are as common as successes. Indeed, foreign technology transplants did occasionally result in resounding failures. Thus, international corporations sought, in the words of G. Bertin, to "secure the key strategic points of lines of technology," such as polyurethane or polyolefins.

2. For certain new branches of activity, including manufacture of polyurethane and polyolefins, foreign countries (more often than not the United States) "could avail themselves of a marked technological lead," to quote from the 1965 DIC report. The preferred mode was to set up a wholly owned subsidiary or a joint subsidiary

with a large foreign majority of equity shares. In such sectors, as early as 1963 (see Table 2) there was an overwhelming preponderance of foreign firms; in some branches, blacks, sensitized supports, and synthetic rubber, control is 100 percent. In others, foreign control accounts for the dominant share; for detergents and soap preparations, control is 62 percent to 80 percent if one considers those companies with a turnover above 30 million francs.

3. The third case characterizing sectors situated well downstream, such as pharmaceuticals, perfumes, paints, and varnishes, mainly takes the form of buying out a medium-sized firm. As the DIC noted in 1965, "this operation is indeed commonly the outcome of a process involving an initial cession of technology, followed by a purchase of equity." I noted earlier how disquieting the vulnerability of such sectors, comprising many medium-sized firms, was in the DIC's opinion.

Yet to what extent was that disquiet justified? For the year 1969, there is no study for chemicals as a whole as detailed as that quoted for 1963. On the other hand, there is a study covering a single sector of pharmaceuticals; in 1969 the 121 French pharmaceutical laboratories with a turnover above 10 million francs accounted for 85 percent of that branch's activity and shared 5,669 million francs between them. Of these 121 laboratories, forty-seven (40 percent) were under foreign control and accounted for 34 percent of aggregate turnover. In this group of forty-seven, twenty-six were U.S. controlled. In 1963 the proportion of aggregate turnover under foreign control in the 10 million-plus turnover class was 21 percent. The vast majority of these laboratories were wholly owned and highly dependent on outside technology. One is therefore led to the conclusion that foreign influence in this sector was quite strong and rapidly growing. This trend, however, has noticeably slackened since 1970. According to G. Bertin, foreign economic control for chemicals as a whole, excluding pharmaceuticals, rose from 15.6 percent in 1962 to 24 percent in 1971, whereas for pharmaceuticals alone the proportion went up from 17 percent to 38 percent. The scale of such an increase warrants the conclusion, in spite of inadequate statistical sources, that there was a sharp increase in the extent of foreign control and a markedly steep swing in pharmaceuticals—a sector in which such expansion is stimulated by the requirement that all drugs sold in France be locally manufactured; therefore, this rise in foreign control is a reflexion of certain inadequacies in French research.

In 1976, according to the data drawn up by the STISI, the "penetration index," worked out on the basis of turnover figures, stood at 25.1 percent in general chemicals, 51.4 percent in parachemicals, and 39.2 percent in pharmaceuticals. The overall trend would therefore seem to have noticeably slackened off. These figures show pharmaceutical chemicals to be one of the most heavily penetrated sectors.

Thus the DIC would appear, in the 1950s and 1960s, to have steered a course corresponding to a consistent purpose whose implementation turned out to be particularly impracticable, owing to the swiftness of technological change, at a time when the opening up of barriers increasingly restricted policy-makers' freedom of action. Faced with these circumstances, the officials at the head of the DIC were not long in grasping that the best way of resisting foreign investments was to make sure investments should not become unavoidable: the process of innovation was to be kept under control rather than allowing it to take control. This choice implied an attempt to specialize to build up a consistent body of truly French technical expertise rather than opting for an all-embracing research policy in the field of chemical technology. But there hangs another tale, which would take me beyond what I have endeavored to recount.

NOTES

1. Archives du Ministère de l'Industrie, IND 22071.
2. *Ibid.*, IND 20511.
3. *Ibid.*
4. *Ibid.*
5. Archives du Ministère de l'Industrie, *Procés verbaux de la Commission des Investissements Etrangers, 1956–1969,* IND 15820, 15821, 15822.
6. Bibliothèque Nationale (Paris), *Premier Rapport de la Commission de Modernisation des Industries Chimiques, October 1949,* Fol. Lf. 290–226.
7. *Ibid.*
8. Direction Genérale de la Recherche Scientifique et Technique,

Report of the Committee on the Research in the Chemical Industry, 1962,
    Archives du Ministère de l'Industrie.

9. Archives du Ministère de l'Industrie, IND 20430 and 20431; Sta-
    tistics from the Bank of France (Banque de France) were kindly
    supplied by the Bank's governor.
10. Couturier, "Les revenus de la recherche scientifique et technique,"
    Cahiers de l'I.S.E.A., vol. II, no. 4 (April 1969).
11. J. Dunning, Technology, United States Investment and European Economic
    Growth in the International Corporation (Cambridge, Mass., 1970).
12. R. Vernon, "International Investment and International Trade in
    the Product Cycle," in Quarterly Journal of Economics, vol. 80 (1966),
    pp. 199–207.
13. Archives du Ministère de l'Industrie, IND 22071.

SOURCES CONSULTED

Bertin, G. Y., L'investissements des firms étrangères en France (Paris: P.U.F.,
    1963).
Couturier, M., "Les revenus de la recherche scientifique et technique,"
    in Cahiers de l'I.S.E.A., vol. II, no. 4 (April 1969).
De Lattre, F., Les finances extérieures de la France (Paris: P.U.F., 1961).
Dunning, J., Technology, United States Investment and European Economic
    Growth in the International Corporation, Edited by C. P. Kindleberger,
    Cambridge, Mass.: The MIT Press, 1970.
Guibert, et al., La Mutation Industrielle de la France: Collections de
    l'I.N.S.E.E., series E, no. 31–32 (November 1975).
Hufbauer, G. C., Synthetic Materials and the Theory of International Trade,
    Duckworth.
Michalet, F., Les in Plantations Etrangers en France, Paris, Calmana Levy,
    1976.
Vernon, R., "International Investment and International Trade in the
    Product Cycle," Quarterly Journal of Economics, vol. 80 (1966), pp. 199–
    207.

COMMENTS

Eisuke Daito
University of Tokyo

Direct foreign investment is the most politically sensitive process the government of the host country is inevitably involved in, and the host country government tends to be tossed about, as was pointed out by Professor Caron, by two imperatives: growth and independence. From these viewpoints, Professor Caron examines changes in French government policies in detail. Regrettably, I am unfamiliar with the French chemical industry. Therefore, I would like to ask some questions on French experiences by taking comparisons with Japanese firms into consideration.

First, in Japan, as well as France, development of the chemical industry in the postwar years relied heavily on imported technologies and foreign direct investments, both of which involve capital transactions in some form. Many firms tried to establish their competitive advantages and diversify their activities by these measures. Since capital transactions were under strict government control, government policies toward firms could play a decisive role in determining their fate. In addition, the power of the Japanese government over private enterprises was strengthened by the keen competition for governmental approval. Government officials have a great variety of companies to choose from and can urge businessmen to make plans in accordance with the government's guidlines and specific instructions. These facts indicate that an analysis of government policies must be followed by an analysis of the policies of private firms. Therefore, I would like to ask Professor Caron to explain the strategies of French chemical manufacturers who introduce foreign technologies and investments.

Second, Professor Caron wrote that the cost of technology transfer is lower when effected through the medium of jointly owned subsidiaries or other means, rather than when they are effected through license contracts with royalty payments. Theoretically, this judgment seems valid for Japan as well. Sales figures of many Japanese firms in the chemical industry grew rapidly every year but, due to the keen competition among them, they sometimes had narrow profit margins. Moreover, they depended heavily on borrowed money from banks. Under these circumstances, we naturally expect that Japanese firms prefer direct investments to license contracts. In reality, however, theory and practice do not always coincide. Actually, technologies have been transferred to Japan mainly through license contracts. To what extent did the French government's experiences differ in theory and practice?

Third, I think that one of the major conclusions of Professor Caron is that while French industrial policies have rested on the myth of basic sectors, foreign firms have shown a marked preference for downstream sectors since the latter half of the 1960s. As a result, foreign corporations penetrated deeply into the field of fine chemicals by buying out "medium-sized firms." Certainly, faced with the overwhelming competitive advantages of foreign firms, medium-sized French firms were totally discouraged. This is a typical example of the negative contribution of foreign direct investment. Nevertheless, the term medium-sized firm is too vague. I would like to know more about the character of the firms and the reasons why they behaved as they did.

Summary of Concluding Discussion

Tadakatsu Inoue

I.

As an aid to the concluding discussion, two tables were prepared on the blackboard. One was designed to outline the problems from the viewpoint of capital-investment countries, that is, the U.S., U.K., Germany, and Japan. The other was arranged to show the problems from the point of view of the capital-recipient countries, that is, France, Australia, and China.

The first table, from the investor's side, provided the following four problem categories in four columns:

1. Basis: capability bases of foreign direct investments in manufacturing.
2. Process: ways of being involved in foreign manufacturing.
3. Area: geographical and industrial areas of overseas operations.
4. Organization and Operation: some managerial problems arising out of foreign direct investment in manufacturing, including ownership patterns, sources of funds, and structural responses to strategic changes.

The second table listed two categories of problems from the receiving side:

1. Environment for receiving foreign direct investments in manufacturing: the attitudes of governments and other conditions in host nations such as market, labor, and cultural and geographical distance.
2. Effects of foreign direct investments in manufacturing on host countries: technological transfer and others.

II.

The squares of the resulting chart were filled in by the reporter or commentator for each country. In the course of discussion, these notations were supplemented or supplanted by new expressions. Words and phrases finally left in each column of the two tables will be reproduced here with some explanations.

1-1. Basis

"U.S. type of innovation directed toward labor-saving and high-income needs," "entrepreneurial ability combined with product innovation," and "technological advantage and entrepreneurial capability" were respectively given as the capability bases of the U.S., U.K., and German firms that early made foreign direct investments in manufacturing. A "monetary system" which could produce a premium on foreign exchange was also emphasized in the case of U.S. firms which spread out direct investments in Europe after World War II. However, some insisted that this should be regarded as a favorable environmental factor for U.S. firms rather than a capability basis built in them.

As to the competitive advantages of the Japanese cotton spinning companies that invested in China after World War I, everyone accepted "managerial or organizing skills," as was well illustrated in a paper read at this meeting. "Continuous improvements in the process of production for standardized goods" were also recognized as the very basis of foreign operations by Japanese firms after World War II.

1-2. Process

Almost the same expression—"from export to foreign manufacturing," "export→sales subsidiary→manufacture," "export→sales agent (engineer with commercial capability)→local production," or "export through active marketing to foreign manufacturing"—was used to describe the U.S., U.K., Germany, and Japan. It should be noted, however, that such sub-phrases as "often defensive, but sometimes offensive" and "time difference" were respectively attached to the U.S. and U.K. In fact, some U.S. firms were aggressive in switching from exporting to foreign manufacturing, while many

TABLE 1 Viewpoint of Investor (Home Country).

	Basis	Process	Area		Organization and operations
			Geographical	Industrial	
U.S.	U.S. type of innovation directed toward labor-saving and high-income needs (Monetary system)	From export to foreign manufacturing—often defensive, but sometimes offensive	DC later added LDC	Machinery, small packaged products (Chemical and information industries)	Ad-hoc organization →International division→Global organization (Break-down of cartel agreement)
U.K.	Entrepreneurial ability combined with product innovation	Export→Sales subsidiary→Manufacture—time difference	Prior 1930 High income market 1930–60 Developed Commonwealth 1960– U.S.A., Western Europe	Consumer goods	Preference for local participation Dual ownership, ex., Shell, Unilever
Germany 1890–1914	Technological advantage and entrepreneurial capability	Export→Sale agents (engineer with commercial capability) →Local production	DC (U.S., U.K.) LDC (Latin America)	France, Chemical, pharmaceutical industries Electrical industry	Banking in New York Tendency to controlling influence
Japan	Managerial (or organizing) skills Imitation plus α—continuous improvement in process	Export through active marketing to foreign manufacturing	LDC (Asia) later added DC (U.S.)	Textiles, electrical machinery later added non-electrical machinery	Joint venture with trading companies →decreasing

Note:

Basis—Capability basis of becoming multinational manufacturing enterprise.

Process—Process of being involved in foreign manufacturing operations.

Area—Geographical and industrial areas of overseas operations.

Organization and Operations—Organizational and operational problems arising out of foreign direct investment in manufacturing.

others were compelled to do so. While some U.K. firms quickly moved from export to manufacture, others took a much longer time in doing so.

1-3. Area

The squares for the U.S., U.K., and Germany corresponding to "Geographical," a subdivided part of the "Area" column, were filled up with such words and phrases as "first and foremost in the neighboring Canada and the developed Europe" (U.S. square), "high-income markets such as U.S., Canada, Australia, and Western Europe (prior to 1930)" (U.K.), and "developed countries (U.S., France, and U.K.) and less developed countries (Latin America), 1890–1913" (Germany). In comparison, Japanese direct investments in manufacturing prewar period were almost limited to China. Even long after World War II, Japanese firms invested chiefly in the Asian countries. It was not until recent years that they began to aim at developed countries.

Under "Industrial," another subdivided part of the "Area" column, the three advanced nations about the time of World War I became full with "machinery and small packaged products" (U.S.), "consumer goods" (U.K.), "chemical and pharmaceutical industries in developed countries and electrical industry in less developed countries" (Germany). In comparison, the major sector that attracted Japanese direct investments in foreign manufacturing in the years prior to the Manchurian Incident was "textiles." When Japan reopened direct investments abroad after World War II, this industry, together with electrical industry, again held a dominant place among the sectors attracting Japanese foreign investments.

1-4. Organization and Operation

While "ad-hoc organization→international division→dissolution of international division (belonging to product division or regional division of headquarters)" was noted in the U.S. row to present the pattern of evolution of the management system of multinational enterprises, most words and phrases given in other rows were related to ownership and financial policies: "preference for local participation" and "dual ownership in the cases of Shell and Uniliver" for the U.K., "banking in New York" and "tendency to controlling influence" for Germany, and "spread and decline of sogo shosha joint ventures after World War II" for Japan. A related problem of "whether to establish a completely new operation or to buy an interest in an existing firm" was a new topic of discussion. A participant pointed out that even in the same country (for example, in U.S. motor companies in prewar days), some decided to go abroad by establishing a new firm, while others combined with existing firms, and that their decision would depend on a number of factors, including the speed with which they desired to set up their local beachheads. A participant indicated that early British investors with novel products had no alternative to building manufacturing plants by themselves. Another stated that Japanese firms generally preferred to establish new foreign plants, partly in order to transfer Japanese wasys of management abroad.

2-1. Environment

In Table 2, for host countries, the "Environment" column was subdivided into "Government" and "Others." For France, "control of industry" and "the will to fill the technological gap" were the guiding principles under which the government controlled strictly capital transactions in the 1950s and 1960s. For Australia, whose row was divided into two periods, pre-1920 and post-1920; "tariffs" that compelled foreign manufacturers to invest there were operative in the early period, while both "tariffs levied by the federal government" and "inducements extended by state governments" were important in the later period. For China, in the years 1842–1937, "partial sovereignty," "no tariff autonomy by 1930," "no complete control over foreign investments," on the one hand, and "suspicious of foreign investments," on the other hand, were written down to present its political atmosphere towards foreign investments.

Under "Others," each row was also filled up with many varieties of expressions. For France in the 1950s and 1960s, "equilibrium of balance of payment," "monetary factor: underevaluation of franc," "cost of labor," "size and dynamism of market," and "structure of market: oligopolistic or not" were enumerated to summarize the factors bearing on a decision to invest there. For pre-1920 Australia,

Table 2 Viewpoint of Host Country.

	Environment		Effect	
	Government	Others	Technology	Others
France the 1950s and 1960s	Control of industry and the will to fill technological gap	1. Equilibrium of balance of payment 2. Monetary factor (valuation of franc) 3. Costs of labor 4. The size and dynamism of market 5. The organization of enterprise (oligopolistic or small size) 6. Political factor (competition with other EC countries)	Development of French technology	1. Growth and share with capital formation 2. Regional equilibrium 3. Oligopolistic structure
Australia	Pre 1920 Tariff	(−) Small population Geographical remoteness Non-capital intensive industries (+) Cultural closeness	New technology in a few industries	Effects—small
	Post 1920 Fed. Gov. Tariff State Gov. Encouragement	Medium population but scattered Capital intensive industries		Vital source of capital Sense of Nationalism Balance sheet
China 1842–1937	Partial sovereignty No tariff autonomy Can not control foreign investment Suspicious of foreign investment	The masses, especially handicrafters, resisted Confined in treaty ports Conduct of business with Chinese compradors in treaty ports through traditional channels	New products and new technology Initial appearance of modern sectors Set up examples for entrepreneurs	Leaving indigenous system functioning Economic structure unaltered

Note: Environment
  Government—The attitude of government for receiving foreign direct investment.
  Others—Market, Labor, Socio-cultural factors, etc.
Effects
  Technology—Effects of foreign direct investment on technological transfer to host country.
  Others—Other effects on host country.

"small population," "geographical remoteness," and "industry: noncapital intensive" were cited as unfavorable factors in inducing investments there, while "cultural closeness" was a favorable one. After 1920, "medium population but scattered" and "industry: capital intensive" were operant factors. The space for China gave "ill feelings against foreigners, especially among handicrafters," "confinement activities of foreigners in treaty ports," and "conduct of business with Chinese comprador in such ports through traditional channels of distribution."

2-2. Effects

One of the most obvious effects was the impact that foreign direct investments had on the development of technology in the capital-recipient economies. But the degree of the benefit observed in each country in a given period was not the same. "Development of French technology" would be a positive expression of the fact that the techniques of foreign subsidiaries were successfully nationalized in the 1950s and 1960s. "New technology in a few industries" and "new products and new technology" given to Australia pre- and post-1920 would seem to say that this effect might be rather smaller than was sometimes imagined. And in the case of China, while foreigners "called forth modern sectors" and "set an example for Chinese entrepreneurs," these effects were essentially confined to treaty ports, leaving the indigenous system functioning.

When we turn from the impact on technology to other effects, we find them spread over a wide range. An important benefit accruing to France in the 1950s and 1960s from foreign direct investments was "growth and share in capital formation" that was oriented to more dynamic sectors. This contribution was also stressed in Australia after 1920. Besides this, "regional equilibrium" and "oligopolistic structure" were observed in France, while "sense of nationalism" was "offended" in Australia. Although a balance-sheet of the effects of foreign direct investments on the latter country has varied decade by decade, "very substantially increased employment," "standard of living maintained," and "capital gains" in such case as foreigners paying too much for acquiring existing companies would be counted on the positive side.

III.

The resulting table was a useful exercise in several ways. If some-one from Japan was interested in the bases of capability on which the Western manufacturers went abroad and got along there, the table listed technological superiority and entrepreneurship. Similar-ly, if someone from the Western countries was anxious to know what competitive advantages the Japanese manufacturers enjoyed over their local competitors, the table listed the ability to organize production and distribution and to make continuous improvements in the technologies obtained from Western sources. At the same time, as the Japanese manufacturers succeeded in catching up with foreign technologies and even in getting ahead of them, their style of multinationalization changed: the direction of their capital ex-ports moved slowly to cover the developed countries in addition to the developing areas of the world; the types of industries that be-came multinational changed also to include non-electrical machin-ery as well as textile and electrical machinery; and their preference for joint ventures with the general trading companies (sogo shosha) began to decline.

The usefulness of the tables was somewhat limited, however, by the fact that different time periods were discussed and characterized for each country, in some cases making comparison difficult.

INDEX